How desperately we in the church need help with our creativity in teaching the good news. The message that we have is thrilling and priceless and life changing. Often it sounds boring because we lack creativity in our methodology. This book is an invaluable instrument for calling forth creativity in our teaching methods.

Bruce Larson
Senior Pastor, University Presbyterian Church,
Seattle, Washington

Preaching is my primary love. But my preaching had better include teaching. **Creative Teaching Methods** calls me to a new creative edge. If a preacher is so stirred by this book on teaching, I can imagine how teachers will benefit. Keep it in a permanent spot on your desk as a reminder to teach better and as a reference book of ideas on how to do it.

Brian C. Stiller
Executive Director, Evangelical Fellowship of Canada

In this book, Marlene LeFever has outlined some tremendous ways to be creative which could bring new depth and excitement to your teaching.

Cliff R. Raad
Executive Director,
Greater Chicago Sunday School Association

It is both encouraging—"I can do that"—and challenging—"I've never tried that, but I could work on it." May I order three copies? One to loan, one to keep, and one for the church library.

Carolyn M. Raffensperger
Director of Christian
Education
First Presbyterian Church
of River Forest, Illinois

I have found **Creative Teaching Methods** a thorough, comprehensive, and illuminating work.

Gardner C. Taylor
Pastor, Concord Baptist Church of Christ,
Brooklyn, New York

The book is delightful and filled with surprises. I think I became a better teacher after reading the first two chapters alone.

Ben Patterson
Pastor, Irvine Presbyterian Church
Irvine, California

CREATIVE
TEACHING
METHODS

Marlene D. LeFever

DAVID C. COOK PUBLISHING CO.
Elgin, Illinois/Weston, Ontario

David C. Cook Publishing Co.
Elgin, Illinois—Weston, Ontario
Creative Teaching Methods
Be an Effective Christian Teacher
© 1985 Marlene D. LeFever

Published by David C. Cook Publishing Co.
850 N. Grove Ave., Elgin, IL 60120
Cover design by Jill Ellen Novak
Printed in the United States of America
Library of Congress Catalog Number 85-071514
ISBN: 0-89191-760-8

My love and appreciation
to my husband, Jack Risley, who
in our team teaching modeled Christian
commitment for teenagers, and who creatively
deals with the struggles and joys of
living for Christ in our marriage
and in his very secular
working environment

Contents

Introduction

I had lost my voice. For two months I croaked along teaching Sunday after Sunday. Each week my throat hurt more and my croaks got weaker. My senior high Sunday school class members were the most lively, verbose dozen I had ever worked with. But during this difficult time, they responded to my need. They stopped talking completely while I presented the content and explained the direction of the class interaction. Then they didn't need to be prodded into action. They immediately took responsibility for the class's success. It was obvious to all of us that without them the class wouldn't work.

I'd always known the principle: participation in the learning process stimulates learning and encourages growth. Negatively, when the teacher is in total control of the class's activities, his or her ego may be the only growing thing in the classroom.

Students need to feel that this is "our" class. "Yes, we have a leader, but without our help, this class would not work." It's the leader who encourages this sense of ownership; it's the smart leader who doesn't wait for a voice loss to implement the shared learning approach.

While I was whispering at my class, I had time to watch students grow spiritually. They became my support group, my "church," during that difficult time. They sent me cards. They told me they were going to pray for me and confirmed that promise each week by telling me how often and for how long they had done just that.

I listened and they talked. I pantomimed and they lived out what they were discovering directly from God's Word. I fell apart, exhausted, and they boosted me: "Thanks for coming. Don't give up. Your voice will come back."

Students are wonderful people. We sometimes forget that in the busyness and frustrations of being a teacher.

This book is designed to help teacher and students work together in the learning process. For the teacher, these methods may mean more work, less ego stroking, and greater affirmation that life learning is taking place. For the students, the processes will help them discover unique ways they can grow in their understanding of what the Christian life is all about. More importantly, they will learn how they can live out that understanding in their Monday-through-Saturday lives.

This study incorporates and enlarges many of the ideas included in my book, *Turnabout Teaching*.[1] It probes new areas: the process of creativity, the use of secular and Christian story, and case study.

How we communicate God's Word should not be static. This book is finished, but the methods we can use to teach will never be exhausted. For example, right now I'm exploring ways video curriculum can be incorporated in Sunday school and Bible study groups. How can we use this unique tool to train the TV generation for Christ? How can we develop programs for video and home computers that will aid parents in training their children?

The authors of *Using Nonbroadcast Video in the Church* articulate the challenge: "Just as the first-century church learned through Pentecost to communicate the Gospel in new languages, the church of today must learn new languages to communicate with its world. . . . The church often resists new technologies and methodologies until pressure becomes so great that it has no other choice but to change. This characteristic provides an excellent balance against fads and gives needed continuity, but it can also become an excuse for seldom acting innovatively when a new and useful technology for communicating the Gospel arises."[2]

Video—a chapter for another book, perhaps. The ways we have to teach will continue to grow. We must grow, too, or as John Peatling cautions, we could find ourselves "the well-meaning antiquarians of the day after tomorrow."[3]

My special thanks to Dr. D. Campbell Wyckoff (Princeton Theological Seminary) and Dr. Charles Bradshaw (Talbot Theological Seminary) for the opportunity to present the ideas in this book through teaching experiences at their schools, and my appreciation to my students who enlarged and honed each area.

Neta Jackson, my editor, went far beyond the jots and tittles of the process. She encouraged me with her enthusiastic responses to content— "Hey, I can hardly wait to try this idea." She also enlarged my thinking by sharing some of the unique worship experiences at her church. I thank her for her craft and her friendship.

1. Marlene LeFever, *Turnabout Teaching* (Elgin, Ill.: David C. Cook Publishing Co., 1973).

2. Daniel W. Holland, J. Ashton Nickerson, and Terry Vaughn, *Using Nonbroadcast Video in the Church* (Valley Forge: Judson Press, 1980).

3. John Peatling, "Science, Wisdom or Wizardry?" in *Religious Education,* Summer, 1983.

CHAPTER 1

The Creative Dare

Where did we get the idea that God loves sh-h-h and drab and anything will do? I think it's blasphemy not to bring our joy into His church.

—Ann Weems in *Balloons Belong in Church*

Barbara had taken the dare and joined an experimental adult Sunday school class. The prerequisite for joining: no student had ever been in a class where a method other than lecture was used. These older adult students were very good at sitting and listening and occasionally responding to questions about Biblical facts and theology. Now they were agreeing to participate in roleplay, work in small inductive Bible study groups, and write personal psalms using the same forms the psalmist did.

"I had never approached a teaching assignment with more trepidation," the teacher said. "The first week I lost two couples, and I had no way of knowing they were the only people who would leave. I was depressed, but then, God gave me Barbara. Barbara was to be my affirmation that new growth in this 40-years-plus group was taking place."

At the end of one session, the group shared acrostics built around the key word it had identified in the Bible study—LOVE. In this acrostic, the first letter of each line helped to spell the identified word vertically. For example:

L ord, I often fail You.
O ver and over, I'm amazed by Your patience.
V ery often I forget to tell You that
E very part of me praises You.

The next week Barbara didn't even wait for the bell to ring before she announced: "I spent the week writing a poem to God. Do you want to hear it? I went through the whole alphabet twice and each line tells God something I love about Him. I never felt so close to Him before in my life."

"For me, the teacher, it was the breakthrough I needed. It was as if God was patting me on the back. Barbara's response broke the barriers the other students had built through the years. They began talking about their relationship with Christ and the new ways they were experiencing Him. I know some of these people had never dared to share a current testimony with their peers."

God used a simple and creative method to help Barbara discover a bit more about Himself and the enthusiasm He had placed within her.

And God used a teacher who dared to try something new, something that could have failed and made him look silly.

As teachers, we all too often act as our own police. "I couldn't try that," we tell ourselves. "My students wouldn't respond." Sometimes that's true; they won't. But sometimes we're wrong, and God takes our creative teaching efforts and turns them into wonderful learning experiences. Adult students feel the presence of God as they never have before. Teenagers realize that the principles in the Bible can be applied in the hallways and locker rooms of their schools. When children and adults participate in the learning process, truth becomes real in their lives.

The potential within a creative teacher is like a dare—a dare to think new thoughts and try new things, not because newness in itself is something to be coveted, but because he or she is following the Master Teacher who used interactive methods to prepare His small band of students to change history.

Jesus used lecture and storytelling. People listened as He told simple stories filled with eternal truths. He used object lessons. The fig tree withered, and His disciples understood. He used small groups to get His 12 involved in the realities of service. Out they went, two by two, to share what they had learned, to experience rejection and success. He used inductive study. He didn't just announce to His disciples, "Fellows, I am the Son of God. That's it—pure truth, and now let's get on with the miracle of salvation." No, He let them hear and watch and come to the right conclusion for themselves.

Am I right to assume that Jesus, were He among us in human form today, would use all the methods available—roleplay, lecture, storytelling, drama, questions, and on and on—to bring people closer to Him? As student teachers for the Master Teacher, we must seek to reflect His every attribute—not just love and truth and mercy that commonly form the basis for sermon topics, but also creativity. The Creator is our model. We must be creative teachers.[1]

People used to think of creativity as a rare gift given to a few. And it's true that in each century only a few incredibly gifted people appear and change a fundamental assumption about some aspect of life. Few of us will be Albert Einsteins, Ben Franklins, or C. S. Lewises. Yet each of us can be more creative than we now are. We can use our adequate amounts of the stuff of geniuses to put life into our teaching and, with the Holy Spirit's help, to change the lives of those students who are learning with us.

What's unique about creative teachers? They have the ability to make the most of every situation. They have a receptivity to change that allows them to greet new opportunities with glee rather than panic. They are curious.

"When I first started teaching junior highs, I never veered from my lesson plan," a teacher said. "My students were from secular families, most with no exposure to spiritual things. I got very good at telling Bible stories, and they were always enthusiastically received. For most of the teens, the stories were new. In the discussion period that followed the stories, I'd get some difficult questions, questions well-churched kids would rarely think to ask. I'd try to answer, but I'd always leave class feeling as if there were more questions than those that had had time to surface.

"Finally I did what for me was a very daring thing. I decided that for one Sunday I would leave the teacher's guide at home. That Sunday would be totally given over to students' questions. My preparation was prayer. 'Lord, don't let the blank spaces be too long, and help me to come up with some answers.' He answered! This was for me the most daring, most creative thing I've ever done."

When you, the teacher, are creative, you are willing to take that step into the unknown. "What would happen in my class if I asked students to develop a mime on salvation?" "How could I use color and form to take advantage of the artistic gifts of some of my students?" A creative teacher is willing to break out of the mold and risk failure because he or she believes that God can use a new idea.

Creativity is part of the Christian's life, part of our journey with the "wild energies of God. . . . At times in my life . . . the numinous Greatest-than-Self whammed me. Awakened previously untapped energies in me. Set me on a 'wild journey' through uncharted wilderness."[2]

BREAKING PATTERNS

"But we've always done it this way" may be the ultimate creativity squelcher. To infuse our teaching ministries with excitement and perhaps to grow our own share of creativity, we need to be willing to look beyond the "always done." We can get so used to the way things are that we forget there may be new ways that are more effective. It's also easier to stick to old patterns and make those patterns better and better rather than to try anything new.

Long before the century of Columbus, man had developed the skills of seamanship and sail craft. When the sailors of that time looked out upon the seas, what they *saw* was a flat surface and not surprisingly, when cartographers ran out of known world before they ran out of parchment, they inscribed the words "Here Be Dragons" on the ominous blankness. Then came Columbus. As he watched sailing ships disappear over the horizon, he noticed that they didn't just "disappear," but that the hull always disappeared first, then the sails and finally the tip of the mast. In very pragmatic, operational terms, Columbus *saw* the oceans differently.[3]

His vision of what might be redefined the world. Our vision of what might be in our Sunday school teaching situations might, with the Holy Spirit's help, change lives. Start by challenging our assumptions.

The lecture has been your teaching horizon; try a simulation. You're an excellent discussion leader; try a lecture illustrated with transparencies. Somewhere within your identity you hear the whisper, "I'm not creative"; try writing a prayer patterned after one of David's, and encourage your students to follow your lead.

Try breaking patterns. Help yourself and your students learn to see differently. Suppose you're teaching a lesson on communion to senior high students in a Sunday afternoon Sunday school class in your home. List three things you might do in your teaching process that you've never done before:

1. _____

2. _____

3. _____

Hard, isn't it? Breaking any kind of pattern that we're used to and trying to come up with a new pattern is difficult. Consider what happens when you unexpectedly lock eyes with someone across the congregation. Even if you had no intention of doing so, you'll find your eyes returning and locking again and again. It can be embarrassing. It takes a conscious effort to break an eye pattern.

Try this experiment. Look at the picture below until you are able to see both the old woman and the young woman in it. When you have seen both, force your eyes to focus on one and then the other and back again every three seconds. What an effort! If it's that hard to break a pattern of eyes, consider how hard it is to break a teaching pattern you've been working on for years. Hard, but certainly not impossible, and worth the effort.

Assignment: Make a list of your teaching patterns. For example: "I always begin with prayer because it settles my ninth graders down." Or, "I always take a student out to lunch after Sunday's class." Or, "My students almost always find that Bible study is the dullest part of my lesson."

When you've finished the list, check those things that you consider excellent patterns that you wouldn't want to break. For those unchecked things on your list, come up with alternatives. Really stretch.

Where do you look for ideas that might be alternatives to weak or overused teaching patterns? One place is in the other patterns of your life. What would happen if you mixed what you do on Tuesday with what you do on Sunday? For example, how might your visit to the Museum of Science and Industry provide ideas that stimulate your teaching? "I had just finished looking at the exhibits," a high school teacher said. "In the museum store, I was intrigued by some unusual puzzles. One was a wooden, Chinese tangram, a square that had been cut into seven geometric pieces. Those pieces could be arranged in numerous ways to form patterns and symbolic pictures. In my class some of the students are interested in architecture, and I thought they might enjoy using tangram pieces to illustrate some concept in an upcoming lesson. I traced the design and have been using it ever since. I often find myself looking for ideas that can be used in teaching, even when I'm not primarily thinking about lesson preparation."

Jesus was that kind of teacher, too. When He saw a sower, He told the story that illustrated the different ways people respond to His message. He was able to mix the different patterns of His life so they contributed to His teaching.

For us, this is hard work. We don't easily take an idea from the experience part of our lives and insert it into the teaching part, yet that mixing will make our teaching more creative.

We also have to be open to things that aren't immediately familiar to us, if we will be creative teachers. The old patterns seem so much more right. Yet, they might not be; they might be just more familiar.

I was leading the same workshop on mime four different times at a Sunday school convention in Maine. There were five other workshops at the same times, so teachers could pick the four throughout the day that most interested them. My first session was successful. Teachers played with several printed ideas and then went on to develop original symbolic mimes to illustrate salvation. They clapped for themselves and the session when the period ended. The second session wasn't quite as good. The third session was dull. By the fourth workshop, people had run out of familiar areas where they wanted to perfect existing skills. A few came because they didn't want to walk to the far side of the Christian education

16

complex to attend one of the other workshops. A few more came to underline their doubts that mime even belonged on the program of a Sunday school convention: "I'm not at all sure about drama in the church. Would Paul have used it?" "Frankly, I was sure it wouldn't work, and I was right." "Maybe with little kids, but for adults mime would be a waste of time."

The more unfamiliar the pattern, the more suspect it is and, because of our bias, the more unlikely that we'll ever successfully use it. It's important to approach new ideas realizing that our initial mistrust is normal and healthy, but not necessarily justified.

On the other hand, in our effort to be different or creative, we sometimes accept an idea too soon. We're tired, or perhaps it's late Saturday night and we're desperate. No teaching method should be used simply because it fills time. An idea must be tested against our aim for the teaching hour. What do we want to do in this lesson? In what ways will God be glorified through the participation of students in this process? Is it time effective?

Edward deBono, in his book *Lateral Thinking*, charges readers to become more creative in their thinking patterns. Usually we think in predictable steps, following a familiar route. We make this week's lesson like last week's lesson, except a little better. This is good. We want each week to be a more effective teaching/learning experience than the last. DeBono calls this type of thinking vertical thinking. It's the traditional process we're used to, and it's very important.

But, challenges deBono, try a different approach. Try lateral thinking. In lateral thinking the teacher tries to move away from where we've always been in order to examine new ideas we may find.

Try it. The ideas in this book will help. Step away from what you are currently doing and look at each new idea. Play with possibilities. Don't make an immediate judgment: "Yes, that's what I'll do" or "This one won't work at all." Practice lateral thinking. Later, with new ideas in hand, we can pick and choose.

Lateral thinking and vertical thinking are complementary. Some people are unhappy about lateral thinking because they feel that it threatens the validity of vertical thinking. This is not so at all. The two processes are complementary, not antagonistic. Lateral thinking is useful for generating ideas and approaches, and vertical thinking is useful for developing them. Lateral thinking enhances the effectiveness of vertical thinking by offering it more to select from. Vertical thinking multiplies the effectiveness of lateral thinking by making good use of the ideas generated.[4]

THE "DO IT" RULE

"I wish I were more creative" is the consistent cry of teachers, and yet part of the wish is within reach.[5] Do it! Pick new ideas and try them. Learn to brainstorm in groups (and perhaps just with yourself) to generate new ideas. And don't give up too quickly. We grit our teeth, and off we go to try something we've never done before, and anything less than a bell-ringing success scares us out of ever trying again.

All the forms of creativity are hard work. Perspiration oils inspiration. (Clichés become clichés because they contain common truth!) We will get what we deserve from our teaching and our Christian education programs. If we haven't put effort into them, they will not be successful. Our ministries will seem dull. Are you bored with God? Maybe that feeling is indicative of the amount of effort that has gone into developing that relationship. Tired of a difficult teaching assignment? Perhaps the yawns grow from your lack of involvement in the process.

Elizabeth O'Connor, in her book *Eighth Day of Creation*, elaborates on the sweat of creativity:

When we have not exercised our own capacity to create, we do not know what it is to wrestle with the angel, or we believe that once the blessing is given, it lasts forever.[6] . . . If your daily life seems poor, do not blame it; blame yourself, tell yourself that you are not poet enough to call forth its riches; for to the creator there is no poverty and no poor indifferent place.[7]

The Christian's creativity is developed through spiritual discipline, not through a do-what-the-mood-dictates process. Freestyle skaters may look to people on the rink side as if they were born in their skates, but no one doubts the hours of practice that fill every week. Good teaching doesn't just happen, either. Teachers need to put in their time: developing spiritual discipline, knowledge of the age level, and understanding the teaching process and the rules governing interpersonal relationships.

Creativity is not a synonym for unlimited freedom. This aspect of creativity is not new to Christians. Perhaps better than our secular counterparts, we realize that true creativity through which God will work is found in the disciplines of our faith—in wholehearted surrender to Christ.

CHALLENGE THE FAMILIAR

Most teachers who honestly *want* to teach creatively are on their way. If the desire is there, you can free yourself up to try new things. You can obliterate the familiar and see what emerges.

Try the following assignment just for fun. Its only purpose is to give you practice in letting go of things that are familiar to you and making them unfamiliar, even ridiculous. Your assignment is to think about what would happen if you combined any three pictures on this page to make something totally new. Don't be serious. Yes, creativity is serious business, but being serious about the end result doesn't negate having fun getting to it. For example, suppose I put the paper clip on top of the chair perched on the mountain to create a lightning rod that would protect the whole valley. Challenge the idea that paper clips always have to hold papers together. Remember how Columbus fared when he challenged the *fact* that the fall-off point of the world was just a little west of that last wave!

Changing patterns, challenging the familiar—move from the silly practice to what the concept could mean in our ministry. When we expose our students to our creative attempts in the classroom and in our lives, we encourage them to polish in themselves the reflection of the Creator.

The congregation was seated and worship began. People from one section of the room began reading the Scripture in English; from another corner, people read the same passage in Spanish. A third group read the Bible in their own African tribal language, and from the fourth corner came two men reading in Greek. Slowly the four groups moved toward the center of the congregation, reading as they came. When they reached the center, they raised their hands in praise toward Heaven and in one voice recited the Scripture in English. The choral reading epitomized the challenge to the familiar homogeneous makeup of most churches, and reflected the dreams of this urban congregation: "That people of many nations will worship God together and we will be a model in Chicago of what Christianity can be." It was the most creative, and spiritually significant worship service I'd ever been a part of.

Creativity. It's a gift that we have from God, and it's a gift that we can give back to Him.

ORDINARY IS NOT SO ORDINARY

I've got ordinary creativity. I've given up dreaming of writing masterpieces such as *Old Man and the Sea* and *On His Blindness*. I've almost given up believing I'll write something that makes the impact of *The Gospel Blimp* or forces questions like *A Room of One's Own*. But I've got that spark of creativity. I know it. When the juices are running, I feel it! When the presses are running, because I work near the presses that print much of what I write, I can see it. I believe that with hard work the spark can be fanned. With hard work I can broaden and increase my creativity. Creativity is not only a characteristic of great people, but of every human being.

Sometimes it's easier to affirm that by looking at people we know. Ask: "Who is the most creative person I know, and why?" In one seminary classroom, a student answered my question by pointing to another student. "He is. He used to be in the theater before he decided to be a pastor. He has shown me ways to communicate the Bible that I never dreamed existed."

Answer that question for yourself. For me, the most creative person I've known was my mother.

We had the only basement in town with a life-sized, motorized whale in it. I was with Mother the day she got it. She went into the supermarket and

20

asked the manager what he was going to do with the big fish opening and shutting its mouth over the tuna display. "Don't toss it," Mother begged. "It would make a great visual aid in the story of Jonah." Mother was always looking for better ways to communicate with children—my brother Jim and me, all the neighborhood kids, and the thousands of children across Lancaster County, Pennsylvania, who had been part of her decades of Bible classes.

I don't think she ever thought, "How can I force my kids to use all the creativity God gave them?" She just loved doing fun things with us and watching in wonder when one of us came up with something unexpected. "I'm so proud of you," she would tell my brother after he built one of his amazing creations. "No one else in this family is the least bit mechanical." He would proudly hold her verbal balloon, and the next time my father announced that something couldn't be fixed, Jim would fix it.[8]

LET LOOSE THE LIMITS

Christians are not always viewed as creative people, either by ourselves or the secular world. We tend to limit ourselves and what we are able to do with the talents and gifts God has given.

For example, for years many magazines and Sunday school publications bought their Bible art from a lithograph service. The little line drawings were safe, predictable, and dull. Then one publication decided to try something different. A Jewish artist was hired to illustrate Bible stories. She did an unusual job. The pictures seemed to come alive on the page. But no sooner had Christians opened their first issue than they began to write protest letters. "These pictures look too Jewish," the letters declared. "They don't feel Christian, you know. Some of the people in them aren't smiling." The artist's work went into storage and the conservative readers breathed a sigh of relief; modernism had been stopped.

In the world of art, we have chosen religious propaganda over genuine creative work. Yes, we are interested in pointing people to Christ, but that noble goal gets rather downgraded when we think the Holy Spirit can't work through excellence. We are growing in this area, of course. Today, several decades after the realistic, Jewish Bible art experience, readers are no longer as unwilling to accept the unpredictable.

A second limiting factor to our creativity is the sacred/secular dichotomy that says beauty is different on Sunday than on other days of the week. There is real history, and there is Christian history. There is fiction and Christian fiction (if not in the word's pure form, we at least understand the difference between the two fiction types). We limit our creative people by insisting that orthodox belief be expressed in "orthodox" ways.

This may be one reason that we lose so many of our creative people to the secular world. We still find those who operate in both worlds suspect. Our creativity is stunted because we don't push ourselves beyond our self-imposed limits.

When teens know that their history teacher is finding more creative ways to teach than their Sunday school teacher, they can make assumptions about their God. Consider the attitude expressed by Christian rock star Larry Norman in *Campus Life* magazine. He knows that Christians often take exception to his music. "My primary emphasis is not to entertain. But if your art is boring, people will dismiss your message as well as your art."

Third, our closed system limits our creativity, because we poorly appropriate the truth behind, "Hath God not said." Yes, He has. We do have important defined limits on what we as Christians may do, but we have yet to explore excellences within those limits.

Perhaps a fourth reason why we haven't explored creativity is our apocalyptic view of our time. Remember, there were no sonnets written on the *Titanic*. Yes, these may be the last days. Many believers feel the signs indicate that they are. But it's possible to become too involved with our immediate state of being, instead of the growing state of becoming.

I was 11 years old when Mr. Donner shared in prayer meeting why he wasn't going to repair his back steps. "Yes, they are falling apart, but why should I fix them? The Lord is coming back soon, and then what will the time spent on those steps profit me?" As a child who was always trying to think of reasons why I should not do dishes until later, Mr. Donner's speech made perfect sense. Years passed, and his wife died. He married again, and instead of just fixing the back step, he built the new wife a whole new house! We may find that as Christians on this ship of life we are concerned about clean decks and flying the right flags when we should be preparing to dock in a whole new world that needs to be written, designed, painted, and danced.[9]

1. The Christian educator ought to utilize both methods of impression and methods of expression. Anthony Mustazza explains in his article, "Staff Training: A Case for Modeling" (*Christian Education Journal*, Volume IV, Number 1, p. 56): "Methods of impression are those learning activities which minimize learner involvement. Some methods of impression are lecture, object lessons, and the showing of films and filmstrips. The student's role is to sit, watch, listen, and learn. Methods of expression are those learning activities in which the student's participation is maximized. Some methods of expression are roleplaying, group discussion, and individual and group projects. The student's role is to be involved in learning through speaking, writing, working, or by being physically active. Since pupils learn through

both methods of impression and expression, there is a danger in limiting education to one approach or the other. Both were used in the teaching ministry of Jesus, and are still needed for education in the church today."

2. Ross Snyder, "Religious Meaning and the Latter Third of Life," *Religious Education*, October, 1981, p. 535.

3. Richard Tanner Pascale and Anthony G. Athos, *The Art of Japanese Management* (New York: Simon and Schuster, 1981), p. 19.

4. Edward deBono, *Lateral Thinking: Creativity Step by Step* (New York: Harper Colophon Books, 1970), p. 50.

5. "To be more creative, . . . all we need is a basic understanding of how creativity works—and a real desire to flex our creative muscles. The encouraging message is that you and I can easily become more creative if we simply put our minds to it." David D. Edwards, *How to Be More Creative* (San Francisco: Occasional Productions, 1980), p. 9.

6. Elizabeth O'Conner, *Eighth Day of Creation* (Waco, Tex.: Word Books, 1971), p. 5.

7. Ibid., p. 64. (O'Conner is quoting from Rainer Maria Rilke, *Letters to a Young Poet*, pp. 18-21.)

8. Marlene LeFever, *Growing Creative Children* (Wheaton: Tyndale House Publishers, 1981), p. 10.

9. Special appreciation to Joseph Bayly, vice-president of David C. Cook Publishing Co., for his help in answering the question, "Why are many conservative Christians uncreative?"

CHAPTER 2

The Creative Process

Nothing would be done at all if a man waited until he
could do it so well that no one could find fault with it.
—Cardinal John Henry Newman

For the highly creative, the creative process may lead them into whole
new realms: $E = MC^2$. But each of us, no matter what the level of our
creativity, participates in this process as we plan for an Easter sunrise
service or work on a new idea for a Sunday school class or write a short
article for our church paper.

THE FIVE-STEP PROCESS

Knowing what happens in these steps can keep us from making
mistakes that limit our creativity or becoming frustrated because things
aren't happening the way we think they should, as we sweat and strain
toward our goal. The steps in the process are: (1) Preparation, (2) Incubation, (3) Illumination, (4) Elaboration, and (5) Verification.

(1) Preparation

Preparation is doing the groundwork necessary to becoming a good teacher. We learn how to study the Bible. We develop the technical skills necessary to use a concordance, Bible dictionary, and other study helps. It's the period when we watch other seasoned teachers and note what they are doing right—what things we might want to emulate and what things we think we might do differently.

Preparation isn't easy. Have you heard the quip: "Becoming an effective teacher is simple. You just prepare and prepare until drops of blood appear on your forehead"? Much of this preparation will not come during the hours when you are consciously preparing to teach. It will happen as you expose yourself to all different aspects of life and become aware of how these things may be helpful in teaching. A good teacher has hybrid vigor. He or she might have skills in counseling, listening, dramatic production, storytelling, brainstorming, group process, and organization. Each skill can be part of the preliminary work that will turn a teacher into an excellent teacher. A good teacher is the person who cares enough to work hard to multiply the natural ability God has given.

The most stable generalization about the creative life is that you work hard, probably for a long time. Of course, in working you transform yourself, and what would be hard for others becomes easy for you. Freeman Dyson, the physicist, describes how as an adolescent he discovered calculus and spent the whole summer working like a madman, solving every problem in a big calculus textbook. After that, the calculus seemed to be almost instinctive.[1]

Hard work begins to sound like fun to the prepared creative person. Didactically stated, if you really want to be a creative teacher, you can't limit your preparation to Saturday night. It's life preparation. Every area of yourself will play a part in the building of a good teacher.

A Teacher-Building Test

Evaluate your growth the way you think your students would. Give yourself a 10 for perfection, 9 for excellent, 8 for good, and so on down the line. A 1 would indicate that you feel a need for total improvement in that area. Work on your low scores. It's important for you to know yourself; it's part of your preparation.

MENTAL GROWTH

____ 1. I have many interests.

____ 2. I would describe myself as having a growing mind.

____ 3. I understand the current educational trends and how they will influence the students I teach.

____ 4. I am a good teacher and getting better.

____ 5. I look for new ways to do things.

____ 6. I enjoy thinking about spiritual things and grappling with difficult concepts contained in Scripture.

____ 7. I am a student of God's Word. I am teaching nothing that I'm not attempting to put into practice.

____ 8. I can admit to myself that I am creative.

____ 9. I could list the ten key concerns or problems of the age level I teach. I have informed opinions about each area.

____ 10. I keep up with current events.

____ 11. I know in what areas I'm not growing spiritually.

____ 12. I know how to lead a peer to Christ.

____ 13. I read.

____ 14. Jesus has control of what my mind thinks about in its "down" or fallow time.

____ 15. I respect the age level I teach.

____ 16. I can accept ideas from my students as well as give them.

____ 17. I am doing my best to nurture my students and where appropriate help them develop their spiritual gifts and talents for God's use.

EMOTIONAL GROWTH

____ 1. I am excited about the next five years of my life.

____ 2. I am fun to be around.

____ 3. I like to converse with people my own age.

____ 4. I know how to listen. I can empathize with other people's problems and joys.

____ 5. I have no problems talking with my peers about my relationship with Christ—what He's doing for me and how I'm growing in my understanding of Him.

____ 6. I accept myself as an adult among my students.

____ 7. I am able to admit my weaknesses to myself and, when appropriate, to my students.

PHYSICAL GROWTH

____ 1. I am pleased with the way God made me.

____ 2. I am as physically attractive as possible.

____ 3. My dress reflects my Christianity.

____ 4. I work at being physically fit.

____ 5. My students aren't ashamed of the way I look or act.

SOCIAL GROWTH

___ 1. I get along with my own family members.
___ 2. I have a healthy relationship with my spouse (or if unmarried, my roommate or close friends).
___ 3. I am concerned about my own children.
___ 4. My own children love and respect me.
___ 5. My peers enjoy being around me.
___ 6. I don't have to be the center of attention to have a good time.
___ 7. Christ is part of all my social activities.
___ 8. I am careful to do nothing that would damage the Christian growth of my students.
___ 9. The family God gave me comes before my church activities.

(2) Incubation[2]

In a busy world where Sunday school comes once every week, this incubation or rest period is extremely difficult. This is the time after some preparation when you let your ideas just sit in your head for a while. This is not do-nothing time. The mind is taking those ideas and moving them around, perhaps changing bits and pieces, perhaps adding something you hadn't consciously thought of. When it's time to come back for final planning, the results will be better, more creative, than they would have been had you worked through your planning all at one time.

Practically, this could mean reading through your lesson on Sunday afternoon in preparation for Sunday morning, a week away. You'll know what your curriculum suggests. You'll have the basic outline of the lesson in your mind. You'll know what Scriptures you'll need to study for yourself before you can teach them to someone else. Ask God to help you personalize that lesson so it has the maximum effect on your students and on you. Then leave the lesson alone for several days. Let your preparation slip to the back of your mind. When you come back to thoroughly study the lesson and put together your final plan, you may find that new ideas have come from seemingly nowhere. You've allowed yourself time.

Does this seem like a waste of time? When you've got your books out in front of you, why not do the studying all at once and have it over with? Try a month's experiment in which you allow incubation time. Evaluate the results and make your own decision.

(3) Illumination

This is the *eureka!* stage. After you have allowed your plans and ideas to be worked through on an unconscious level, something very special might happen. In original creativity this stage is absolutely imperative.

Suddenly you know the solution. A light bulb flashes. Or illumination may come in bits and pieces all through the week. But suddenly there is something there that wasn't there before.

Archimedes demonstrated this *eureka* experience. His king gave him the task of determining whether a crown did not, in fact, have more silver than gold in it. In the third century B.C., mathematician and inventor Archimedes had no idea how to solve the problem. The crown, after all, did look like gold. One day, however, as he was taking his bath, he realized that his body displaced a certain amount of water. In a flash he knew how to solve the problem. "Eureka!" he yelled. He would weigh the crown against equal weights of gold and silver and compare the amount of displacement when each was placed in water, and the suspicious king would have his answer.

Carol Orsag Madigan, coauthor with Ann Elwood of *Brainstorms and Thunderbolts: How Creative Genius Works*,[3] was asked in an interview, "Where does the inspiration for creativity come from?"

A variety of sources—from visions, voices, dreams, and drugs to a grapefruit or a migraine headache. In the case of Buckminster Fuller, some toothpicks and dry peas inspired his geodesic-dome designs. When he was in kindergarten, his teacher told the class to use toothpicks and peas to make structures. The other children made rectangular barns and houses. Fuller, who had very bad eyesight and wasn't familiar with the outlines of things, formed a triangle because it seemed very sturdy to him. The teacher made such a fuss over it that he realized he had discovered something important. It later became the basis for the geodesic dome.

Lewis Carroll suffered migraine headaches, which inspired parts of *Alice's Adventures in Wonderland*. For instance, there are quite a few episodes in the story when people change sizes and when a blind spot appears to someone trying to focus his vision. Size distortion and blank-spotting are two classic symptoms of migraine headaches.[4]

In Archimedes' case, he recognized a lucky accident, as did the makers of Ivory soap, when too many air bubbles got into a batch. It floated, users loved it, and the accident is still marketed.

I enjoy writing short stories and occasionally accept an assignment for a Christian publication. The trick is to develop a story line that presents Christian principles as integral to the story, not simply tacked on the story's end or stuck to the story's surface like the dots on inexpensive dotted Swiss fabric. Occasionally when I was driving an hour to work, right between watching the police car in my rearview mirror and stopping at a yellow light I would realize that the story I had intended to write was flawed, and I'd have an instantly formulated solution to the problem. *Eureka!* In a very insignificant way, my mind was following the same creative pattern that Archimedes' mind did. Illumination ended incubation.

Of course this didn't happen with every story, and it certainly won't happen with every Sunday school lesson. But when it does, the results are special. As a Christian I feel that the Holy Spirit works through these special experiences—illumination—and perhaps He chooses to work through us more often when we give Him time.

(4) Elaboration

Now the process is fleshed out. We have our idea and we're going to see exactly how it works. This is the preparation of the complete idea. We write or plan it.

But first, a caution. Sometimes we can be so excited about an idea that we hold on to it too tightly. A creative teacher needs to develop a tolerance for ambiguity. The idea should not be forced into a preconceived mold. Something may happen that almost begs you to take your idea and run a different direction with it.

A teacher decided to use roleplay as part of a lesson on witnessing. Her teacher's guide did not provide a roleplay, so she tried her hand at writing one—a great idea. But as she wrote, her mind went back to the people who had shared Christ with her—how their faces had looked, what their body language had said to her. For example, there had been one lady sitting next to her on the pew. The pastor preached on the importance of sharing faith. At the end of the sermon, the woman had turned to the teacher and without so much as an hello, looked hard into her eyes and barked, "Are you saved?"

"Maybe it would be helpful," the teacher thought, "not to have any words in this practice, but to simply illustrate what we say to people by our body language." She threw away her roleplays and began to reconstruct her idea. She had relinquished some control. It would have been easier for her to say, "Oops! I must get back to this job of writing a roleplay or I'll never be ready for Sunday."

Writers very often report this experience. They'll announce after something is completed, "I didn't intend to have that character play such an important role, but he just ran away from me." If the writer had held on too tightly, she might have called that character a mistake and gone back to the original idea.[5]

(5) Verification

Now is the time, before anyone else sees what you have planned, to look back over what you've done and evaluate it. It's the self-test period, and it will probably lead to some refinement. I had a creative writing teacher who was big on the phrase, "Kill your darlings." What she was saying was that we can sometimes be so uncritical, so in love with our own work, that we skip this verification stage.

For example, you and your team are planning a worship service in which the youth of the church lead. You've outlined the service; everything is planned. But don't skip verification. With your plans in hand, you need to review who is going to be part of the worship experience. What does the group want to happen? Will the planned service accomplish those goals? A creative team needs to answer honestly. No matter how wonderful an idea is, if it won't meet goals, it should be discarded and the process started again.

A skit may be the best skit ever written by two senior high students, but if it doesn't add to the impact of the service, it should be cut. Get rid of irrelevancies and excesses.

TOO SOON IS BAD

Now skip ahead in time. Suppose you have presented a worship service. It was the best you could do and it's over. One of the mistakes we often make is to evaluate too soon. Ten minutes after the service, the team is devastated because, for example, no one in the congregation responded when a student asked for volunteer praise prayers. "If only we hadn't done that. How could we have been so stupid as to assume that people would participate extemporaneously. Let's never try that again." And at this point you limit your creativity.

Wait to evaluate the final product. Wait a week and hear the kids talk about the difference their participation made in their lives. Wait a week and hear how parents felt when they realized that, contrary to what they saw at home, their kids were growing in their understanding of their faith.

I spoke recently on the gifts of the Spirit, a difficult subject made even more difficult because I was speaking to a group of people I knew well. I had no sooner uttered my last word when I was evaluating. I decided that I would never do anything like that again. I was terrible. I had just wasted all those people's time. Several days later, a friend said, "I was listening to the Christian radio station, and a teen called to say he had heard you speak on spiritual gifts. He said you helped him realize that he had been doing nothing to develop the areas in his life he suspected God wanted to use. One of those areas was hospitality, so he spent the afternoon visiting people in the hospital." I soared. One person had been helped and my time was worthwhile. I had evaluated too soon.

31

Another mistake: sometimes we set our expectations so high in our ministries that we end up disappointed and discouraged. There's a hard balance to maintain here. We need to aim a little higher than we can reach in our own strength. This allows God to do wonderful things in our lives and forces us to give Him the credit He deserves. For example, it would be wonderful to set as this year's goal raising the attendance of the college class from 10 to 20, but it would be total discouragement if we set the goal at 75. (With God's help, you just might reach 75, but let Him surprise you so you're not devastated if He doesn't choose this time or place for a miracle.)

Expectations should also be set with God in mind. It's so easy to get wrapped up in self so that the creativity of God never shines through. "I want to have the best Sunday evening youth group this church has ever seen." I may reach that goal, but God may not have been part of the process. And then, what is the worth of all my efforts and pretty displays of human energies?

A third mistake: we get discouraged because we force our work before it is ready. Sunday school teachers have to have a lesson for each Sunday morning, so there are limits to the amount of time they have. But very often, we church people aren't good planners. We set goals and design programs without allowing enough time. Our creativity takes a backseat to the clock when, if we had started earlier, that wouldn't have had to happen. Can it be that we wing it because we feel, but never say, that most Christians don't know the difference between excellent and very good?

A salesman who had been a pastor for five years said, "When I was in the pastorate I could wing it. I knew enough about my subject that if I didn't have preparation time, I could do a snow job on the congregation. But now every word is important. It's a lot harder."

BRAINSTORMING

We work within the community of faith. We set the development of church family as a goal. We each contribute our special functions to the body. If we operate on these premises, it is not difficult to accept brainstorming as one important technique for meeting some of those objectives. Quite often God uses our team efforts in a far greater way than He uses our individual accomplishments.

Brainstorming: we work in small groups of five to ten people who are determined to meet the same goal. It might be to reach the neighborhood for Christ, start a junior high ministry, or provide homes for damaged youth and adults. Our efforts together can be more creative than our individual efforts.

Brainstorming is fun. It separates two brain processes so that neither one is quite as unreachable as before. First, it allows us to deal imagina tively with ideas—lots of ideas—in fact, any silly, half-serious, or totally serious idea anyone cares to throw out to the group. Then it allows us to deal critically as we pick out the idea or combination of ideas that seem most workable in this situation.

In setting up a brainstorming situation, you might want to follow this process, or adjust it to fit your needs.

1. *Pick your people.* In a group that is too small, one person's ideas might become too dominant. In a group that is too large, people may find the numbers intimidating. There are two mind-sets on the preparation of the people who will participate. Some leaders like to give the topic ahead of time so people can think about it. It allows time for incubation to play a part in the creative process. I prefer this approach. Its primary drawback comes when one or two people have spent a lot of time thinking through the issues and getting excited about ways the project might go and others have spent little or no time. Those most involved, especially if they have strong personalities, can dominate the brainstorming and negate its effectiveness.

The second approach is to simply ask people to show up at a meeting. Each knows the topic, but very little planning has gone into the process ahead of time. These types of meetings can be lots of fun but they can add to the time necessary between idea inception and project completion. This second approach makes the purest use of the brainstorming technique.

2. *Each person must know and understand the goal of the group.* A goal can be very specific: To develop ways to raise money for this year's Sunday school mission's project that will depend on the teens' contribu tions rather than their parents'. It can be general: To list ways our church might enlarge its impact in this town.

3. *The process of brainstorming should be explained to everyone in the group.* In brainstorming there is a formal setting; the five to ten people are all together for a specific purpose. Each person brings his or her unique perspective so there will be cross stimulation of ideas. People understand that they will be separating the *quantity* and the *quality* of ideas.

a. *Quantity* At the beginning of the brainstorming process, everyone suggests all the ideas he or she can think of. The idea here is quantity. The challenge is to be as unique as possible. People use one idea to build upon another. A wild idea from one person might spark a tame one by someone else.

During this part of the brainstorming, all judgment is suspended. People should not make statements about the worth of any idea as it

33

relates to the goal. All ideas are of equal worth. The ideas stand alone or become stepping-stones to other ideas. Everyone agrees that for meeting a goal, there are usually dozens of ways to get there. There isn't one right answer. There may be six perfectly effective ways to raise money for missions. It is better to have more ideas than could ever be used than to come to the end of this activity and not have enough.

This imaginative thinking should be fun. In many ways, it's like play. "If we had the whole world of ideas before us, no boundaries whatsoever, what would we do to change our city for Christ?" The process should be unthreatening. Don't be timid. Explore, suggest, dare. Go beyond all your previous ideas. Break some habits. Play. (The telescope and the microscope were at first considered playthings. Who knows what spiritual inventions will come out of this time of play?)

Keep a list of all the imaginative ideas that are suggested. Set a time limit for this time of free thinking—30, 60, even 90 minutes. Then stop.

If possible, break completely at this time and set another time for the last part of the brainstorming process where ideas must be critically evaluated. Some people even find it helpful to have one group of people play with ideas and another group sort them out.

If it isn't practical to have two meetings, at least have a break here for a half hour and don't talk about the project. During this time of rest the brain may come up with a unique idea. Or perhaps the time will allow people to return and look more critically at all the ideas without being hurt by feelings of idea ownership. ("That's my best shot, buster. How dare you say it's totally off target?")

b. *Quality* Now is the time to look critically at what has been suggested. Risk is involved here. So is the possibility for success. When we do not allow ourselves the possibility of failure, the Spirit cannot work in us," said Elizabeth O'Conner in *Eighth Day of Creation*. "We are controlled by perfectionistic strivings that inhibit the mysterious meshing of divergent lines within us. Spontaneity dies and the emergence of the unexpected ceases to be a possibility. We are tied and bound."[6]

During the evaluation, go over the list that was made during the first part of the session. Pick ideas that are possible with a little stretch. Put these into the primary list.

Completely weed out those ideas that couldn't possibly be useful. (Coming up with these ideas wasn't a waste of time. They could very well have been the ideas that sparked some of those on the primary list.)

Start a second list of those ideas that might be helpful later. They might serve as beginning points for the next brainstorming session. By the end of the evaluation session, the group should choose which idea or combination of ideas it will use.

"I'm part of a worship service planning committee," Joyce said. "I meet with a group of church members and the pastor about once a month to talk over ideas that might be helpful in guiding people toward making a response to Scripture and to God. We start by just throwing out ideas. At one planning session, we talked about doing a radio-type drama built around Lewis's Narnia Chronicles; handing out evaluation tests to everyone in the congregation; reading some sections from I John using a choral reading to emphasize the book's symphonic outline. The list went on and on. Most of us would have had to give up our jobs and devote our full time to implementing some of the ideas, but we finally hit on exactly the right way of saying to the congregation: 'We're here to worship God; let's move toward Him.' "

Because Joyce and her group are actively involved in brainstorming, the worship in her church remains fresh, unusual, and God centered. "I don't feel so much like a one-man show," her pastor admitted. "I've got a group of people who are committed to helping me."

What happens if you don't have a group to help you with brainstorming? Do it by yourself. Just sit at a table and list ideas as they occur. Don't evaluate the ideas or make plans to implement them. Set a time limit for yourself. If you don't, you will quickly write all the ideas you have and assume you have found all the ideas that are possible. Commit yourself, for example, to about 45 minutes for the idea search. Stick with the process. When the time is up, take a break, a day or two if possible. Then return to make the necessary selections.

1. Howard Gruber, "Breakaway Minds," *Psychology Today,* July 1981, p. 69.

2. D. N. Perkins in *The Mind's Best Work* (Cambridge: Harvard University Press, 1981) examines a number of accepted propositions about creativity and suggests revisions. His arguments merit careful consideration but not blanket acceptance. For example: "Proposition: Mental leaps depend on extended unconscious thinking. During the experience we call a mental leap, the results of that thinking suddenly become conscious" (p. 50). "Revised proposition: Extended unconscious thinking does not occur. Deferring a troublesome problem and returning to it later occasionally helps for reasons that have nothing to do with extended unconscious thinking" (p. 57).

3. Ann Elwood and Carol Orsag Madigan, *Brainstorms and Thunderbolts: How Creative Genius Works* (New York: Macmillan Publishing Co., 1984).

4. Cheryl Lavin, "The Fast Track," in *Chicago Tribune Magazine,* Feb. 12, 1984, p. 6.

5. Novelist Anthony Burgess wrote, "No novelist who has created a credible personage can ever be quite sure what that personage will do. Create your characters, give them a time and place to exist in, and leave the plot to them; the imposing of action on them is very difficult, since action must spring out of the temperament with which you have endowed them. At best there will be a compromise between the narrative line you have dreamed up and the course of action preferred by the characters." Anthony Burgess, "Modern Novels: The 99 Best," in *The New York Times Book Review,* Feb. 5, 1984, p. 37.

6. O'Conner, *Eighth Day of Creation,* p. 48.

CHAPTER 3

The Creative Person

Often the Creator takes us where we do not want to go, trampling over our stereotypes in an effort to show us what we have not seen before.

—Elizabeth O'Connor

"Who wants to waste a Saturday at the Contemporary Art Museum?" a senior high fellow asked his Sunday school teacher. In spite of his protests, the group decided the museum trip was better than no class event at all. The 15 teens lived in a middle-class neighborhood about 45 minutes away from one of the best museums in the country, but none of them had ever been there.

Some of the kids were bored by the museum, but most were delighted with the participative art that was on display. The most popular activity was to sit at a card table that was actually a movie screen. The tabletop film showed a meal being eaten. Students sat at the table as if they were participating; the screen showed a hand move the fork and a bit of mashed potatoes disappeared. Not great art, but an interesting experiment. Three of the boys in the class entered a film-making class at their high school the following year, wrote and acted in their own half-hour film, and sponsored a class meeting to show the finished product. Maybe five years from now, they will be doing innovative things in Christian video. But without exposure, possibilities are never birthed.

Silvano Arieti in his book, *Creativity: The Magic Synthesis*, suggests possible characteristics present in a society that are likely to promote creativity among its people.[1] An openness to new experiences, like a Saturday at a contemporary art museum, is one of those characteristics.

When the following characteristics are true of a society, it tends to grow a large number of geniuses of the first rank, many more than can be explained by simple genetic factors. Some of these characteristics cannot be controlled by a society; they either exist or they do not.

GROWING CREATIVE CHRISTIANS

Apply Arieti's list to the Christian society, both families and church, and we may increase the possibility of developing creative people who set as their highest goal the desire to excellently glorify God. As Arieti has said for society at large, some of these factors cannot be controlled. However, as we look at them, they provide possible answers to some of our more difficult questions about how to foster creativity.

(1) Exposure

In order for our children and our students to be creative, they must have cultural and some physical means available to them. In addition, they must be open to that stimuli.

If a person has never seen a creative teacher or read a book on creative teaching, it is unlikely that the person will become a creative teacher. If a student has never seen a mime, that person will probably never develop one to the glory of God. If great paintings remain outside a Christian's world, that person will probably not paint pictures that give the world a new understanding of its condition without God.

If we adults aren't open to the creativity in our world, we stifle it in our children. One young man decided to go to Bible school instead of accepting the scholarships in art that had been offered by two secular schools. "For me, it was the wrong decision, made from a position of guilt rather than from a desire to develop as a unique Christian. I realized my mistake when I asked for permission to attend the ballet. It was denied. 'You're not a music major. Why would you want to attend the ballet?' I left the school, and quite honestly, left God, too. If music and form belonged exclusively to the secular world, then so did I. I was almost 30 before I realized my mistake."

Money plays a role in our exposure to the cultural experiences around us. For example, it costs to get into a museum. Paper and paints are expensive. Special classes add to the expense. Jack's parents were missionaries and had barely enough money to get to the end of the month. "I could tell when things were getting low," he said. "We ate lots of noodles. But I always had paper and crayons, and as I got older, paint. My parents had identified my talent and were doing everything they could to make certain I had what I needed to develop. At the time, I took my supplies for granted. Now I wonder how many of those noodle dinners were the result of my new pad of watercolor paper."

Some areas that the world labels creative are outside the limits Christians should place on themselves. Any form can, when given over to evil, be perverted, and be anti-Christian. It's important to train our children to be discerning. In creative areas this discernment is not easily developed. The Amish community in my hometown of Lancaster, Pennsylvania, does not allow electricity into its homes because the lines are connected to worldly establishments; modernism can lead its children away from the community. But in some Mennonite homes next door to the dark ones, pastors and Sunday school teachers use electricity to study the Word of God. It's important not to label things too quickly. In the area of the arts, some Christians in panic have lived the old cliché and thrown the baby out with the bathwater.

(2) Vision

To grow creative Christians our churches will have to switch their stress from *being* to *becoming*. We are so involved in programs for today and what we are going to do this week, that we forget that we are not permanent residents in the present. We can't get caught up in the gratification and comfort of the immediate, forgetting that we are in the process of building the now and future Kingdom of God. Arieti sounds almost like a preacher when he says: "The creative man is conscious of the fact that creativity is something that grows, has duration, and requires a future as well as the present. . . . A society that promotes nothing but being will lead to decadence and not to growth."[2]

Harmon Smith, a colleague of mine and fellow Episcopal priest, tells of a visit to Dachau, in Germany. Sick from the experience of seeing what Christians did to Jews, he was reflecting on the Holocaust with Pastor Reiger, a member of the Lutheran Confessional Church who had been himself a prisoner at Dachau. He said to Pastor Reiger, "How could this have happened in the land of Luther and Bach?" The old man responded, "That is easy to understand. The Christian church had become concerned with the here and the now, it had lost its visions and forgotten what the Bible teaches—'without a vision the people perish.' But," he continued, "Hitler remembered and he gave our people a vision."[3]

---

(3) Equal access

We must give everyone free access to cultural situations, if our churches are to grow creatively. We dare not discriminate. We grow in challenging situations. These challenges should be as open to men in our churches as they are to women, as open for Blacks as they are for Orientals.

Throughout history men who were unusually creative far outnumbered women. Perhaps women are less creative, or perhaps the end result had something to do with society's unwillingness to allow most women to participate in learning and in cultural situations that would have encouraged them to develop their talents. What a lot our world may have lost because half of its population was not encouraged.

In our churches today, an opposite discrimination may be at work. *Creativity* has become a feminine word. Women are usually thought of as being more creative than men, more at ease sharing their emotions through drama, song, and teaching. Is it unmasculine for a man to have a gift for teaching very young children? "Of course not," we say, but our attitudes don't always back up our words. "Men should teach teens and adults. It's more fitting."

Look a little deeper. Most creative people are both sensitive and independent. In our society sensitivity is a female characteristic, and independence is considered a masculine characteristic. It is possible that the creative girl may seem more masculine than her counterparts and the creative boy more effeminate. Many people who work with adolescents either ignore or try to program these traits out of creative children. So some find their talents, and in fact, their whole selves, unaffirmed by the church. They leave the church, and many more than we like to admit find their affirmation in the artist community within the gay society.

"My junior high teacher kept trying to teach me to throw a ball," one Christian adult in his early forties said. "I wanted to paint murals for the worship service and plan dramas for our class. But somehow those activities weren't treated as important. I knew I was different. I didn't fit. I was the wrong kind of guy. I left the church and spent a decade in the homosexual community. With my conservative church background and the constant reminders by my parents, I knew what I was doing was wrong. But my art was more important to me than anything else.

40

"Throughout the whole period, a youth leader kept in touch with me. He let me know he was praying for me, even when that was the last thing I wanted to know. Pascal wrote, 'There is a God-shaped vacuum in the heart of every man that can only be filled by God Himself.' That was true for me, and when I got empty enough, I returned. I found a church that respects my gifts, and yes, I do consider the artistic talents God has given me as gifts to be used for Him.

"In my church, I'm currently working with three young men, all with talents in various creative fields, all from church backgrounds, all trying to break away from the gay community that accepts them as valuable people when their own churches did not."

(4) Moderate stress

Freedom, or even retention of moderate discrimination, after severe oppression or absolute exclusion, is an incentive to creativity.

If this is true of a creative society, it could explain the difficult questions being forced on the church and our Bible schools and seminaries by women and minorities. A church ministries student told me, "Would you believe that when this seminary was built a decade ago, there was no ladies' room included? It just never occurred to any of us that such a facility would ever be necessary." An Oriental pastor asked, "Why can't I be a full member of a mission that serves in the country where I'm a national? I'm not angry at God, but I wouldn't extend that statement to include some of the people who claim to be close to Him." As teachers and leaders, we have to listen to the questions—and the pain beyond the questions that are never asked. We need to search Scriptures for principles on which to base decisions, and then we must, in love, lead our students to their fullest possible development of their own creativity.

Why is discrimination a stimulus to creativity? Perhaps one answer is the stress that discrimination adds. Moderate stress is a stimulus to creativity. Place the emphasis on the word *moderate*. Too much stress will hinder creativity, generating fear and rigidity.

(5) Cultural differences

Creativity grows as we expose ourselves to different and even contrasting cultural stimuli.

I went to a church that opened the building for a Vietnamese service on Sunday afternoon. I was on the service planning committee, and it never once occurred to any of us on that committee to combine services one Sunday to see what the two groups could share with each other. Our languages are different, but our God is the same. I suspect we missed out on a growth experience because we were unable to see an exciting possibility.

For the last several years as part of my job responsibilities as a Sunday school curriculum editor I have participated in a Christian education tour with one of the largest black denominations. The only white woman, it was an education for me because I was allowed to be part of worship and learning experiences that were new to me. In many of the teaching meetings, I felt a warmth and acceptance that I don't often feel in my more familiar church experiences. These people are used to punctuating what their speakers say with words of encouragement, and I find that those words, as I am teaching, make me do better than I do! From the back of a room, a woman will say, "Tell me more." Others agree. A man will say, "That's right. That's right." Teaching becomes a pattern of give-and-take. I provide some of the teaching content, and the students provide me with immediate affirmation that what I am saying is helpful.

(6) Tolerance

We need to develop a tolerance for and interest in people who don't believe exactly the same way we do. Here we are not talking theology. We have certain Biblical absolutes, and we dare not develop a tolerance for heresy or watered-down religiosity in our churches. But there are some styles that we know better than others, and they usually seem more right, more Christian.

What can I learn about separation from the world from Mennonite women who wear white prayer caps? Or do I just reject that symbol as odd, old-fashioned? Tolerance means that we develop an inquisitive interest in things that are different from our set patterns.

Franklin was invited by his next-door neighbor to pray at the opening of a Pentecostal service. A Sunday school teacher in a conservative independent church, he was pleased to accept. He rose to give the prayer and the people around him started softly praying aloud. He waited for them to be quiet and they waited for him to get started. Tolerance and appreciation: which prayer approach was more right?

(7) Modeling

Our children and students will become more creative as they are exposed to creative people. In an adult setting, significant people must interact. We work together and the impact of our ministry grows as well. Excitement is contagious; and so, we suspect, is creativity. Arieti points out that people "who reach the rank of genius appear in particularly large numbers in certain periods of history in given geographical areas. This uneven distribution suggests that special environmental circumstances

42

determine the occurrence of creativity, rather than exclusively biological factors."[4] The American anthropologist Kroeber stated that

". . . genetics leaves only an infinitesimal possibility for the racial stock occupying England to have given birth to no geniuses at all between 1450 and 1550 and a whole series of geniuses in literature, music, science, philosophy, and politics between 1550 and 1650." . . . If Kroeber is correct, we must accept the fact that the possibility for the development of a large number of creative people always exists in certain populations.[5]

One creative person draws another and they challenge each other. Genius attracts genius. No, most of us aren't geniuses, but our abilities do grow when we are surrounded by people we can admire and emulate. In the early 1970's a Chicago church illustrated this growth. Circle Church was the dream of its founders, David and Karen Mains. In this church, people wanted to worship God creatively and to help people grow in the identification and use of their gifts. It started with several highly motivated, creative people. Then there were a few more who attracted a few more. People who didn't know how to spell *mime* found themselves excited about writing and participating in a full-length mime drama, *Norman Newcreature*. People who knew that they might someday write, started writing. Musicals were developed. Missionaries went out. Experiments were tried and when they failed, they were evaluated and tried again. Talented person after talented person packed into the rows. Today those creative people are spread across the world. Many are in significant ministries—many more than the law of averages would allow.

Exposure to creative people helps us demand more of ourselves. "My parents believed that we would learn to understand our world better if we met people who lived beyond our little sphere," one missionary teacher said. "So when I was a child every missionary who came through our church was invited to eat or sleep at our home. Usually I loved it because many of these people would talk to me as if I were important. Some would ask me questions and would, in turn, take my answers seriously. I admired some of those people, and I wanted to be like them. They seemed to know what they wanted from God and they were willing to work hard to force His hand. Those people helped me set my sights higher. I was the first one in my family to finish high school, the first to graduate from college, and the first to serve God overseas. My present is due in large part to those encounters my parents so carefully structured."

(8) Honor

If we are to grow creative people in our churches, we must show that we honor creativity. Plato underlines this: "What is honored in a country will be cultivated there." The church must offer incentives and awards for creativity. For some people, we will help them grow when we give them honest praise. For our church professionals, we must pay them enough to allow them the time and means to participate in their own growth.

Praise for the creative person is not just a nice thing to do. It may be imperative. It's not difficult to find examples of people who were fires of activity in the church for several years and then just disappeared as burned-out workers. How could anyone with so much potential just walk away from jobs that need to be done? The answer, at least in part: creative people are often overachievers. What a difference it can make to these people to feel our affirmation and our prayers, and perhaps our cautions when they take on more than they should. Creative people are a valuable church resource, and it's a wise congregation that realizes this resource can either be quickly used up or productively increased.

We might want to consider some ways in which honor would be given to people who are involved in creative endeavors. Would it make sense, for example, to form a high school drama team? Should we offer a church scholarship to a student who chooses to study literature or journalism? Should we set up a task force to brainstorm how to make our corporate times together more meaningful? The list of questions can go on and on.

Will our churches be characterized by creativity? What direction are we heading? Perhaps we are in the process of setting that direction. Many cultures are mixing in some of our churches. People from all races and both sexes are making significant strides. We are learning to enjoy each other and our differences.

I was speaking at a youth workers' convention sponsored by the Seventh Day Adventist Church. As usual, I was wearing earrings, although I certainly would not have worn them if I had known that Adventist women usually do not wear jewelry. I was one of the few women at the convention, so I hadn't noticed how out of place my added sparkle was, until I bent over to say hello to a little child. "What's that?" she asked, pointing at my ears. Her father was embarrassed. "She doesn't see people outside our church very often," he explained. "We're so glad you could be with us for this convention." I was impressed. He could have just as easily said, "And, frankly, we would have enjoyed you a lot more if you had taken the time to find out how we feel about decorated ears." Instead I learned of our differences and felt affirmed. Differences and yet acceptance, a sign of potential creativity.

But there are some negatives when we consider the direction we are heading. Our Sunday school teaching doesn't always reflect the creativity we dream of our students having. We don't plan enough for the future, perhaps because the noise and bright lights of the present distract us. We aren't disciplined in our faith and in the development of our gifts. No real creativity can be developed without discipline. We are losing touch with who we really are—a people set apart by God. We ineffectively fight our assimilation into contemporary society.

Milton Rockmore, in a printed interview with Arieti, asked him how he would assess the direction of our society, and his words carry a challenge for Christians: "I'd say we're in transition and can move either to an historic creative era or decadence. It's up to us. We haven't found the direction yet."

THE CREATIVE PERSON

"Instead of counting sheep," Dale said, "I make up ten-sentence stories. The first sentence has ten words and the second nine and so on to one. I'm not sure that I wouldn't fall asleep faster if I counted sheep, but my stories are so much more fun."

Creative people. It makes sense for teachers not only to cultivate their own creativity, but also to know enough about creative characteristics to be able to spot them in their students and to cultivate them.

Gordon Cosby in his sermon, "The Calling Forth of the Charisma," reprinted in *Eighth Day of Creation*, says:

No matter how much we love a person, accept him, give him support, have warmth and affection for him, no matter how much we help him in so many ways, unless we can actually call him forth so that he is himself exercising the uniqueness God gave him, then the love is incomplete; he is not free, he is less than human.[6]

When we see the possibility of creativity in our students, we must help those people develop. If we don't, we are not fully "teacher."

One of the most universal characteristics of a creative person is curiosity: into everything, questions you wish wouldn't be asked, insights that just don't dovetail with the thought you have been trying to communicate. The creative person is also imaginative. He or she actually cultivates imagination. The creative person is enthusiastic and discerning, knowing what's good about his or her creations and what needs to be rethought. He or she will stick to ideas and productions that personal assessment affirms are worthwhile.

"I remember the person who first named me creative," Richard said. "She was my baby-sitter when I was in my early elementary years. She would encourage me to use scraps of material from her sewing basket to make women's hats. I kept making creations for her until I was in my middle teens. By then I had decided I was pretty good. I once gave her an Easter bonnet, and she wore it to church. Hats weren't in fashion that year, but there she was with an amazing green creation that dipped a little to the right. I was so proud. It took nerve for her to do it, and a massive amount of love. With that kind of backing I wouldn't have dared not to continue in the field of design as an adult."

The creative person has a strong will. This often makes the student hard to teach. Creative people are convinced they know a better way, and it's frustrating for us leaders to admit that they sometimes do.

Howard Gruber, psychologist, has studied the creative lives of scientists of the first rank. His description, of course, applies to the highly gifted, but to a lesser degree to our students, too.

The people I've studied all tend to be strong, robust, energetic. They have an overall sense of purpose, a feeling of where they are and where they want to go. That goal-directedness guides the choice of a whole set of enterprises and dictates which enterprise to focus on at a given time. Creative people have a network of enterprises. They become the sort of people who can easily handle seemingly different but intimately related activities. They become highly skilled jugglers. Of course, it's not all entirely conscious, but a great deal of it is. . . .

Creative people have a sense of problem bracketing. That is, they know that when an issue is fundamental but cannot be settled that they must put it aside—bracket it—at least for a while, and concentrate on the work that can be done. . . .

Taking a step into the unknown is serious business, but exhilarating, too. Over and over again, I discover that creative people love their work and would not dream of doing anything else. They have very high levels of aspiration, and it excites them to feel they are doing great things.[7]

Now, go back and read Gruber's statement with yourself in mind. How many of his descriptive points could be describing you as teacher? You know something is happening in the lives of most of those students, and you have an inner excitement that makes all the hours of studying worthwhile. You wouldn't want to be doing anything else in the church. Are you a problem bracketer? Every teacher eventually has a student who just doesn't respond. We work and pray and nothing happens. Perhaps at this point the bracketing abilities of the gifted can be a clue to the rest of us. One unresponsive student doesn't mean we haven't been effective. That student should not cause us to turn away from the assignment God has given us, the assignment we love. Instead we continue praying—not only for that student, but also for our own development as a teacher. And we move ahead. When God's time is right and that student is willing, something wonderful will happen.

We may not be around when that time comes. Joseph Bayly, author and Sunday school teacher, tells a story of a woman who had gone through her Sunday school years without having it touch her much at all. No doubt her teachers felt they had failed in their work with her. But as a young adult she suddenly faced an experience that she couldn't handle by herself. "I came to the end of my rope," she said. "Suddenly I remembered some of the things my Sunday school teachers had shared with me all those many years ago, and Christ became real to me. How I wish I could find those old teachers and give them a big thank-you hug."[8]

Creative students are independent in their thinking. They will not bend to the opinion of others. They enjoy being different. That marked independence often makes them leaders. This lack of bending adds some stress to their lives—and often to their teachers' lives as well. However, this stress is one of the spurs to creativity.

"When I have a creative student, I have to bend the rules, and sometimes common sense, in order to meet his or her special needs," a junior high teacher said. "I had a brilliant student in seventh-grade Bible and English class at the Christian school where I taught. He would get straight A's and was so well liked by his peers that he had been class president for the last three years. However, he flunked true/false tests. Really failed. Hardly any answers would be right. The first time this happened I thought he was trying to be funny. Seventh graders can have weird senses of humor. His face when he picked up his paper, however, let me know that humor wasn't involved at all.

"When he flunked the second test I realized that his thinking process was different. If I really cared for him as a student and truly affirmed the special gifts God gave him, I had to make some adjustment. So after school, he and I talked through all the questions he had gotten wrong. He would start with the answer I wanted. However, he would then look at it from a different perspective. That could mean the statement was just a little false. Maybe I, the teacher, had meant for him to add a little phrase to the end which would make it totally wrong. He attributed a lot more thought to my test development than I had. I excused him from true/false tests. How much preparation for life does a true/false test give, anyway!"

Creative people see things as other people do, but they also see things as others do not. And they are likely to say so.

Creative people daydream a lot—moving far out in their thoughts and coming back again, sometimes bringing with them the ideas and possibilities that were part of their minds' freedom. It can be frustrating to the teacher when the daydreamer chooses the middle of the Sunday school hour to disappear mentally. It's hard to say as we're teaching, "Don't worry; Annette will return." But it's true. Our creative students are less rigid and

47

less controlled than others, and it's fun when we are able to capture their fantasy thoughts and direct them back toward the lesson. The rest of our students will be raised a little in their creative consciousness because they have been exposed to the few. Of course, it's disconcerting to feel we've lost students while we're teaching. But moving with them, allowing them to operate in the ways God made them, is worth the effort.

Creative students won't accept your authority as easily as most of the other students. They often see authority as conventional rather than absolute. They want reasons for rules, and they delight in finding loop-holes in that reasoning. Many will do the same thing with Scripture, and with theology. They challenge us. Right in the middle of the Christmas lesson, for example, with the class filled with visitors, Mr. Divergent Thinker drawls, "What logical person could believe the Incarnation?" You panic as you try to put together all the points that restructure the question into "What logical person would not?" Where is C. S. Lewis when you really need him? More love and modeling than polemic is required with these thinkers. They must accept God's truths if they are to contribute to His work. And sometimes that means accepting one of the difficult answers we give: "This is truth, this is absolute, because God has said it."

Many creative students have a good sense of humor. They value what is funny and what can be punned or twisted in interesting ways. The story is told of Spurgeon who would share jokes or humorous anecdotes as part of his sermons. Although he made his point, from time to time his board would question the use of humor to communicate the morning message. "Ah," he said, throwing his head back and roaring, "if you only knew how much I restrained myself, you would praise me rather than censor me."

TWO CREATIVE TYPES

Most creative students you teach will be the type that Abraham Maslow calls self-actualizing. They are fun to be around. They enjoy life and are often childlike and fresh in the ways they approach life. They tend to be natural leaders—filled with energy and daring. They aren't hard to pick out of the group and encourage. They are often the class leaders, perhaps the ones with which teachers have Timothy relationships, special mentoring friendships in which the students are given more of the teacher's time. More is expected of these students, and they deliver.

But a few of your creative students may not fit this pattern. They are easily missed and perhaps even avoided. Maslow calls this group special talent people. These creative students are not at ease with themselves. They often isolate themselves from the group. They exercise a high degree of control over impulse, but not over their imaginations.

48

When we have students we believe fit into this category, we must find ways for them to be accepted by the group and to be affirmed as people. They will have little trouble developing their areas of high creativity. In fact, they will far surpass their teachers and peers. However, they will need our help as they work to become more at ease with themselves and with others. Perhaps with special talent people, the following ideas will be helpful to the teacher:

- Establish a friendship with this person. It won't be easy, and very often it won't be all that enjoyable for you. He or she may have difficulty with conversation, may not trust you, may feel you're only trying to do your Christian duty.

- Let that person know you are aware of his or her talent. Affirm the student. Sometimes the talent will be obvious—for example, the teen who does nothing but practice the piano. She plays for all the youth meetings and perhaps for the worship service. Every waking moment she chooses to practice. It's an obsession, an escape for her. Careful here. In our ministries excellently skilled people are a real asset. Who doesn't want a terrific pianist in the group? We can use this person's skills to the advantage of our ministries and not accept our responsibility to help this young person grow in other life areas.

We need to work toward helping special talent people to like themselves and trust others. This must happen if they are ever to grow to spiritual maturity. Of primary importance is their relationship with God, but their relationship with their peers is also important. We all grow horizontally and vertically; the special talent people may need your help in both directions.

- Extra prayer time for this student is time well spent.

These people may feel pain, annoyance, and fear about life rather than excitement and joy. Those feelings of alienation may drive them on to greater achievement in their creative fields, but they will not be whole people.

WHO TOOK THE 90 PERCENT?

Little children are so creative. Why do so few grow up taking with them those vast reservoirs of thought, idea, and play? Our society and our parents, and even our own policing of our thoughts are partly to blame. Perhaps we in the western world are too action and product oriented to allow time for creativity to develop. As a people we have difficulty allowing people to be creative—no matter what we say about respecting or even coveting the quality.

I remember being amazed when a friend told me he was paid to play with a computer. He didn't have to program anything. He didn't have to discover anything. He just played with possibilities all day long, and at the end of the week, the lab gave him a fat paycheck. I thought, "What a waste when he could actually be doing something!" However, it's thinking like this that sets limits.

Perhaps as many as 90 percent of all children are highly creative until they reach the age of five. Many continue to develop in creative abilities from kindergarten through third grade with boys taking the creative lead. There is a sharp decline between the third and fourth grades. Many students give up their creativity in the fourth grade and never reacquire it. The next decline occurs in seventh grade, after gains for some in fifth and sixth grade. The four years following seventh grade can also be characterized by some growth.[9]

That first decline comes when children enter school. For the first time they have to conform to the classroom. For the first time, a group of people have to work as a team. They are leaving the carefree days of childhood and entering their primary stage of growth.

It would be easy to blame the school systems for this loss of creativity, but that would be too simplistic. In order for education to take place, there must be a certain amount of discipline. We do operate, not as individuals on life islands, but as a society. Perhaps we can find ways that will limit this loss.

During the elementary years, the home seldom does a better job than the school in holding onto children's creativity. Parents tend to worry if their children are different from their peers. It's easy for parents to be more concerned about external success and popularity than about inner growth and creativity. There's a lively tension between what is creative and what is practical.

Brian loved to take things apart. From the time he could crawl, his trucks never remained the way they had been when he was given them. Wheels were taken off and exchanged. Strings were tied here and there. Tinkertoys stuck out in amazing places. As he continued to grow so did his augmenting—and so did his father's consternation. Brian worked on old cars people would give him, even before he was old enough to drive. He played with electricity, with pumps, with machines that made gurgly noises in the night. The basement and the littered backyard were his world. And through it all, his father would protest: "Nobody else takes things apart like you do. You're destructive; they are never the same again. How could you ruin that TR-4 by souping it up so high that it can't be run on the highway?" Brian had the fortitude that only very creative children do. His father worried about the things he ruined, but he delighted in the creation of things that never were before and probably never would be again. Now, as an adult, he holds a responsible job with a computer company, and his own backyard is still filled with ideas that are in various stages of development. Now his father calls Brian to come fix anything that breaks, and Brian often hears his father brag to others about his achievements. Someday a person like Brian may discover a way of holding our complex world together a bit longer.

For most children, when a worried parent says verbally or with actions, "Why can't you be like other children?" the child will conform. A measure of creativity will be lost.

The sharp decline in creativity that comes between the third and fourth grades arrives at the beginning of the preadolescent stage. Children are beginning to strive for peer acceptance, to do anything to be like their friends. They want to dress, walk, talk, and comb their hair exactly like everyone else. The stretch to remain creative, which in most cases means to be different, is just not worth it for most children. The decline at the beginning of the adolescent period comes because of the increased tension to be liked and accepted by peers. With this is the added stress of handling all the new things that are part of this stage of development—the opposite sex, emotional fluctuations, getting acquainted with this new self.

HELP OUR STUDENTS BE MORE CREATIVE

What can a teacher do to help students use the creativity they have and encourage them to stretch and perfect?

● First, *give your students a model of a creative growing adult.* If we are not growing ourselves, we have a lot of nerve expecting students to aim high. Try a new approach to Bible study and share it with the class. Learn something new; do something different.

Dr. Charles Bradshaw, chairman of the Department of Christian Education, Talbot Theological Seminary, teaches a course in creativity. As part of the course requirements, students must try something they have never tried before. "Stretching is difficult," Bradshaw explained, "and yet it's imperative if they are going to go beyond where they currently are. I've been amazed at some of the ways my students fulfilled their assignments. One man checked himself into a mental hospital for a weekend. Several students went skydiving. Another student started working on his real estate license. We are not all challenged by the same things. But in each challenge we personally accept, our horizons are enlarged."

Trying new things will help you remain open and growing. There are other ways to grow, as well. Allow yourself some time alone. Our busy lives program out quiet time. Make an appointment with yourself, for

51

example, to do nothing for ten minutes a day. Let your mind float. Where does it go? What dreams float by? Consider what might be. Play with building pictures from clouds in the sky. It doesn't matter so much where your mind goes during this quiet time. Just get in touch with what is in you: without kids or spouse or job or housework or television or background music! We all use those things to keep us from thinking, perhaps because free thinking can lead us into areas that challenge us.

Keep in touch with your emotions. It will help you be more empathetic toward your students, and more important, it will keep you a complete person. "I remember thinking when I was in seventh grade," said Marilyn, "that adults seemed to forget how things were when they were my age. I decided right then that I would be different; I wouldn't forget. I kept that promise to myself, and even today nearly three decades later, I can go back to those old feeling tapes and play back the emotions I felt as an adolescent. I remember how I felt when one of the boys in my class offered to illustrate the first book I wrote. I remember the anger I felt at a teacher when I realized that she didn't read the spelling sentences that we wrote on assignment each week. I would put mine into a story, and for the longest time I couldn't understand why she didn't say anything about my achievement. When I realized why, I never liked her again."

"I work with kids in my church, and they don't have the same experiences I had," one teacher said. "But they seem to have the same emotions. I don't tell them the stories of my past very often, but remembering the real feelings they are having as part of their current stories makes me love and understand them better."

A creative teacher is disciplined. It is possible to wing it from time to time. Most of us bring a lot of knowledge to our classrooms. But holy shoddy is still shoddy. Sunday school teaching is hard work. We can't wear that title honestly without also accepting the sweat that goes with it.

● Second, *affirm differentness in the classroom.* It's a lot easier to teach students who are normal, predictable—but not half as much fun. The fact that a little stress makes people more creative applies to teachers, too. Those creative teens can add just enough stress to the teaching situation so that we will grow as we deal with them.

● Third, *don't tie achievement to affirmation.* Everything a creative person does won't be creative. Brian really did ruin an expensive TR-4, but in the process he learned how to do things that would be helpful in his next tinkering trip into the unknown. He needed to be affirmed in his learning process, not necessarily praised for treating a car as a plaything.

You don't want your students to be doing things simply for your affirmation. If they are not gaining some personal satisfaction from their

52

trips into the unknown they may not continue when you are no longer part of their world.

You want your affirmation to mean something. If you gush over the wonder of something both you and the students know is second best, you damage your credibility. It's also possible that your students will feel that if second best pleases you all that much, why work hard to do their very best?

● Fourth, *make times with your students as much fun as you can.* Vary the way you teach. Some students learn best by doing, others by hearing, some by talking themselves. So if you vary your methodology, you'll keep all your students actively involved.

And there is value in variety simply for its own sake. Industry did some experiments on ways to increase production. They added music and production went up. They added extra lighting and production went up. They took away music and production went up. They lowered the lighting and production went up. It became apparent that it wasn't the individual changes that were making the difference. It was change itself.

So break habits. If you've never given a good lecture, plan one. If you have never dared to do anything with roleplay, structure one. Habit and predictability in your teaching will lock your doors to creativity.

You certainly won't be equally good at each method you try. You may decide that you'll just never give a good lecture. (It's easy to give a poor one, but the real thing is hard work.) You may decide that no matter how excellent it would be for some teachers to use a color-inspired Bible study, you have no color sense. The whole idea—even after you've tried it twice—just isn't right for you. Fine; move on to something else.

Learning is rarely easy. We're not trying to turn our one-hour session into playtime. But learning can be diverse, effective, and often fun.

One way to increase the enjoyment of your students is to try unusual assignments, both in class and out. One teacher during a unit on parables encouraged her students to write parables. She gave the eighth graders several examples of contemporary parables, including one that she had written. A number of the girls picked up their teacher's challenge and wrote original parables. Here's one written by a 13-year-old daughter of missionaries to Japan.

YAKE IMO MAN

(Yake imo are the Japanese words for hot sweet potatoes.)

The evening was dark and cold, but in spite of this, the yake imo man was pulling his cart down the narrow street. "Yake imo! Yake imo!" he called.

A few people who heard his cry came to try his hot, delicious sweet potatoes. Those who came found them so good that they took extra potatoes back to their families and friends.

But most people weren't interested. Some said, "I can do without yake imo this time. Maybe some other day." Others said, "I want the potatoes, but it's too cold to go to the trouble tonight."

The yake imo man kept calling until he was sure everyone on the street who was interested had gotten potatoes. Then he turned and started down a new street calling, "Yake imo! Yake imo!"

She did it! She wrote a parable illustrating the responsibility Christians have to share the Gospel, no matter what. And now it would be a little more difficult for her to say about future ideas, "No way! I could never do that." I suspect the student, Melody Jamisson, got her missionary parents involved in the completion of this parable. Perhaps together they were reaffirmed in the special, difficult job God had given them to do for Him in Tokyo.

- Fifth, *encourage difficult, unusual questions.* Respect them.

I was teaching a course in creativity, and after the third or fourth question from students, I realized that each was prefacing his question or opinion with an apology. For some in the predominantly male class, I was the first female teacher they had had for a graduate course. "I don't mean to challenge what you said, and please correct me if I'm wrong, and I certainly wouldn't for a minute disagree, but . . ." Finally I knew I had to say something after this statement: "I don't think that everyone has some creativity," the student began, but then came the extender: "Please don't take this personally, and I'm sure you based your comment on good information, and actually you're probably right, maybe"! His opinion was good and short, but he certainly couched it in so much fluff that the essence was almost lost. It was time for my mini-lecture on the value of good questions. No teacher of a class that doesn't ask difficult questions is totally satisfied that he or she is teaching, or that the class is thinking.

After that same class a student came up. "Please forgive me for my comment and I know you're probably in a hurry to get somewhere, but . . ." I groaned. "But I'm a lot more at ease in a course where we get a list of stuff that is true and we just memorize it. Some of what you're expecting us to do I've never dreamed of doing. I'm afraid I'll flunk."

Now there was an honest student. If we teachers do not encourage independent critical thinking, we are limiting our students, whether they are in seventh grade or graduate school. We are also limiting the ways they are able to interpret Christ to their worlds. (The student got a B-.)

There are only two times when I don't want questions, and both are a discredit to me as a teacher. The first is when I'm not totally prepared, and I'd prefer my students not know that. The second is when I'm taking a little ego trip. Something inside me says, "I've got all the answers, and I'm now going to dump them on you. Sit still, take notes, and soak up all the wonderful knowledge I'm about to present."

● Sixth, *watch for blocks* that we and our students use to keep ourselves from being as creative as possible. The following nine blocks are suggested by Don Koberg and Jim Bagnall in their book *The Universal Traveler*.[10] As you read, check those you use and write the initials of any students you currently have whom you suspect is stymied by the block.

☐ Fear of making mistakes.
☐ Fear of being seen as a fool.
☐ Fear of being criticized.
☐ Fear of being alone. A person with an idea toward change can stand in a very empty spot.
☐ Fear of disturbing traditions and making changes.
☐ Fear of being associated with taboos. "Does drama really belong in the church?"
☐ Fear of losing the security of habit.
☐ Fear of losing the love of the group.
☐ Fear of truly being an individual dedicated to God.

"Being afraid is both natural and normal," say Koberg and Bagnall. "It would be a mistake to think we could eliminate it altogether, nor would we want to. Fear is simply the reluctance and anxiety to deal with the unexpected, or the result of lack of preparation to deal with the expected. But fear deters progress toward creativity through misdirecting our energy and by restraining us from the action necessary to its development. But changing our focus from 'I don't want to be wrong' to 'I will try to be more right,' the positive point of view can overcome our fear block to creativity."[11]

● Finally, *creative teachers believe they have something to offer.* We are important. God can certainly use us.

HOW CREATIVE ARE YOU?

No creativity test can perfectly identify the amount of creativity you have. Or if it could tell you where you are today, it would not predict where you could be next month as you work with the skills God has given you. Still, tests can be fun.

"How Creative Are You?"[12] is a helpful exercise, if (and that's an important *if*) you don't take the results as definitive. The answers to the test are found on page 60.

HOW CREATIVE ARE YOU?

Researchers have developed a number of tests to determine whether someone is predisposed to think creatively. The following test was designed by Eugene Raudsepp of Princeton Creative Research, Inc., after studying characteristics of highly creative people. To take the test, indicate after each statement whether you: (A) agree, (B) are in-between or don't know, or (C) disagree. Answer as accurately and frankly as possible, trying not to guess how a creative person might respond. There is no time limit.

___ **1.** I feel that a logical step-by-step method is best for solving problems.

___ **2.** It would be a waste of time for me to ask questions if I had no hope of obtaining answers.

___ **3.** I always work with a great deal of certainty that I'm following the correct procedures for solving a particular problem.

___ **4.** I concentrate harder on whatever interests me than do most people.

___ **5.** When trying to solve a problem, I spend a lot of time analyzing it.

___ **6.** I occasionally voice opinions in groups that seem to turn some people off.

___ **7.** I spend a great deal of time thinking about what others think of me.

___ **8.** Complex problems and situations appeal to me because I find them challenging.

___ **9.** It is more important for me to do what I believe to be right than to try to win the approval of others.

___ **10.** People who seem unsure and uncertain about things lose my respect.

___ **11.** More than other people, I need to have things interesting and exciting.

___ **12.** On occasion I get overly enthusiastic over things.

___ **13.** I often get my best ideas when doing nothing in particular.

___ **14.** I rely on intuitive hunches and the feeling of "rightness" or "wrongness" when moving toward the solution of a problem.

___ **15.** I sometimes get a kick out of breaking the rules and doing things I'm not supposed to do.

___ **16.** I like hobbies that involve collecting things.

___ **17.** I feel I have capacities that have not been tapped as yet.

___ **18.** Daydreaming has provided the impetus for many important projects.

___ **19.** I like people who are objective and rational.

___ **20.** I see myself as more enthusiastic and energetic than most people I know.

___ **21.** I can get along more easily with people if they belong to about the same social and business class as myself.

___ **22.** I have a high degree of aesthetic sensitivity.

___ **23.** I have a highly developed capacity for self-instruction.

___ **24.** I like people who are most sure of their conclusions.

___ **25.** Inspiration has nothing to do with the successful solution of problems.

___ **26.** When I'm engaged in an argument, the greatest pleasure for me would be for the person who disagrees with me to become a friend, even at the price of sacrificing my point of view.

___ **27.** I tend to avoid situations in which I might feel inferior.

___ **28.** In evaluating information, the source of it is more important to me than the content.

___ **29.** I resent things being uncertain and unpredictable.

___ **30.** I like people who follow the rule "business before pleasure."

___ **31.** One's own self-respect is more important than the respect of others.

___ **32.** I feel that people who strive for perfection are unwise.

___ **33.** I prefer to work with others in a team effort rather than solo.

___ **34.** I believe that creativity is restricted to specialized fields of endeavour.

___ **35.** It is important for me to have a place for everything and everything in its place.

___ **36.** Sometimes I'm sure that other people can read my thoughts.

___ **37.** The trouble with many people is that they take things too seriously.

___ **38.** I have a great deal of initiative and self-starting ability.

___ **39.** I have retained my sense of wonder and spirit of play.

___ **40.** I can maintain my motivation and enthusiasm for my projects, even in the face of discouragement, obstacles, or opposition.

___ **41.** People who are willing to entertain "crackpot" ideas are impractical.

___ **42.** I'm more interested in what could be rather than what is.

___ **43.** Even after I've made up my mind, I often can change it.

___ **44.** I enjoy fooling around with new ideas, even if there is no practical payoff.

___ **45.** I think the statement, "Ideas are a dime a dozen," hits the nail on the head.

___ **46.** I don't like to ask questions that show ignorance.

___ **47.** Once I undertake a project, I'm determined to finish it, even under conditions of frustration.

___ **48.** I sometimes feel that ideas come to me as if from some external source and that I am not directly responsible for them.

___ **49.** There have been times when I experienced an "avalanche" of ideas.

___ **50.** I try to look for ways of converting necessities to advantages.

___ **51.** It is wise not to expect too much of others.

___ **52.** I am able to more easily change my interests to pursue a job or career than I can change a job to pursue my interests.

___ **53.** Many creative breakthroughs are the result of chance factors.

___ **54.** People who are theoretically oriented are less important than are those who are practical.

___ **55.** I feel it is important to understand the motives of people with whom I have to deal.

___ **56.** I can see things in terms of their potential.

___ **57.** When brainstorming in a group, I am able to think up more ideas more rapidly than can most others in the group.

___ **58.** I am not ashamed to express "feminine" interests (if man), or "masculine" interests (if woman), if so inclined.

___ **59.** I tend to rely more on my first impressions and feelings when making judgments than on a careful analysis of the situation.

___ **60.** I can frequently anticipate the solution to my problems.

___ **61.** I often laugh at myself for my quirks and peculiarities.

___ **62.** Only fuzzy thinkers resort to metaphors and analogies.

___ **63.** When someone tries to get ahead of me in a line of people, I usually point it out to him.

___ **64.** Problems that do not have clear-cut and unambiguous answers have very little interest for me.

___ **65.** I usually work things out for myself rather than get someone to show me.

___ **66.** I trust my feelings to guide me through experiences.

___ **67.** I frequently begin work on a problem that I can only dimly sense and not yet express.

___ **68.** I frequently tend to forget things such as names of people, streets, highways, small towns, etc.

___ **69.** I have more capacity to tolerate frustration than does the average person.

___ **70.** During my adolescence I frequently had a desire to be alone and to pursue my own interests and thoughts.

___ 71. I feel that the adage "Do unto others . . ." is more important than "To thine own self be true."

___ 72. Things that are obvious to others are not so obvious to me.

___ 73. I feel that I may have a special contribution to give to the world.

___ 74. I find that I have more problems than I can tackle, more work than there is time for.

___ 75. Below is a list of adjectives and terms that describe people. Indicate with a check mark *ten* (10) words that best characterize you.

___ energetic	___ quick	___ alert
___ persuasive	___ efficient	___ curious
___ observant	___ helpful	___ organized
___ fashionable	___ perceptive	___ unemotional
___ self-confident	___ courageous	___ clear thinking
___ persevering	___ stern	___ understanding
___ forward-looking	___ thorough	___ dynamic
___ cautious	___ impulsive	___ self-demanding
___ habit bound	___ determined	___ polished
___ resourceful	___ factual	___ realistic
___ egotistical	___ open-minded	___ modest
___ independent	___ tactful	___ involved
___ good-natured	___ inhibited	___ absentminded
___ predictable	___ enthusiastic	___ flexible
___ formal	___ innovative	___ sociable
___ informal	___ poised	___ well-liked
___ dedicated	___ acquisitive	___ restless
___ original	___ practical	___ retiring

ANSWERS TO CREATIVITY TEST

Scoring instructions: To compute your score, add up the points assigned to each item. For each question, the first value is for A (agree), the second is for B (in-between or don't know) and the third is for C (disagree).

1. -1, 0, 2,	19. -1, 0, 1	37. -1, 0, 1	55. 2, 0, -1
2. 0, 1, 2	20. 2, 1, 0	38. 2, 0, -1	56. 2, 0, -1
3. 0, 1, 2	21. -1, 0, 1	39. 2, 0, -1	57. 2, 0, -1
4. 3, 0, -1	22. 3, 1, 0	40. 2, 0, -1	58. 2, 1, 0
5. 2, 1, 0	23. 2, 1, 0	41. -1, 0, 1	59. 1, 0, -1
6. 2, 1, 0	24. -1, 0, 1	42. 2, 1, 0	60. 2, 1, 0
7. -1, 0, 2	25. -2, 0, 2	43. 2, 1, 0	61. 2, 0, -1
8. 2, 1, 0	26. -1, 0, 1	44. 2, 1, 0	62. -2, 0, 2
9. 2, 0, -1	27. -1, 0, 1	45. -2, 0, 1	63. 2, 1, 0
10. -1, 0, 2	28. -2, 1, 2	46. -1, 0, 1	64. -1, 0, 1
11. 2, 1, 0	29. -1, 0, 1	47. 2, 0, -1	65. 1, 0, -1
12. 3, 0, -1	30. -1, 0, 1	48. 2, 0, -1	66. 2, 1, 0
13. 2, 0, -1	31. 2, 1, 0	49. 2, 1, 0	67. 2, 1, 0
14. 3, 1, 0	32. -2, 0, 1	50. 2, 0, -1	68. 2, 0, -1
15. 2, 1, 0	33. -1, 1, 2	51. 1, 0, -1	69. 2, 1, 0
16. -1, 0, 1	34. -1, 0, 1	52. -2, 1, 0	70. 2, 0, -1
17. 2, 1, 0	35. -1, 0, 1	53. 2, 1, 0	71. -1, 0, 1
18. 3, 0, -1	36. -2, 0, 2	54. -2, 1, 0	72. 2, 1, 0
			73. 1, 0, -1
			74. 2, 1, 0

75. The following have values of 2: energetic, observant, persevering, resourceful, independent, dedicated, original, perceptive, courageous, enthusiastic, innovative, curious, dynamic, self-demanding, involved, flexible.

The following have values of 1: self-confident, forward-looking, informal, thorough, open-minded, alert, restless, determined.

The rest have values of 0.

Scoring: 125-150   Exceptionally Creative
90-124   Very Creative
55-89   Above Average
35-54   Average
15-34   Below Average
-56-14   Noncreative

60

1. Silvano Arieti, "The Creativogenic Society," in *Creativity: The Magic Synthesis* (New York: Basic Books, Inc., 1976), pp. 312-336. Arieti suggests two important conclusions about the creative society: "First, some societies and cultures have enhanced and some others inhibited creativity. Second, although the creative process is an intrapsychic phenomenon, it is part of an open system. The magic synthesis does not occur without input from the external world, and it is greatly facilitated by a proper climate or milieu" (p. 312).

2. Ibid., p. 315.

3. John Westerhoff, "The Church and the Family," in *Religious Education*, Spring, 1983, p. 263.

4. Arieti, *Creativity*, p. 294.

5. Ibid., p. 295.

6. O'Conner, *Eighth Day of Creation*, p. 101.

7. Gruber, "Breakaway Minds," in *Psychology Today*, July 1981, pp. 64-70.

8. Illustration from the video, "Successful Sunday School," produced for David C. Cook Publishing Co., 1983, by Domain TeleMedia, Wheaton, Illinois.

9. From studies done by E. Paul Torrance, department of Educational Psychology at the University of Georgia, and published in *Forum*, Winter, 1973.

10. Don Koberg and Jim Bagnall, *The Universal Traveler: A Soft-Systems Guide to Creativity, Problem-Solving, and the Process of Reaching Goals* (Los Altos, Calif.: William Kaufman, Inc., 1976).

11. Ibid.

12. "How Creative Are You?" from "Business Probes the Creative Spark," by Niles Howard, *Dun's Review*, Jan., 1980, pp. 34, 35. Reprinted with the special permission of *Dun's Business Month*, (formerly *Dun's Review*), January 1980, Copyright 1980, Dun & Bradstreet Publications Corporation.

CHAPTER 4

Acting Up—
Drama in the Classroom

Puff, puff, chug, chug, went the Little Blue Engine. "I
think I can—I think I can—I think I can—I think I can."
—from *The Little Engine that Could* by Watty Piper

Many Christians have a difficult time viewing their bodies in a positive
light: "Yes, God made me for His enjoyment, and He announced after the
making, 'This person is well made.'" While we accept "and it was very
good" as a Biblical truth, we have trouble with it experientially. We are all
too fat, too skinny, too flat, too tall, too . . . . Why, if we were only well made,
we would have no trouble getting up in front of our classmates, or the
whole church, for that matter.

I can still remember feeling eight feet tall in high school. I never got to
be in student productions because I really did tower over the rest of the
kids. My size just didn't fit any of the parts—until I was in eleventh grade. I
was chosen to play the overbearing wife of a mousy, little husband. I was
so tall I could add just the perfect visual comedy. I loved plays enough to

think even that part was wonderful. I never for a moment doubted, however, that when He planned me, God got the height wrong. For me, and I suspect for most people, a desire not to try something new in front of classmates has pride at its base. "I'm not perfect," a student thinks, "but as long as I sit here vegetating, perhaps others won't notice. I'm not going to get up there and make a fool of myself. I don't give a rip how much I would learn." So we limit ourselves and our ministries.

Spend a few minutes thinking about your body. What does the word *body* make you think of? Doodle some of your thoughts about your body. Do your doodles concentrate on the parts of you that you don't like?

Read the following psalm aloud. Stop and do the mental exercises it suggests. Make this simple step in restructuring your thoughts about your body. It's a necessary step if you are going to ask students to take a chance with their bodies—to stand in front of people and participate in classroom dramatic experiences.

Excerpt from
PSALM 139

O Lord, you have searched me
    and you know me.
You know when I sit and when I rise;
     you perceive my thoughts from afar.
You discern my going out and my
     lying down;
     you are familiar with all my ways.

Let your mind's eye view your body. Put an X on the parts of your body that you are dissatisfied with.

Before a word is on my tongue
    you know it completely, O Lord. . . .
For you created my inmost being;
    you knit me together in my
     mother's womb.

Now go back and put stars on the parts of your body you really like. Do you have as many stars as X's?

I praise you because I am fearfully
    and wonderfully made;
    your works are wonderful,
    I know that full well.
My frame was not hidden from you
    when I was made in the secret place.
When I was woven together in the
    depths of the earth,
    your eyes saw my unformed body.

Thank God for the way you were made. Praise Him for the parts of your body you have rejected before. Emphasize the stars. Thank Him for what He can do with all of you when you are totally given over to Him.

All the days ordained for me
    were written in your book
    before one of them came to be.

DRAMA IN THE CLASSROOM

Why should Christian teachers use drama, plays, and skits in their classrooms? It takes a lot of time to find dramatic works that fit into lesson plans and students who can present the lines effectively. With perhaps a bit of overstatement, Paul Burbridge and Murray Watts provide the answer:

> The Bible shows that powerfully written stories, vivid pictures, parables and acted-out illustrations have often been God's method of communicating to man.
>
> Drama is a gift from God to help us explore the world, enjoy it, and to be moved by suffering, to laugh at the funny side of life, to provoke ourselves and others to thought.
>
> Drama has become the most popular form of entertainment and communication today. Television and radio have brought drama, once an occasional form of entertainment, into the vast majority of homes on a day-to-day basis. . . .
>
> If the church fails to come to terms with drama in our present age, it fails in its mission.[1]

Consider what might happen in a senior high Sunday school class if the following dramatized segment of *The Singer* by Calvin Miller were read by good readers at the beginning of a lesson on salvation. Before the reading, students are told that the Singer represents Jesus who can put a new song of joy in our hearts. The Hater is Satan who does his best to make us dance to his tune, a tune that will chain us like the giant is chained in this reading. The giant represents all of us before we accept Christ.

A *dramatized excerpt from*
THE SINGER[2]

GUIDE: The World Hater came up to the Singer in a woods. They stopped by a shaded spot beneath the fortress wall. A heavy set of chains hung from a great foundation stone that held the towering wall. Manacles hung bolted on the wrists of a burly, naked man. He slept or seemed to.

SINGER: Is he mad?

HATER: Senselessly.

SINGER: Who brings him bread and water?

HATER: I do.

SINGER: Why?

HATER: To see him dance in madness without a tiny hope! Imagine my delight when he raves and screams in chains. Would you like for me to wake this animal?

SINGER: He is a man. Earthmaker made him so. What is his name?

HATER: The crowd.

SINGER: Why such a name?

66

HATER: Because within his sleeping hulk there are a thousand hating spirits from the Canyon of the Damned. They leap at him with sounds no ears but his can hear. They dive at him with screaming lights no other eyes can see. Then he rises and strains in fury against the chains to tear them from the wall.

GUIDE: The Hater took the silver pipe out of its sheath. The tune began—a choppy, weird progression of half tones. The sleeping giant stirred, screamed, and tried to tear the chains that held him to the wall.

SINGER: Stop, Hater!

GUIDE: But the Hater played more loudly than before. At the precise and ugly moment, the pinion on the left gave way. The chain fell loose. Then with his one free hand, the monster tore the other chain away. In but a second he stood unchained before them. The Hater took his pipe and fled into the trees. The Singer then began to sing and continued on until the Madman stood directly in his path. With love that knew no fear, the Singer caught his torment, wrapped it all in song, and gave it back to him as peace. And soon the two men held each other. In their long embrace of soul, the spirits cried and left.

GIANT: *(Perplexed)* What year is it?

SINGER: It is the year of the troubadour. How long have you hung upon the wall and writhed in madness?

GIANT: I cannot tell the years.

SINGER: Will you come with me into the city?

GIANT: Yes. *(Then remembering)* I cannot, for I am naked.

SINGER: Not if you love me. He whom the Earthmaker loves is hidden from his shame forevermore.

GIANT: I love you more than life.

GUIDE: And when they turned to leave the two of them were dressed. In the city a woman recognized the Madman. "You are the Madman." *(pause)* "No, you are sane."

GIANT: I am the Madman, but the Singer has come and I am full and whole.

GUIDE: Who is this Singer?

GIANT: He is the Son of Earthmaker. Listen to me. I hung upon the wall until this very hour. I could kill and would have many times except for the great chains which held me. I cried and wished to die. I tore at every band and tried to set my own brutality toward freedom, but never did the chains give way until today.

HATER: Stop! You are still mad. Listen to me, Madman. Listen to me play the silver pipe.

GUIDE: Beads of perspiration appeared upon the Madman's brow. Fear tore at him—could he stand the melody that formerly had driven him insane? The weird progression of shrieking notes began. But the Madman's tension soon began to ease. In the frustration of his losing, the Hater played more loudly than before. Soon the Madman was entirely at peace. He exulted in the confidence of total sanity.

GIANT: It's no use, World Hater. The Singer has come. I learned a new song from the Singer for whom the world has waited.

The high school students who participate in this reading may have heard the salvation story twice a month for most of their lives. Yet this presentation forces them to look at what may have become common-place. Suddenly some will see their salvation in a new light. They will feel the wonder of no longer being slaves dancing to an evil tune. In Christ they are free, unchained. In listening to the reading and participating in the discussion that should follow it, growth may take place.

Drama is an intimidating word to teachers who have never tried it. But don't you suspect that if the Biblical writers were leading our classes, they would make wise use of it? The Old Testament was spoken before it was written. Are we wrong to assume it was spoken with fervor and strength, with dramatic explosions and pregnant pauses? In ancient Israel if the rabbi whose duty it was to teach had a poor speaking voice, he used a herald, someone who could act as a loudspeaker, or an effective messenger of the Word.

Move to the New Testament. Have you ever thought about the expression Jesus probably used when He spoke? A lackluster monotone would be hard to believe. Consider the following verses. Say them aloud with the kind of expression you think Jesus might have used:

- *Gentle reprimand* from John 21:22:

    "If I want him to remain alive until I return, what is that to you? You must follow me."

- *Slight humor* in Matthew 14:16:

    "They do not need to go away. You give them something to eat."

- *Anger* from Matthew 15:6-8:

    "You nullify the word of God for the sake of your tradition. You hypocrites! Isaiah was right when he prophesied about you: 'These people honor me with their lips, but their hearts are far from me.'"

- *Love and understanding* from Mark 5:34:

    "Daughter, your faith has healed you. Go in peace and be freed from your suffering."

- *Gentleness* from Luke 5:10:

    "Don't be afraid; from now on you will catch men."

- *Sorrow* from Luke 13:34:

    "O Jerusalem, Jerusalem, you who kill the prophets and stone those sent to you, how often I have longed to gather your children together, as a hen gathers her chicks under her wings, but you were not willing!"

READING PLAYS—GREAT TEACHING TOOL

Consider some of the benefits of reading a play as part of the teaching plan:

• As they read a play, *students will look at familiar truths in new ways.* The short segment from *The Singer* is one example. Or imagine what might happen in an adult Sunday school class on Easter Sunday morning. Instead of the familiar reading of Christ's death and resurrection, members read and discuss the play, *Christ and the Concrete City.* In this modern verse drama, they find themselves at the foot of the Cross examining the part their sins played in the death of the Lord. Christ forgives them. Suddenly many experience anew the celebration of Easter. Adults are ready to participate, perhaps for the first time in many years, in the joy of the Resurrection.

• When we read plays in class *we equalize people's experiences.* Visitors along with regular class members are able to participate in both the presentation of the play and its discussion. People who are familiar with Christian concepts can add depth, but those who are new to the faith may infuse the discussion with emotion, meant in the best sense of the word. Shy students are often able to participate in reading a play with as much enthusiasm and success as those who are more outgoing. With a script in front of them, they feel more secure. Stage fright that accompanies most dramatic productions doesn't enter in here. Performance is not the primary objective.

• Play reading *exposes the group to a wider range of experiences* than they would ordinarily have. Through drama they can go back to the Crucifixion or become part of another culture.

It's a good thing to remember that not everyone, especially in adult classes or in churches where drama has never been used before, will be as sold on this method as you may be. It's wise to think about objections before you are hit with them.

It is a form of art and can be used in very many different ways. Like atomic power, for instance, drama can be used for good and for evil.

To say that "drama is of the devil" is willingly to hand over to the devil the control of many people's leisure hours, to discourage young Christians from wanting to write thoughtful plays for television and to dampen the desire of acting groups in churches to communicate God's truth with freshness.

Nonetheless, some people's experience of drama may have involved watching violence, corruption, sexual immorality, without any form of judgment passed on these negative sides of human experience. They may also have seen badly and thoughtlessly put together sketches in their church which have failed to convince them of the positive potential of drama.

Those interested in drama should have respect for those who are either opposed to their work or cautious in their attitude towards it; they should never be unable to take helpful criticism, even when accompanied by unhelpful criticism; always seek for the "soft answer that turns away wrath" when differences arise inside or around a drama group; and prove by the quality and commitment of the work, rather than by arguments, that drama can play a vital part in the life of the church.[3]

BUILDING COURAGE

A few simple exercises can help remove the scare factor from reading plays, and they can also help your students do a better job in class. The first few times you use play reading in class, use about five minutes of your class time for exercises like these that follow. After the first several experiences, this warm-up period will not be as important.

This first exercise helps students play with expression, develop their voices and interpretive skills. For a reading to come alive, students must read with expression—emotions that make the characters into real people.

Ask different students to say the sentence, "Peter is at the door," using the emotion you assign. The line is based on the story in Acts 12:5-14. Read the story ending at verse 14, "When she recognized Peter's voice, she was so overjoyed she ran back without opening it and said: 'Peter is at the door.'" Read the following attitudes without any expression in your own voice. You want students to be original in their development of the attitude you assign:

- *Inattention* (I want to get back to the meeting in the living room.)
- *Disbelief* (I thought you were in prison.)
- *Shock and fear* (Maybe it's Peter's ghost.)
- *Excitement* (He's here!)
- *Disgust* (He always shows up and bothers everyone.)
- *Wariness* (Maybe the soldiers have been following him and he's guided them right to us.)
- *Fury* (Go away and let us pick up our lives where we left off.)

Expression can change a dull reading into one students will hear and remember.

Quality is the sound that is peculiar to each reader. Loudness, rate, and pitch add variety as a reader speaks. Ask students to say, "How about coming to church with me next Sunday?" in the way they think it might be said by the following characters you will assign. You might want to announce the character first and allow a few seconds for everyone to mentally portray him or her before you call on someone to do the interpretation for the whole group.

- An elderly gentleman
- An affected society woman
- A small child with bubble gum in his mouth
- A man with a bad cold
- A woman with a very sore throat
- A whining teenager
- A bashful boy

In some class readings, students will be able to insert a few actions, especially if they have had the script for a week to prepare the reading. This next exercise can help people get used to using facial expressions and hand movements that help interpret what is going on. In each, no words are to be spoken.

- A teen who has just decided her date has stood her up . . .
- A little boy who just realizes that he's brushing his teeth with shaving cream . . .
- A woman getting up the nerve to tell her husband she is sorry for being angry at him . . .
- A man changing a very dirty diaper . . .
- A teen who has just been benched for the rest of the game . . .
- A woman trying to build up the courage to share her faith with a teen sitting next to her on a bus . . .
- A man who has just found a fly in his soup . . .

EYE CONTACT

When a reader can make eye contact with the listeners, or even with other people who are participating in the reading, the end result is more interesting. Yet it's difficult to look up from a script that the reader probably doesn't know very well. Suggest this technique to your students: use the left hand as a moving marker. As they read they should move their hand down the page marking the exact line that is being read. No matter how often they look up from their parts, they can find their place in a split second.

People can train themselves to look up from material they are reading. The eye is reading several words ahead of the mouth. If the readers push their eyes just a little further ahead, they will know what the next phrase, or five to eight words are, before they have read them aloud. They can then look up during those words, establishing contact with the listeners or with the other appropriate readers. (With the hand bookmark in place, they will have no trouble returning their eyes to the correct place.) The more they practice, the longer the phrases they will master.

Often when a reader does this, his or her mind will put together the right sense of the next several words but will substitute another word for one that is written. It's usually a substitution that makes no difference in the reading of the script. For example, the script says: "I have no desire to complete this shortsighted conversation." The person reads ahead, looks up for the entire sentence to the person she is speaking to and says, "I don't really want to finish this shortsighted conversation." Encourage students not to go back and correct themselves. As long as the sense remains, what was spoken is correct, and probably more natural to the speaker than the printed words.

Sometimes you'll have a student who wants to participate in a reading, but his or her reading skills will be less than adequate. Often this student will be a boy. (Boys' eye focus matures from six to eight months behind girls', yet during first grade they are taught reading at the same time. Many boys are not physically ready to read. Perhaps this is one reason high school boys outnumber girls in remedial reading classes 16 to 1.) If poor readers are willing to participate, give them the scripts early. You might even call them during the week to practice. Some students can increase their ability to read aloud by reading children's books. They can simply read to themselves, but that's not nearly as much fun or affirming as reading to a neighborhood child who will benefit from the stories' content and the extra attention.

HOW TO PICK A PLAY

Evaluate each play or skit or reading before you use it in the classroom. It must be a teaching tool. Use the following questions to rate its effectiveness, and any selection that doesn't get a positive rating should not be used.

1. *Is the subject matter important enough to rate the time my students will spend reading and discussing it?*

Ask yourself, "How will my students benefit from the reading?" If your only answer is, "I think they would enjoy it," your answer is not strong enough. Most Sunday school teachers have just 50 minutes to train students to put Biblical truth into life responses.

2. *Is the subject matter consistent with what I want to teach?*

If you are considering a short Biblical drama and the portrayal of Jesus' deity is weak, don't use it. It may teach but certainly not what you want it to teach.

In secular readings, you will want to be extra careful about what is said. You can't expect the subject matter to be Christian. In fact, secular readings can gain their greatest advantage because they don't say predictable Sunday schoolish things. They challenge the Christians' presuppositions and often force them to think about why they believe what they do. Still, there are limits. There is no excuse for bringing questionable language, for example, into the classroom, no matter how well the segment might illustrate what you're trying to teach.

3. *Is the play suited to the age level I teach?*

In the play segment from *The Singer,* several words were changed with the permission of InterVarsity Press to eliminate words that would not be part of a normal high school student's vocabulary. These word changes didn't destroy the meaning of the story, and without them, the segment would have been too difficult for many teenagers to understand. (For example *burly* was changed to *large.* Burly is the better word, but young people are often unfamiliar with it. Our primary purpose in Sunday school is to communicate, not to increase vocabulary.)

4. *Is the plot interesting enough to hold my students' attention?*

After you've found a play that you think you might use, read through it several times and get acquainted with it. Think about which students might best do each role. Consider what questions you might use to spark discussion after the reading. (If the reading came as part of your Sunday school curriculum, excellent questions will probably be included. However, you know your students better than any curriculum writer ever could. Personalize the printed ones.)

Assume you are going to be formulating questions to go with *The Singer.* You can't take for granted that the reading will be understood by everyone in the class. Many students are used to watching television situations. These don't require much thinking and certainly no discussion. You may need to draw thinking responses, questions, and observations from your students. Good questions will help you do this. Consider some of the qualities of good questions:

● A good question asks for a paragraph answer, rather than single-word answers. Poor question: "Did the giant understand what happened to him immediately after he and the Singer met?" Better question: "How do you know that the giant only partially understood what happened to him immediately after he and the Singer met?"

● Some questions should make sure the listeners understood the reading, while also giving them an opportunity to add some of their personal understanding. Examples: "What characteristics in the Singer do we also see in Jesus?" "Why do you think the Singer took the man into town?"

• Some questions should force the listeners to take what they heard and share the implications for their lives today. Examples: "Suppose someone came up to you after class and said, 'I'm like the giant still chained to the wall.' What would be your response?" (This might lead into a natural roleplay situation in which students review how to share Christ's salvation message with their peers.) "How did you feel when you realized that you had passed from a chained giant to a close friend of the Singer's—passed from death into life?"

LESS SERIOUS, JUST AS EFFECTIVE

"The Singer" is a serious reading and is effective with high school, college age, and adult students. But not all teaching tools have to be as serious. Consider the following skit by Dean Nadasdy, and as you read, structure some questions you might use with a class of teenagers.

TIME TO TAKE OUT THE GARBAGE[4]

Characters: Narrator
Julie
Kristin

Bible Text Base: Proverbs 28:13 (KJV)

(*read by narrator*) He that covereth his sins shall not prosper: but whoso confesseth and forsaketh them shall have mercy.

NARRATOR: Julie is spending the afternoon at Kristin's house. For some strange reason, she has noticed that they haven't gone into the kitchen the entire time. Being curious, Julie decides to take a peek. What she saw she couldn't believe. So . . . (*enter Julie and Kristin*)

JULIE: Kristin! What happened to your kitchen? What is all that stuff?

KRISTIN: Oh, that's our garbage. But you weren't supposed to look. We hide it in the kitchen so no one will see it.

JULIE: What?! You hide your garbage in the kitchen? Now that's dumb!

KRISTIN: Dumb, is it? What makes you say that?

JULIE: Well, you've heard of garbage trucks, haven't you? Why don't you just take out the garbage?

KRISTIN: Too lazy, I guess. Anyway, who wants the whole neighborhood to see our garbage? Our garbage is our business!

JULIE: It sure looks that way. Looks to me like you've been in the garbage business for some time.

KRISTIN: Julie, if you don't like it, you . . .

JULIE: Really, Kristin, doesn't the smell get to you? How do you eat anything? The garbage is up to the ceiling!

KRISTIN: I have to admit, banana peel sandwiches are starting to bore me.

JULIE: How about the rest of the family? Do they feel the same way, about keeping the garbage, I mean?

KRISTIN: I guess so. We've agreed not to talk about it anymore, though. Since the pile got so big about six months ago, none of us is home much. In fact, we hardly even see each other. I haven't seen Dad for weeks. He just couldn't handle the stench anymore. My big brother, Bill, joined the army last month to get away. That leaves Mom and me.

JULIE: And what does she think about the garbage?

KRISTIN: I don't know. She misses Dad . . . and Bill, too.

JULIE: What happens when you run out of room here?

KRISTIN: Sooner or later I guess the garbage will get the best of us. We'll probably just have to move and start all over again.

JULIE: With the garbage, you mean?

KRISTIN: Right. Say, Julie?

JULIE: What?

KRISTIN: Could I spend next weekend at your house?

JULIE: Sure.

KRISTIN: And the next one, too?

Now practice your question-developing skills.

● Write a question that asks students to give a paragraph answer about the skit's content.

\
\

● Write a question that combines the skit's content and the listeners' understanding of the Christian life.

\
\

● Write a question that will help students apply the skit's lesson to their personal lives.

\
\

If you use secular plays, they will need to be very carefully woven into your lesson plan. I've found sections from the tragicomedy, *Waiting for Godot*, extremely helpful. I used it in a senior high English class at a Christian school. The students studied the play and discussed it in terms of their own experiences in finding God. I also used it in a Bible study with other Christian workers. For me, this Theater of the Absurd masterpiece underlines the fullness and certainty we Christians can have. We know that Christ is with us, and that He is coming again—absolutely, with no guesswork. In this play, two clown tramps wait for Godot to arrive and give some meaning to their lives, but Godot never comes. It's a contrast we "cradle Christians" easily forget.

As you read this edited section, ask yourself what questions you might use with a class of teens or adults.

Excerpt from
WAITING FOR GODOT[5]

ESTRAGON: Let's go.
VLADIMIR: We can't.
ESTRAGON: Why not?
VLADIMIR: We're waiting for Godot.
ESTRAGON: *(despairingly).* Ah! *(Pause.)* You're sure it was here?
VLADIMIR: What?
ESTRAGON: That we were to wait.
VLADIMIR: He said by the tree. *(They look at the tree.)* Do you see any
       others?
ESTRAGON: What is it?
VLADIMIR: I don't know. A willow.
ESTRAGON: Where are the leaves?
VLADIMIR: It must be dead.
ESTRAGON: No more weeping.
VLADIMIR: Or perhaps it's not the season.
ESTRAGON: Looks to me more like a bush.
VLADIMIR: A shrub.
ESTRAGON: A bush.
VLADIMIR: A—. What are you insinuating? That we've come to the wrong
       place?
ESTRAGON: He should be here.
VLADIMIR: He didn't say for sure he'd come.
ESTRAGON: And if he doesn't come?
VLADIMIR: We'll come back to-morrow.
ESTRAGON: And then the day after to-morrow.
VLADIMIR: Possibly.

ESTRAGON: And so on.

VLADIMIR: The point is—

ESTRAGON: Until he comes.

VLADIMIR: You're merciless.

ESTRAGON: We came here yesterday.

VLADIMIR: Ah no, there you're mistaken.

ESTRAGON: What did we do yesterday?

VLADIMIR: What did we do yesterday?

ESTRAGON: Yes.

VLADIMIR: Why . . . (*Angrily.*) Nothing is certain when you're about.

ESTRAGON: In my opinion we were here.

VLADIMIR: (*looking round*). You recognize the place?

ESTRAGON: I didn't say that.

VLADIMIR: Well?

ESTRAGON: That makes no difference.

VLADIMIR: All the same . . . that tree . . . (*turning towards auditorium*) that bog . . .

ESTRAGON: You're sure it was this evening?

VLADIMIR: What?

ESTRAGON: That we were to wait.

VLADIMIR: He said Saturday. (*Pause.*) I think.

ESTRAGON: You think.

VLADIMIR: I must have made a note of it. (*He fumbles in his pockets, bursting with miscellaneous rubbish.*)

ESTRAGON: (*very insidious*). But what Saturday? And is it Saturday? Is it not rather Sunday? (*Pause.*) Or Monday? (*Pause.*) Or Friday?

VLADIMIR: (*looking wildly about him, as though the date was inscribed in the landscape*). It's not possible!

ESTRAGON: Or Thursday?

VLADIMIR: What'll we do?

ESTRAGON: If he came yesterday and we weren't here you may be sure he won't come again to-day.

VLADIMIR: But you say we were here yesterday.

ESTRAGON: I may be mistaken. (*Pause.*) Let's stop talking for a minute, do you mind?

Continue practicing your question-developing skills. You may find it's even easier to write good questions for this secular material than it was for the skit that was overtly Christian.

● Write a question that requires students to give a paragraph answer dealing with the content. Example: "Suppose a Christian and a non-Christian went out for coffee after seeing this section from the play. They discuss what the play was about. Contrast and compare their answers."

- Write a question that combines the excerpt's content and the listeners' understanding about Christian life. Example: "In what ways did the two tramps resemble non-Christians you know?"

- Write a question that will help students apply the skit's lesson to their personal lives. Example: "Would a volunteer please share a recent joyful, growing experience in the Christian life that separates his or her experience from the monotony and despair the two tramps feel?"

Waiting for Godot could easily lead to the renewing of joy for who Christ is. "But Zion said, 'The Lord has forsaken me, the Lord has forgotten me.' Can a mother forget the baby at her breast and have no compassion on the child she has borne? Though she may forget, I will not forget you!" (Isa. 49:14,15). "Behold, I am coming soon! My reward is with me, and I will give to everyone according to what he has done. I am the Alpha and the Omega, the First and the Last, the Beginning and the End. . . . Come! Whoever is thirsty, let him come; and whoever wishes, let him take the free gift of the water of life" (Rev. 22:12,13,17).

Perhaps for many in our society, the response to the Christian message is better explained in the following sketch[6] by Paul Burbridge and Murray Watts than it is by the tramps.

VOICE OF CHRIST: Listen. I stand at the door and knock. If anyone hears my voice and opens the door, I will come into his house and eat with him and he will eat with me. (*Knocking*)

DAVE: Can't get any peace even to read the paper these days, can yer? Who is it, anyway?

VOICE OF CHRIST: The person you've been waiting for.

DAVE: I haven't been waiting for anybody, mate.

VOICE OF CHRIST: Can I come in?

DAVE: What do you mean, 'can I come in?' This is my home. You can't just come in here. I didn't invite you. (*He continues to read the paper. Pause. The knocking begins again.*) Push off, will yer? Some people won't take no for an answer, will they? (*He gets up and goes across to the door.*) Look, mate, I don't want to seem unfriendly . . . if there's anything you want . . .

VOICE OF CHRIST: I want to come in.

DAVE: Well, you can't. I'm busy. Try again when I've got more time. Try Wednesday.

If you're enthusiastic about using plays in class, it won't take you long to collect some that are easily adapted to a number of teaching situations.

Notice the place that humor plays in many of these examples. In some cases students may recognize themselves and laugh a bit nervously, but a lot of learning takes place behind a smile. Many humorous pieces work across the age levels. "If God Talked Back," printed in *Moody Monthly*, was aimed at a mature adult readership. It was also published in *Looking Ahead*, a Sunday school paper for young teens. (Two students—voice of God and person—can present this dramatic reading.) As you read this excerpt from Clyde Lee Herring's conversation between God and a person saying the Lord's Prayer, see if it doesn't speak to you, too.

Excerpt from
IF GOD TALKED BACK[7]

"Our Father which art in heaven . . ."
Yes.
Don't interrupt me. I'm praying.
But you called Me.
Called You? I didn't call You. I'm praying. "Our Father which art in heaven . . ."
There, you did it again.
Did what?
Called Me. You said, "Our Father which art in heaven." Here I am. What's on your mind?
But I didn't mean anything by it. I was, you know, just saying my prayers for the day. I always say the Lord's Prayer. It makes me feel good, kind of like getting a duty done.
All right. Go on.
"Hallowed be thy name . . ."
Hold it. What do you mean by that?
By what?
By "Hallowed be thy name"?
It means . . . It means . . . Good grief, I don't know what it means. How should I know? It's just part of the prayer. By the way, what does it mean?
It means honored, holy, wonderful.
Hey, that makes sense.

People are drawn to comedy. They don't feel as preached to or as threatened by it as they might by a teacher bringing out the same point in a more traditional way. The next skit shouts at the students: "You're puffed up with pride and God isn't going to stand for it!" Yet senior high and adult students would listen and learn—and perhaps change.

NATURAL MAN[8]

Natural Man (NM) comes to the center of the classroom. Three students on one side of the classroom make up the chorus.

CHORUS: Blessed is the man who walks not in the counsel of the wicked.

NM: I never do anything like that.

CHORUS: Nor stands in the way of sinners.

NM: I never do things like that either.

CHORUS: Nor sits in the seat of scoffers.

NM: Well, hardly ever.

CHORUS: But his delight is in the law of the Lord.

NM: The Bible really is a wonderful book.

CHORUS: And on his law he meditates day and night.

NM: Someday, after I retire, I'm really going to take more time to read the Bible.

CHORUS: He is like a tree planted by streams of water, that yields its fruit in its season.

NM: That sounds like a slow process.

CHORUS: And its leaf does not wither.

NM: Leaves? Fruit?

CHORUS: In all that he does, he prospers.

NM: Now that's the part I like!

CHORUS: The wicked are not so, but are like chaff which the wind drives away.

NM: Serves them right.

CHORUS: Therefore the wicked will not stand in the judgment, nor sinners in the congregation of the righteous.

NM: It's nice to know that God is going to give them what's coming to them.

CHORUS: For the Lord knows the way of the righteous, but the way of the wicked will perish.

NM: I'm glad You know which of us are righteous, God. If only everyone were as good as I am. *(Exits very haughty and proud.)*

Humor works. It allows us to see ourselves from a different and non-threatening perspective. A student might admit, "Natural Man sounds a lot like someone I'm very attached to—me."

A high school teacher shared a concern common to many people: "I used to complain that there aren't enough dramas around. I'm solving that problem myself. I'm training myself to look beyond those pieces that are labeled 'Drama' or 'Skit.' I've found that there is a lot more drama to be used—in magazines, books, songs, and, of course, curriculum itself. All I have to do is divide the copy into different speakers' parts." Right, and it's not difficult. "Natural Man" and the adaptation of "The Singer" were not originally scripted. "If God Talked Back" was first published as a magazine article.

BIBLICAL DRAMA

Dramatized Biblical material is a valuable teaching tool for several reasons. First, students are exposed to content. People who have known the Bible story for years review it, and people who have little Bible background get a quick overview that can lead them into deeper study.

Second, it helps students look at familiar material in new ways. Just as reading a modern version of the Bible helps people see new ideas in verses they have memorized in the King James Version, so a dramatization can help them rethink a familiar passage.

"I was amazed at the play *Godspell,*" a college student said. "I'd always been skeptical about the Bible containing any humor until I saw that collection of dramatized parables. I've had whole months of Sunday school lessons on the parables and not a twinkle in sight. Then the secular world gets ahold of Jesus' parables, and they come alive. The lessons Jesus was sharing through them with His followers hit me like a lemon pie in the face. I laughed and I learned. I realize that *Godspell* was secular and the view of Jesus was not as the risen, only Son of God. But I learned, and I was honestly sorry that no Christian had come up with as excellent a production containing the whole truth."

The following reading by Jerry Chip MacGregor has to be read aloud to be enjoyed. Three people read lines quickly and with expression that overemphasizes what is happening. Slapstick motions will best capture the mood of this version of the Prodigal Son.

THE PRODIGAL SON[9]

1: Once there was a rich man.

2: A rich man?

3: A rich man.

1: Who had two sons.

2: Two. Me . . . and you.

3: Two!

1: Two. One day the younger said to his father:

2: Father! I want my share of the estate now.

1: Now?

2: Now! I don't want to wait 'til you die.
I want it now—my share of the pie.

1: So his father divided his wealth asunder. Gave half to one and half to the other.

3: Half of his money.

2: Half of his share.

1: He took the amount that was left to his care.

2: Ooo-wee! All that money.

3: Yeah.

1: The younger son moved to a distant land.

2: Gone with my money!

1: Oh, he took his money all right.

2: Money! Ah ha! Money-money-money-money (continues with the word *money* until next speech).

1: He took it and spent it. He had quite a time.

3: I'll bet he spent it on women and wine.

1: Oh, he did; he blew it.

3: Didn't use it.

1: Didn't use it. (Pause) And then it ran out.

2: Money-money-money . . . money . . . no money . . . oh, no.

1: And famine struck.

2: Oh no, oh no.

1: And now he was hungry.

3: He'd blown all his dough.

1: He found work at a farm, feeding pigs their mess.

2: Feeding pigs?

3: Feeding pigs?

1: Feeding pigs, no less. Then one day he finally came to his senses.

2: At home even hired men eat their fill.

3: And there you are with your pigs and their swill.

2: And dying of hunger.

1: He said to himself,

2: I'll go and ask if they'll have me still.

1: So homeward he went. He practiced his speech.

2: Father, I've sinned against Heaven and you. No . . . Father, I'm not worthy to be your son . . . Naw . . .

1: While he was still some distance away

2: Father, I've sinned against Heaven and you.

1: His father took notice.

2: Father, I've sinned against Heaven and you.

1: And ran out to greet him.

3: Greet him?

1: Greet him.

3: Meet him and greet him?

1: Quick, bring us something to eat!

3: What, rings for his fingers?

1: Shoes for his feet! He was dead and now lives. My son has come home.

2: Oh, praise you.

1: Said the younger son to his father.

3: Bah!

1: Said the other.

3: I think it's a bother.

2: A bother?

1: Why, son, tell me, what is the matter?

3: I have worked on your land and been faithful and true.

1 and 2: True.

3: So why do you throw a feast for my brother?

1: My son, said the father. What I have is yours. But my son, my son, my son has come home. He was dead and now lives; my son has come home.

2: Brother!

3: Bother!

1: My son has come home.

One of the easiest ways to read Biblical drama in class is to announce that the characters are part of a radio program. No props are needed. Students use expression, rather than movements, to communicate the message. (Teen groups, when they have had time to prepare a reading, often add sound effects.) Even in a radio format, the reading will be more effective if the readers use eye contact.

The following radio drama excerpt was written for an Easter worship service, the product of creative worship planning. In this drama, "He Is Not Here!" several reporters are following and reporting on the events in the

83

last days of Jesus' life. The play follows the story through Jesus' resurrection. In this excerpt, we hear about the events surrounding the triumphal entry.

Excerpt from
HE IS NOT HERE[10]

REPORTER I: This will be a test. *(To one side.)* A little more cable please, Bob. This is a test. One. Two. Three. Ted, I'm at a good vantage point for the entire procession. I hope the background noise isn't too much for the pickup, but the crowd is really packing in. The mobile unit is completely surrounded. I just hope they don't snap our connecting cables. *(Crowd noise rises.)* The word we have here, Ted, is that He's still about a quarter of a mile away. According to our best estimates, the crowd is about two thousand. I'll be ready to go live as soon as He comes in sight. *(Crowd noise.)*

DIRECTOR: *(For live performance, sign in studio reading ON THE AIR is displayed.)* Good evening, ladies and gentlemen. My name is Ted Andrews. Welcome to W·A·D News. We are coming to you live from Jerusalem. As you know, crowds are gathering in Jerusalem for the Feast of the Passover. The one person making all the news today, though, is Jesus of Nazareth, whom many claim to be the Messiah. For the latest report on this astounding miracle-worker, let's go to Susan Gregory in Bethany.

REPORTER II: Susan Gregory in Bethany. We heard here yesterday that Jesus might go to Jerusalem today. That raises the old question: Will He confront the Sanhedrin? Whether He does or not, there can be little doubt now that He is moving very much in the open with a large group of followers. We believe word of this development first came from Jesus' close friend, Lazarus. This is the Lazarus whom Jesus reportedly brought back from the dead. We asked him if he knew Jesus' plans.

LAZARUS: This morning word got around that He was going to the city today for the Passover Feast so we were all up at sunrise. He sent two of the fellas ahead to get Him a donkey, and they'll meet Him at Bethphage. That's about all I know.

REPORTER II: We have word that one or more of His inner circle is already inside Jerusalem. Is there any substance to this rumor, and can you say if there will be any move toward direct confrontation with the Sanhedrin?

LAZARUS: Let me tell you something—no one has ever been able to tell what Jesus is going to do next. To answer your first question, I think Judas is in Jerusalem, but he's just taking care of all the expenses for the feast.

REPORTER II: Susan Gregory in Bethany. Now to Jim Matthews who, I understand, is with someone from the Sanhedrin. Jim?

REPORTER III: Yes, Susan, we've reached a spokesman for Caiaphas here just outside the room where deliberations are going on right this moment. Sir, it appears to us that Jesus is coming directly into the city with a very large group of His supporters. How do you react to this?

SPOKESMAN: I can only say that we don't want any trouble. We have enough to do what with hundreds of pilgrims pouring into the city every day. Whatever we do, it will be to keep the peace.

God set the stage for drama at creation. In His colors and forms and noises He showed His sense for the dramatic. Into us He placed the love of words and actions and feelings. When we read plays set within the Biblical context, we put personal life into the event. We are emphasizing the content, of course, but we are also emphasizing how the Bible characters may have felt and spoken.

Job is the perfect story in the Bible to set in play form. Consider this dramatic excerpt of Job 1, 2.

Excerpt from
PROLOGUE—JOB[11]

JOB: (*Looking up in prayer*) O glorious God, my Lord, accept these offerings on behalf of my sons and daughters in case they have sinned in their hearts against Thee. Forgive them, O Lord, our God. (*He continues offering sacrifices during the following dialogue.*)

VOICE OF GOD: Satan, have you noticed my servant Job in your travels across the earth? There is no one on earth as devout as Job is.

VOICE OF SATAN: Oh, I have noticed Job. But would he worship You so faithfully if he weren't so prosperous? Of course, he worships You. But what if everything he has were taken away from him? I bet he would curse You then.

GOD: What? Job? Curse me? Not Job. In fact, I'll show you. You may take everything away from him. You will see, he'll still bless me. Only you can't hurt Job himself.

SATAN: It's a deal. I'll have Job an atheist before I'm through.

Many students are capable of writing and presenting their own plays based on Biblical events. Although these are rarely of professional quality, they do have merit, giving students the opportunity to study the story for themselves.

To dramatize a passage, follow these steps:

1. *All students should become thoroughly familiar with the Bible story.* This means, quite simply, studying the source. It's amazing how many people

feel they completely know a story and will even attempt to teach it in Sunday school or script it without checking their memories against the Bible.

2. *All who are involved should talk about why they are doing the dramatization.* More than likely, if a group of students go to all the work of writing a play, they will want to expose it to more than simply one Sunday school class. The group should know:

Who is going to see what we write and perform?
Why will these people be coming to see us?
What things might they be expecting?
What things might they need?
How can we best meet those needs, with the Holy Spirit's help?

3. *Write goals for the play.* Make sure that each goal is measurable. Students will be able to evaluate what happened against the goals they have set. Some sample goals:

Goal: That there be a part of the play for each person in our senior high class.
Goal: That the plan of salvation will be presented clearly.
Goal: That people will get a complete overview of the events in the story we are presenting.

4. *Decide what form the story will take.* Will it be a radio drama? Do students want to act out events? Will the play use a narrator? Will mime be used?

5. *Consider the tone of the story that will be performed.* The tone should fit the story's content. It would be crass, for example, to present the story of Stephen's death with the same flippancy as the story of "The Prodigal Son" was told.

6. *Put words on paper.* If this is a major group project, people might want to talk through the conversations and tape them. From a transciption it's easy to cross out phrases that don't fit or lines that don't come alive.

When the play is finished, students should read it aloud, and ask themselves, "Does this sound like real talk?" If lines are stilted, rewrite. Usually it's a good rule, one that masters like Shakespeare could break, to keep conversations short. People interact; they don't talk at each other.

If students are doing a section from the life of Christ, you'll want to discuss whether to put words into Jesus' mouth. Many people prefer to have Jesus speak only the words that are recorded directly from Scripture. No matter what decision is made here, take care to be Biblically true to the story.

7. *Practice reading the play.* Use lots of expression. Overdo it. In front of an audience, what feels overdone to the reader often sounds effective. Decide how readers will position themselves on the stage. Radio drama readers may want to stand in front of microphones. Or, readers might sit in a semicircle in the stage area so everyone in the audience will be able to see all participants. The more important characters should be in the middle of the seating arrangement with supporting readers on the outside. Whenever possible, readers should sit near those with whom they have the most interaction. This may make it necessary for readers to switch seats from time to time. When those onstage are not in on the action, they could bow their heads and shoulders to show the audience they are not participating in the scene.

Some students enjoy walking through the action of the play as they read. However, for this to be effective, each student must be skilled in the use of eye contact. Otherwise scripts hinder the production.

8. *Throughout the activity, pray together that the Lord will use you to present His message effectively.*

9. *Several days after the play has been presented, evaluate how things went.* Evaluation should center on what the group might do differently next time, rather than on who did a great job and who was just awful. Evaluation questions might include:

● To what parts did the audience react positively? Why?
● Which goals were met? How do we know?
● What were some of the good comments you heard people make after the play?
● If we were doing this again, how could we do a better job?

(Write these ideas down. Read them to the group before the next planning meeting starts.)

---

1. Taken from *Time to Act,* by Paul Burbridge and Murray Watts. © 1979 by Paul Burbridge and Murray Watts and used by permission of InterVarsity Press, Downers Grove, IL 60515.

2. Reading developed from *The Singer,* by Calvin Miller. © 1975 by InterVarsity Christian Fellowship and used by permission of InterVarsity Press.

3. Burbridge and Watts, *Time to Act.*

4. Reprinted from *Resources for Youth Ministry,* a quarterly publication of the Board for Youth Services of the Lutheran Church—Missouri Synod, 1333 S. Kirkwood Road, St. Louis, MO 63122. Used by permission.

5. Samuel Beckett, *Waiting for Godot* (New York: Grove Press, 1954). Used by permission.

6. Burbridge and Watts, *Time to Act.*

7. Clyde Lee Herring, "If God Talked Back." All rights reserved by the author.

8. From an adaptation of Barbara Jurgensen's book, *The Lord Is My Shepherd, But . . .* by Ramona Warren.

9. "The Prodigal Son," by Jerry Chip MacGregor, was written as partial requirement for the course, "Creativity and Art Forms," Talbot Theological Seminary, 1983.

10. "He Is Not Here!", a radio play by Gil Moegerle, was first presented at Circle Church, Chicago, and later printed by David C. Cook Publishing Company as part of the *Senior High Creative Teaching Aids* packet.

11. "Job," adapted by Douglas Olsen, in the **Christian Growth Elective** course, *Why Me, Lord?* by David Howard.

CHAPTER 5

Roleplay:
Do-It-Yourself Drama

Tell me, I forget.
Show me, I remember.
Involve me, I understand.

—Ancient Chinese proverb

During the French Revolution, a general looked over his balcony at a river of people rushing through the streets toward the Bastille. Spinning on his heels, he shouted to his aide, "Quick! My tunic and my sword. I am their leader; I must follow them."

Quite often those teachers who lead teens and young adults have this experience when they work with impromptu drama. Teachers show students the Bastille—the possibilities of drama—and before we know it, teachers are in the rear of their column running in delighted amazement to get back into the action.

The primary aim of the Christian leader should not be to cram knowledge into students' heads, but to help them *apply and use* what they have learned. Dramatics—plays, roleplays, simulations, mime—have tremendous potential for helping us reach this goal.

In this chapter and the next two, we will be concentrating on impromptu drama in which script ideas may be given, but the scripts aren't simply read and the actions prescribed. These types of dramatic teaching methods can be used in youth group meetings, Sunday school classes, prayer groups, and released time classes. They are adaptable to many different teaching goals.

SETTING THE STAGE

The following steps will help reduce anxieties in yourself, as well as your students:

1. *Establish a climate in which your students feel secure.* They must want to share their feelings, emotions, and opinions with the group. They must know that you will appreciate anything they attempt, and will not put them down in any way. This is not so much what you do or say in the classroom as it is who you are. Do your students see you as an accepting, innovative person who will be delighted with an imperfect try?

2. *Be personally enthusiastic.*[1] Be at ease with what you are doing. You may find it helpful, for example, to work through a roleplay with another teacher before you use it in class, at least the first few times you try this process.

3. *Be prepared for an imperfect first experience.* This is true with any new method. The first week Mr. Dye tried roleplay in his teen class, for example, the two students he had chosen stood in front of the group looking helpless.

"I can't think of anything to say," one girl said. "I don't know what you want me to do."

"I can understand," Mr. Dye sympathized. "Why don't I play the part of the girl who has been shoplifting? You play the Christian friend who has seen me break God's rule. That way we can help each other keep the conversation going."

A few students giggled when their male teacher took the role of a thief and a girl, but they soon forgot personalities as they listened to their classmate use principles and verses she had learned to confront and show love to the thief.

You may find it helpful the first Sunday you use roleplay to select a few gifted students before class and go over the dramatic form with them. This will assure a successful first experience. But after the class is familiar with the impromptu forms, discontinue the preclass sessions. They hinder the spontaneity which is such a valuable part of this teaching tool.

4. *Maintain control over your students during the experience.* If you have set a serious atmosphere for learning, most discipline problems will be eliminated. Students will realize that these activities are part of the learning process, not a time-consuming spot of entertainment.

One teacher explained the value of roleplay to her high school class like this: "The situations we are dealing with are the types you may have in real life. If you learn to handle them, you will be better prepared to live the Christian life. Roleplay may help you become a more effective Christian. This may be God's training ground for all of you, getting you ready for the work He has for you. So have fun, and be serious. Yes, those two things can go together."

5. *Use dramatics frequently.* Obviously, if you stop after the first poor experience, you will never have the joy of seeing reality step into the classroom. A group of adult Sunday school teachers were attending a seminar in learning how to use roleplay. One woman was assigned a role, and she began to talk through the issues that were important to the character she had assumed. The conversation was realistic, and she began to cry. "I'm sorry," she said. "This is a problem that I genuinely have. I need to have someone else take this part and I'll listen. If this group can come up with some answers, you'll give me a new lease on my life. Right now, I'm just not sure what direction to take."

6. *Encourage as many students as possible to participate.* Match what you are asking with students' abilities. Remember that even though some students may never be able to comfortably get up in front of the class, they are participating as they watch. After you have done roleplay or mime several times, disassociate yourself with the content and watch your class. Those few who are putting concepts into action in front of the group are obviously involved. Those who are the audience, the learners, are usually riveted in their attention. Dramatic forms demand as close to 100 percent attention as you'll get with any group method.

7. *Always follow a roleplay, mime, or simulation with discussion.* This will double the impact of the dramatic venture. "Why do you think that character acted the way he did?" "Why do you think we often act the same way in similar situations?" "What things would have to be different in order for us to change our approach?" "What difference would being a Christian make?"

8. *The first couple of times you use impromptu drama, you may want to use warm-up exercises,* especially if this is something new to most of your students. These warm-up experiences should take no more than four minutes of class time. They are fun, and they force people to use their hands, legs, and faces in new ways. Make sure students know you are expanding their thinking when you introduce them to these exercises. You

91

want them to explore areas within themselves that they may not be in touch with. Out of these silly little exercises can come the freedom to do unique things for God.

WARM-UP EXERCISES

Students should work in pairs or small groups so that everyone in the room is participating. This takes away the feeling that "Everyone is looking at me." Adults may want to do these exercises in a chair or standing in one location. Often teens and young adults will get so thoroughly involved that they will squat on the floor to more fully participate in the activity.

Leaf Development

Pretend you are all seasons of a leaf. A fourth of you will be the budding spring leaf. Another fourth will be the full and blowing green leaf of summer. A fourth will be the changing and coloring leaf of fall. The final fourth will be the dropping, drying, pulverizing leaf of winter. Use your bodies to illustrate each aspect of the cycle.

For example, you might kneel as a spring leaf. Curl your body into a tight knot. Slowly begin to expand the knot; the bud is forming. Your fingers reach out little by little. You grow a bit more. You are hit by an unexpected cold spell. You shiver and shake, but gain strength through the experience. Finally you stretch into your final newness.

This type of experience is fun. Again, no more than three of four minutes should be used here. As everyone in the class participates, no one has time to look at anyone else. Or, as people work in pairs, they can give encouragement to each other. It's also fun to explain to the partner exactly what you were trying to do as a leaf. (You may want to read the illustration of the spring leaf to the group just to give students time to collect their own ideas and stretch their thinking.) As people participate, even four minutes a week, they will become more free and daring in their expression.

Doorbell

Different people have different experiences that eventually lead them to walk up to a house and ring a doorbell for help:
- A man who has just had his wallet stolen.
- A lady who has locked her car key inside her car. (It's interesting to watch people play this one. Nearly always, the character will kick the car!)
- A neighborhood child who wants help fixing his bicycle chain.

Mother Goose Rhyme

Select a Mother Goose rhyme that everyone knows. Ask students to work in small groups to present it in three ways. They should use movements that are appropriate to the age level as they recite the rhyme.

"Mary had a little lamb" is a familiar couplet. How might it be recited by a first grader in front of parents at a school program? How might a group of teens recite it? Finally how might the rhyme be presented by a professor? (College students enjoy this; usually they will rewrite the simple words, delivering it in a sonorously didactic style.)

Table Talk

You will need a table. People should take turns standing behind the table and using their feet and hands to communicate the following things:
- I've just had a terrible day.
- I'm very nervous about this test.
- It's so good to finally be home again.
- I hate housework.
- I can't believe they accepted me into the aviator program.

Drama! From these short, freeing exercises, it's just a short distance to doing things in the classroom that can revolutionize people's concept of Christianity. The Sunday school stops being an exciting event that everyone enjoys to varying degrees each Sunday and becomes instead the training group for real conflict between the Christian within the Kingdom of God and the world around him or her.

THE PLUSES OF ROLEPLAY

Janet obviously didn't want to be in summer Bible school. She was 13 and, until that summer, church had played little part in her life. When she was placed in a foster home, her guardians insisted that she follow the patterns they had established, and that included being at the little white church on the Maine hill every time something special was planned.

The junior high course for the two-week school was on faith sharing, and the primary method that was used throughout the course was roleplay. Students were placed in various situations and asked to share their faith as practice for the real thing.

Janet loved playing the part of the non-Christian. In fact, she was one of the best non-Christian players the other students had ever had to contend with. For each of their reasons for accepting Christ, she had two for why that was the silliest thing she had ever heard. Little by little, the students got better in using Scripture and applying what they had to say to the special needs of the person in the roleplay.

Traditionally there was a closing show-and-tell meeting for parents. Each age level demonstrated what it had learned during the two weeks. The students decided to let the teacher give them roleplays they had not done in class, and they would demonstrate what they had learned. They voted on who should participate and Janet was one of the winners. It was perhaps the first time she had ever been awarded anything positive by her peers. She was delighted.

The teacher panicked. What if Janet swore in front of the parents? What if the other students couldn't answer her arguments? "Janet," the teacher said with self-preservation as her motive, "tonight I want you to play the Christian."

Silence. A bit of rebellion. But Janet had won the vote, and she agreed to do it the teacher's way. That evening at the show and tell, Janet was excellent. She handled the verses and the Christian concepts perfectly. The teacher breathed a sigh of relief and suspected that the young girl had spent the afternoon learning those verses, determined that her classmates would not be ashamed that they had chosen her.

After the program, Janet came up to the teacher. "I guess you know I'm not a Christian." The teacher nodded. It hadn't taken brilliant analytic skills. "But tonight as I was saying the verses, it made sense," Janet said. "I'm going to think about it."

Roleplay—a powerful tool in the hands of a teacher who is willing to try this unique process. Roleplay is the process of assigning group members roles of people who are involved in real or hypothetical situations. The students talk back and forth, looking for solutions to problems, exploring the feelings of the people whose roles they have assumed, learning to articulate their faith and their own growth experiences.

What are the benefits of roleplay?

● *Roleplay stimulates inductive learning.* Most Sunday school students believe in theory that God's Word supplies answers. In roleplay they must find those answers and use them in classroom situations. These practice sessions often make it easier for students to carry what they have learned into their own lives.

Consider what might happen to teens who participate in the following roleplay. The teacher's aim is to help students discover how to exercise Christian friendship in difficult situations.

SITUATION: William is obnoxious and rude, so naturally students rarely include him in their activities. John begins to see that his rejection of William is unchristian and decides to ask William to join the youth group's basketball team. He shares his decision with two Christian friends.

Roleplay the conversation among the three boys. Assume that Friend 1 rejects the idea of making friends with William and including him in their activities. Friend 2 begins to see John's point.

In the classroom, the teens would assume their roles. (Because the roles are done in a church setting, students may mouth more Christlike conversations than they would in real life.)

> FRIEND 1: You're crazy if you ask William to play with us. He can't get along with anyone. He'll ruin the team spirit.
> FRIEND 2: No, wait. Maybe John's right. Christ would probably let William play.
> JOHN: That's my point. If we're going to be Christians, we have to follow Christ even when it's inconvenient.
> FRIEND 1: Maybe you do, but I'm not interested. You make the choice. Either you're friends with creeps or you're friends with me.
> JOHN: I want to be your friend. I really like you, but I don't want to let Jesus down. I love Him.
> FRIEND 2: If you invite William, I'll try to make him feel welcome.

After the three boys have carried the roleplay as far as they can, their teacher would cut the action and begin class discussion. It could go something like this:

Teacher: Steven, how did you feel playing the part of the Christian who was unwilling to be friends with William?

Steven: Cruel. I hope I wouldn't act like that in real life.

Class Member: I've got a problem something like this in my school gym class. There's one kid who always gets picked last for teams. He's a wipeout at everything. Maybe the next time I'm captain, I should pick him first.

Teacher: Even if your choice angered others you chose to be on your team?

Class Member: Maybe, if I were convinced I had done what Christ wanted.

• *By evaluating what students say in their roleplays, the teacher is able to determine where students are and concentrate his or her teaching in the areas of greatest need.*

• *Roleplay demonstrates to students that, from a human perspective, everything won't always turn out perfectly for the Christian.* There will be people who won't like them; their witness may be rejected; they may face problems which will never be resolved. Roleplay can prepare them to handle these difficulties without becoming discouraged or doubting that God cares.

- *Through roleplay and the discussion that follows it, students may find answers to their problems.* Too often older teens and adults repress their true feelings during the Sunday school hour. Even though they might want help or clarification, they may be ashamed or afraid to ask for it. But in a roleplay, they assume identities of imaginary people. Through these people, players are able to vocalize their own negative or divergent attitudes in the security of a play situation. As the class deals with "imaginary" problems, it can help students who are facing the same or similar difficulties in real life.

Consider the adult who feels bitter toward God and other people. Perhaps he refused to take part in a shady business deal and consequently went bankrupt. What insights might he gain from the following roleplay, even if he only participated by listening?

SITUATION: Joseph has been unjustly accused and thrown into prison.

Roleplay the debate that might have taken place in Joseph's mind during those years in jail. One student will play Joseph's doubting self, and another, Joseph's trusting self.

The roleplay might begin like this:

DOUBTING SELF: But, God, I followed You. Is this the way You reward me? I don't understand.

TRUSTING SELF: No, I don't understand, but I remember hearing the stories of how You led Abraham through difficulties. Surely You will do the same for me.

Group Magazine printed a transcript of teens working together on a difficult situation one of their members was really facing. They used roleplay to help that teenager deal with her problem. The true situation as Nancy perceived it was this: her parents wanted her to stay home and spend time with the family, but she wanted to attend a work camp during her Thanksgiving break. A real conflict built up. Nancy brought her frustrations to her youth group. The group used roleplay to help her look at the situation and consider the implications of her decision.

In the roleplay, Nancy was able to practice talking with her "parents" in an effective way, excellent preparation for talking with her real parents. She learned to control her feelings better. The group members were able to give her support for her problem. They were able to make positive suggestions. Nancy was able to see her situation more clearly because she was standing apart from it. She set goals for her approach to her parents. She got rid of some of the problem feelings she had been having toward them and felt much more confident about solving her problem.

• *Roleplay gives people a chance to experience new, unusual, or problem situations in a protected, caring environment.* They can try new approaches and correct mistakes. Unlike real life, if they make a mistake or suddenly have a better idea, they can go back and replay situations.

In Nancy's situation, she described what was happening. Actors were chosen. Nancy acted her own part the first time around, but she had difficulty controlling her feelings under pressure from her "mother" to stay at home. The leader asked Nancy to change roles—to take the role of mother. In this role reversal, Nancy had a new look at the situation.

What follows is a section of the roleplay and discussion that followed it:[2]

"Please, Mom, this is really important to me!"

"I know it is, Nancy, but this may be your last Thanksgiving dinner at home. We really want you to spend it with us."

"Besides, Nancy, you went to a work camp just this last summer. I can't see why you need to go on another one so soon. Your mother and I like to have you around some of the time."

"Dad, this camp is set up only for the kids who went to last summer's camp. I was chosen for my enthusiasm in helping others. It's something I've always wanted."

"But, Nancy, your Aunt Martha is coming just to see you, and she'll only be here at Thanksgiving."

"Mom, you know Aunt Martha just gives me a big hug and a kiss. Then she talks to you all the rest of the time."

After the roleplay continued for another minute or so, the leader cut the action and asked the group to talk about what had happened.

Leader: Nancy, what was going on inside while you were playing the part of the mother?

Nancy: Well, once I got into it, I began to understand how my parents felt so strongly about holidays.

Leader: What about you, Julie; how did you feel in Nancy's place?

Julie: I felt ganged up on. It's hard trying to answer one point after another with two parents firing at you.

In the continuing discussion, Nancy was able to affirm in front of the group how much she loved her parents and what a great thing it was to be able to hold conversations with them. She came up with a few new ideas to share with her parents. After the discussion the group played the roles again, and this time Nancy played herself.

Leader: Okay, who would like to play Nancy's mom this time around?
Shari: I know her mom pretty well, so I'd like to try.
Leader: Excellent. Nancy, give Shari some idea of how your mom might react to new suggestions and firmness on your part. Roy, think through your role again with the new information about her dad. We'll start in a few minutes. The rest of you continue to observe so you can make suggestions and share what you see happening. Remember, Nancy's goal is to stick to the issue and not get upset.

● *Roleplay allows players to experience a release of feelings.* Negative ones are often replaced with more positive ones.

● *Roleplays often deal with problems group members have had but haven't dared to mention.* It's a relief to students to know that others feel the same way they do, or are struggling in similar areas.

● *When students place themselves in the roles of other people, they learn to identify with them, and in this way they gain information about why others behave the way they do.* Role reversal, as Nancy's situation demonstrated, often assures this advantage.

Consider a roleplay in an adult class on family communication problems. Each person brings out his or her point of view. As the roleplay is slowing down, the teacher asks the men to take the women's roles and vice versa. When students gain increased understanding of themselves and others, they have paved the way for behavioral changes. The old Indian motto says, "Never judge a brave until you have walked a mile in his moccasins." That's true, and roleplay allows each of us to put on others' moccasins for a few minutes.

● *Participating in roleplays may help students use their intellectual potential more fully in other areas.* Poor interpersonal skills or feelings of low self-esteem can affect students' intellectual development. If through roleplaying they come to understand their own and others' behavior better, they could move on to a higher all-around intellectual performance.

● *Roleplay can guide students into Scripture.* It can show people who have been Christians for years just how important continuing Bible study is. It can demonstrate just how poorly prepared many of us are to live our faith in difficult situations.

POINTS TO REMEMBER

1. *Not all students will be effective roleplayers.* Some who have never tried it will assume they can't do it. Most can; they are just afraid of the first try. Some really can't. Be sensitive to the limitations of those few people. There will be other areas in which they can contribute to the class.

2. *Roles vary in difficulty.* Suppose you have a Christian with a problem and a Christian who is trying to help. The first role is easier (in roleplay, not in real life). Match the roles to the experience and spiritual maturity of students. It's ideal when a student will volunteer for a role.

Occasionally, there are characters necessary to a roleplay with which no one wishes to be identified. This is particularly true in young teen classes where the young people are working on picking and owning their identities. It would be all too easy for the class to pick up the term "fatty" and apply it to the girl who plays a role of someone who is overweight. In the first few roleplay situations, you may want to avoid this type of roleplay completely, unless one of the students brings up a real situation that he or she needs help with. Later, unfavorable roles should go to people with enough personal security to carry them off.

Or, use "The Chair" technique. If a situation is too emotional or a character too threatening for a student to play without overacting or causing the class to think of him or her as the type of person in the role, assign that role to "The Chair." The students in the roleplay would direct all their comments to "The Chair" as if it were a real person.

3. *Prepare the class audience before the roleplay begins for its part in the presentation.* Suggest that each student identify with or try to experience the feelings of one or more of the characters. Explain that everyone is included in the discussion following the roleplay and that students may be asked to give their feelings about certain responses or suggest alternate ways the roleplay might have been developed.

4. *In difficult roleplays, or when the players do not have a strong Bible background, consider assigning class helpers to each player.* These helpers meet with their player before the roleplay begins to decide what position will be taken. At points during the roleplay, you may stop the action and allow players to ask advice from class helpers before resuming the play.

Or, as an alternate to the class helper idea, you may want to send an additional student into a roleplay to help a player who is having difficulty. For example, if the "Christian" player is unable to answer the questions of a "non-Christian," you might introduce a second "Christian" to the situation to keep the conversation progressing.

5. *Cut the roleplay* when:
- the group has seen enough of the situation to analyze the problem and make helpful suggestions.
- the group can project what would happen if the roleplay were continued.
- the players have reached an impasse, and it would serve little purpose to send in additional students to prolong the play.
- there is a natural closing.

6. *Always follow up the roleplay with a discussion of what happened during the roleplay itself.* This will include questions such as: what do you think each character was feeling? Why did characters react the way they did?

7. *Lead the students from the discussion of the roleplay into a personal application of what they learned from the experience.* Questions such as, "Why do you think the characters acted the way they did?" might change to "What makes us act like that sometimes?" This application is actually an inductive guide designed to help learners transfer what they learned in the classroom roleplay to their own life situations.

Also, as part of this final step, the students might suggest ways they could improve the roleplaying technique and give suggestions of other problem areas they would like to deal with through roleplay.

To summarize the entire roleplaying process: first the teacher presents the situation and instructs his or her students so they will be able to get the maximum benefit from it. Second, the dramatic action is presented. And finally, there is the application. Not one of these steps may be excluded if the roleplay is to be completely effective.

NOW IT'S TIME TO ROLEPLAY

Study the following situations. Each can be used to help introduce your class to roleplaying. Read or tell the situation to your class. Then follow the directions at the end of each roleplay.

The first, "How to Ditch a Friend," is designed for junior high and senior high girls. It is especially effective when it is used in lessons that center around living the Christian life.

HOW TO DITCH A FRIEND

SITUATION: The Group had been "The Group" ever since school began. It was unofficially composed of the prettiest girls in the class. Girls from this clique always got elected to class offices. They laughed a lot and seemed to enjoy life more than any of the girls who weren't a part of The Group.

From the beginning of the year, Cory had made up her mind that she would break into The Group, even though she thought it might mean seeing less of Lois.

Lois was her best friend. They could share their thoughts and special secrets. Often they planned their devotions together. But Lois was dumpy looking, and somehow her clothes always seemed out-of-date. The Group would never accept Lois.

So Cory began her infiltration plan. She started sitting at the same lunch table with The Group. And when her mother asked who she wanted invited to her birthday party, she mentioned only the names of the girls in The Group and the fellows they talked about.

The Monday after the party, Cory was talking to Lois when Sandy, a girl from The Group, walked by. "That was a great party, Cory," she said. "I'll save you a seat in the cafeteria this noon."

Sandy walked away without saying a word to Lois. It was just as though she hadn't seen her at all.

---

(1) *Roleplay* the conversation Cory and Lois might have immediately following this incident. How does Cory explain the party and how does Lois react? Each girl should try to share honestly with the other how she feels in such a way that their friendship will not be permanently damaged. Each girl should learn something about herself and about friendship through the conversation.

(2) *Roleplay* the conversation between Cory and Sandy as Cory explains the importance of her friendship with Lois. Cory might attempt in this conversation to break down the clique she has tried so hard to join.

Note that "How to Ditch a Friend" leads students to a crisis point. At that point, participants should have little trouble reacting to the situation. And because the problem itself is specific and not too complex, students will be able to solve it successfully.

Nearly every girl will identify with at least one character in this roleplay. This identification will make it easy for her to participate in a discussion following the roleplay.

Opening discussion should center on the roleplay itself:

- "How do you think Cory felt about herself throughout this roleplay?"
- "If Cory had to choose between her friendship with Lois and her friendship with Sandy, which do you think she would choose? Defend your answer."

Then help the students personally apply what they have learned through the roleplay by asking questions like these:

- "Why is it so easy for Christian teens to form cliques? What could our class do to help dissolve existing cliques and keep others from forming?"
- "How do you think Christ might finish the following sentence? One of the qualities I would like to find in Christian friendships is _____, because _____."

During the discussion, the teacher acts as a guide, asking questions, listening to comments students make, usually keeping the students on the lesson topic.

Occasionally, however, a student will ask a question or make a comment that the teacher knows will change the lesson's focus. For example, suppose that during the discussion of the above roleplay, a girl would say, "What's wrong with being popular? As far as I can see, Sandy wasn't the villain here. Why are Christians always against success?"

The teacher should evaluate the question—in this case, what is the Christian's view of success? If the teacher feels the student genuinely wants an answer, he or she should allow the discussion to switch directions. Real needs of students and their questions should take precedence over lesson plans.

The roleplay, "Home Is Hate," is designed for junior high, senior high, and adult students. It should be used in lessons that center around witnessing and living the Christian life.

HOME IS HATE

Situation: About three months ago this same time of night, Tor had sneaked out the back door and was determined never to return home again. Now he stared at that door, waiting for courage to knock.

He could almost hear the fights and the sobbing, and see the hypocritical pecks on the cheek his parents gave each other when others were watching. Tor often wondered what kept them together. He'd even hoped for divorce so the bickering and pretense would end.

Then that night for no specific reason, no big fight, he had just reached his end. He couldn't live in that house anymore.

"Why come back?" he reasoned. "After the welcoming scene, everything will be the same. The walls will close in on me again."

But he'd promised God he'd chance it, so he had to knock.

Through Kurt, a guy he'd met on a beach, Tor had discovered Jesus Christ. He'd been accepted at a Christian hostel and, for a perfect month, he had learned about his new God.

Then last week at dinner, Kurt said, "Tor, don't you think you ought to go home and tell your folks what's happened?"

"My home is hate," he answered. Then with vivid illustrations, he shared his parents with the group. He wanted to convince them it would be wrong to return, but by the time he finished talking, he knew what God expected of him regardless of circumstances.

Now back home, he prayed a final time, "I wish You hadn't asked, Lord." He knocked. Seconds later a light went on upstairs.

---

(1) *Roleplay* the conversation that takes place between Tor and his parents. Try to capture the feelings each might have. Develop the questions the parents would have about Tor's running and Tor's explanation. Include how Tor would give his testimony and the reactions the parents might have to his newfound faith.

(2) (For adults) *Roleplay* the conversation between Tor's parents after Tor goes to bed. Assume that, in spite of Tor's witness, their attitudes remain the same. Then replay the conversation assuming that their attitudes are beginning to change, and they are evaluating their relationship with each other and God.

In roleplays like "Home Is Hate" in which emotions play a large part, the teacher may want to stop the conversation at an emotionally charged point and ask players to remain in character while they soliloquize on how they feel at the moment. By reflecting out loud, the actors are better able to evaluate their responses, and this additional data helps the other players and the audience participate more completely in the roleplay.

Discussion questions on a teen level for this roleplay might include:

● "Suppose the same pressures Tor ran away from build again. Now that he is a Christian, how might he handle them?"
● "In what ways other than through his spoken testimony might Tor witness to his parents?"

On the adult level, a discussion leader might ask: "How might these parents work to build a new relationship between themselves and with their son?"

The purpose of the lesson will determine the type of application questions that would be most effective here. If the purpose is to train teens to witness to those around them, an application question might be: "Why is it often harder to witness to those we know than it is to tell strangers about Christ?"

But if the adult class is studying interpersonal relationships, they would gain more from a question like this: "If you could share with a new Christian just one principle on successful Christian family living, what would it be?"

The next roleplay, "Small, Round Compact," was designed for senior high and some junior high students. You may want to assign the part of Julia to "The Chair." Assign the roles before the situation is read.

SMALL, ROUND COMPACT

SITUATION: Charlene sat stiffly on the edge of the bed and stared at her bulletin board. It displayed all the treasures of her senior year—Stu's rose, a picture of a blond holding gas-filled balloons, the cover of "TIME" which was a collage of things associated with women. She had used that cover to illustrate her women's lib paper for social problems class. Then it had meant an A, but now the little, round compact in the corner of the collage seemed to fill the room.

In her hand she held an identical birth-control compact she had found in her 15-year-old sister's drawer.

"Julia's sleeping with John!" Charlene said out loud as if the connection of the case with real life just hit her. "How could You let her do it, God?

"I wish I'd never gone looking for her green scarf," she thought. "Now what am I supposed to do?"

Soliloquy: Charlene should share how she is feeling right now about herself and her role as older sister to Julia. She might include some of the fears she has about confronting her sister.

Roleplay Charlene and Julia's conversation. How might Charlene show her kid sister she is ruining God's plans for her life? What reasons, now that there is little danger of pregnancy, could Charlene give for saving sex for marriage? How might Julia counter her arguments?

Class discussion could be started with questions such as: "How would you answer Charlene's question to God, 'How could You let her do it, God?' " "If you had played Charlene, what additional things would you have said to Julia?" A question such as "What happens when we knowingly go against God's plans?" would guide the students toward personal evaluation.

Some roleplays are designed primarily to develop students' skills. For example, roleplay is one of the most effective ways of helping students articulate the reasons why they believe as they do. In these skill development roleplays, one person might share why his or her beliefs make sense and another person would keep the conversation going with questions.

Theology Practice: Roleplay a conversation between a Christian in confirmation class and an elementary kid who says, "How come those classes are so important anyway? What difference do they make?"

Theology Practice: Roleplay a conversation between a Reformed Jew and a Messianic Jew on the reasons why the one accepts Jesus as God's Son and the other does not.

Theology Practice: Two high school students share their views of creation. One believes in God as Creator and the other does not.

Theology Practice: Two adults discuss different ways communion is viewed by Christians by taking two different positions. Each should be a spokesperson for one position. "I believe this because . . ."

The whole class can be involved simultaneously in skill-development roleplays like the four above. Number the students in pairs: 1, 2, 1, 2. For the first skill-development roleplay, number 2 might play the role of the Christian who is going through confirmation class. This is the harder role, of course. For the second roleplay, the pair should reverse roles.

Don't discuss skill-building roleplays after each one. Instead, wait until you have done four or five of them, and discuss them as a unit. A question like this might be a good discussion starting point following the roleplays above: "In what areas did you feel that your answer was weakest? Strongest?"

The type of application questions you use will depend on your students' involvement in the topic. If they are just beginning to learn why they believe as they do, to study their church's doctrine, the teacher should keep the roles simple. The more aware of the subject the students are, the more complex the roleplay setups can be.

The following roleplays are part of a course on witnessing designed for students in the last two years of high school.[3]

Focus: Felt needs

SITUATION: David knew it was Jeff's first day back at school since his mother had died of cancer. So he made a special point to stop by Jeff's locker on the way to his first class. But he hadn't expected a reaction quite like the one he got.

"Hey, man," said David, "I just wanted you to know I'll be praying for you today. I know it's going to be a rough one."

"Oh, get off my case," snarled Jeff. "What do you know about death? Not even enough to be afraid of it. And don't bother talking to your Friend upstairs. What does He know about it, either?"

Continue the roleplay as David tries to show Jeff how Christ can meet his felt need.

Focus: How to become a Christian

SITUATION: Annalise has stopped by her friend Karen's house. She finds Karen isn't at home, but Karen's mother, Mrs. James, invites her in anyway for a Coke.

At the kitchen table she talks admiringly of her daughter, then says suddenly, "You girls both have so much faith. I wish I could have as much faith as you do."

Roleplay the conversation that develops as Annalise explains to Mrs. James what real faith involves and how she can exercise it.

105

SITUATION: Pete and Al are at it again. They've had this friendly debate going about Christianity. Pete brings up an argument for Christianity; Al counters and brings up a point against Christianity; Pete counters it, and so on. All perfectly good-natured. Pete knows Al is serious about finding Christ—this is his way of checking things out. Today, though, Pete is in for a surprise.

"OK, we've talked facts long enough," says Al. "Tell me, what difference does being a Christian make to your life?"

Roleplay the conversation as Pete shares personally from his Christian experience. (Note: Person playing Pete may use his own real experiences.)

WHAT YOU DON'T KNOW

In some roleplays, the players are given different information about their situation. Player 1 will not know some of the hidden issues that Player 2 knows. This is a lot like what happens in real life. People often show us only part of what they are feeling or worried about.

As an example, read the following roleplay by Mark Olson: "Carmen and Maribel."

CARMEN:

Your name is Carmen.

You are the guest of honor at a slumber party given by your best friend Maribel to celebrate your 15th birthday. You admire Maribel for being so friendly and at ease with people. You are very happy that she is having a party for you and you want to please her.

But Maribel wants to play a levitation game. You are a Christian and you believe that it is wrong for Christians to dabble in the supernatural. It seems harmless enough, but you feel sure it would be wrong.

Your job, as Carmen, is to convince Maribel not to fool around with levitation. If she won't give up, refuse to take part. But try not to be preachy or goody-goody. Show Maribel that you value her friendship no matter what.

MARIBEL:

Your name is Maribel.

You are 15. You are having a slumber party for your best friend Carmen, who's having her 15th birthday.

You are anxious to have the party turn out well, both for Carmen's sake and to boost your popularity at school. Carmen is a Christian and a little shy. You're anxious to have the other girls see that she can be a lot of fun.

At another party you were at, some kids were fooling around with levitation. They actually seemed to lift a person off the ground without touching her. You want to try it at your party since it was so much fun.

Your job as Maribel is to tell Carmen what you want to do, explain to her that it's just a case of "mind over matter" and that all everyone has to do is concentrate on the word "up." Try to convince Carmen that levitation is harmless and fun and that since it's her birthday, she should let you try to levitate her.

"Carmen and Maribel" was developed for use in a teen Sunday school class. Individualized information given to different roleplay characters can be very little, as in the roleplay above, or it can be extensive, as in the roleplay simulations in Chapter 5. These types of roleplays are both more difficult and more helpful than many of the simple ones. People almost always have more happening below the surface than they are willing to immediately share. If Christians deal only with what is immediately apparent, they will come across as superficial, predictable, and unloving. When there is more to the role than any player individually knows, players must become interested in the other players as people. People, not just the situation or just leading a "soul" to Christ, become primary.

Abraham Maslow constructed a human needs pyramid[4] which can be helpful to teachers dealing with students. You may want to explain the concepts the pyramid illustrates to students before they get too involved in roleplay situations.

Maslow's pyramid has a lot to teach the roleplayer—in actuality, the Christian who is serious about putting Christianity to work.

1. *People generally move up the pyramid only as they get their needs met on each lower level.* For example, you meet a neighbor at the grocery store and invite her to a special musical at your church. She responds, "It's so cold out." That's not a logical answer. What does the cold have to do with the church musical? She may be telling you that the heater in her car doesn't work, so if she comes you'll have to pick her up. She may even be telling you that she doesn't have heat in her home, and until that Level 1 need is met, she just isn't interested in church musicals.

2. *People work all their lives to reach and maintain Level 5.* At this level, Christians may be developing their gifts for Christ's use and learning what it means to model Him more perfectly.

3. *People move from one level to another.* People are motivated by their lowest unfilled need. A person might be doing just great when he suddenly loses his job or finds out that his 13-year-old daughter is drinking heavily with her friends. Suddenly he slips on the pyramid. He can't work on self-esteem or personal growth until he handles the love, safety, and security needs first.

In a roleplay, as in real life, the helper can't deal with any problem until he or she first takes care of the needs that are primary in the other person's life. If roleplay can teach us this type of sensitivity, we will move ahead a giant step.

Level 5
Self-Actualization Needs
Using your potential, abilities.

Level 4
Self-Esteem Needs.
What you think of yourself,
Self-image, self-worth.

Level 3
Love Needs.

Level 2
Safety and Security Needs.

Level 1
Physiological, Biological
Needs.

Although roleplays are often limited to two people, they don't have to be. One of the benefits of having more people involved is that the responsibility for the success of the roleplay is shared. When one person can't think of another word to say, a second or third person can step in.

Another benefit: there is the possibility that people are drawn to reasoning that is slightly more advanced than their own. Young people in particular vary widely in their ability to reason and make moral or Christlike decisions. As they hear each other speak in roleplay dilemmas, they will be exposed to thinking patterns that are different, often more complex, than their own.

The following roleplay[5] has three players, and each player is given slightly different information:

FATHER:

Your daughter, Sharon, has been dating a nice young man, Ralph, for several months. You and your wife think he's a fine person. Lately, however, you notice that Ralph hasn't called or come by the house. Sharon no longer talks about him, and seems withdrawn. Then you overhear Sharon and her mother talking about the reasons for the situation. You break into the conversation, angry with Ralph, angry with Sharon, and angry with your wife for sympathizing.

MOTHER:

Your daugher, Sharon, has been dating a really nice young man, Ralph, for several months. You and your husband think he's a fine person. Lately, however, you notice that Ralph hasn't called or come by the house. Sharon no longer talks about him, and seems withdrawn. You ask her what the problem is. As she tells you, you react sympathetically and with love. You try to help her talk about her feelings. As you talk with Sharon, your husband overhears the conversation.

SHARON:

You really like Ralph and like being with him. You've been dating him for several months, and were friends with him a long time before that. Your parents have always welcomed him in your home. On your last date, however, you feel he went too far sexually. You told him you don't want to see him or talk with him for a while, until you sort out your feelings. Your mother notices that Ralph no longer calls you or comes by the house. You finally tell her what happened on the date, and your need to decide whether or not to keep seeing Ralph. As you talk with your mother, your father overhears the conversation.

PICTURE ROLES

For a change of pace, show the class a picture, and ask students to develop a roleplay around it. The picture could depict a situation or show a close-up of a face.

When students look at a face and are asked to feel with that person, they can put quite a bit of themselves and their own feelings into their comments without feeling exposed. "She's worried," a junior high might say. "Her parents have been fighting a lot and last night she heard her mother say that she was tired of being stuck in the marriage and she had no intention of remaining stuck. Let's roleplay what the girl tells her youth leader about her fears."

Some pictures tell stories. The students are given a picture and asked to develop roleplays based on the situation.

Study the following situation. What issues might the situation bring up for an adult class?

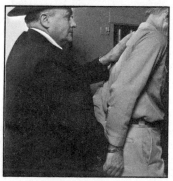

Review: So You're Going to Lead a Roleplay

If you're going to lead a roleplay:

● *Make certain everyone understands the situation.* Are there difficult words or concepts that need explaining? Don't assume too much. One teacher tried a roleplay with adults on discretionary income, and the roleplay was a complete flop. He didn't find out until several weeks later that the people involved had no idea what the word *discretionary* meant, and they were too embarrassed to say so.

• *Don't forget that you understand more about the teaching situation than the students do.* You have an aim in mind. You know where you want the class session to go. You know why you decided to use this roleplay on this particular Sunday. But don't be rigid here. Be open to the Holy Spirit's leading and be willing to change your plans when you become aware of an unforeseen need.

• *Play out the situations until the roles are effectively presented.* This rarely takes more than two or three minutes. If things aren't going well, add another character to the situation or step into a role yourself.

• *Don't forget the value of role switching.* It's not necessary that a father always play a father. He might learn by playing a mother or a son.

• *Always debrief.* Let people tell how they felt about their roles and responses. Have some questions prepared that may stimulate discussion. Caution: never evaluate the people in the roleplay ("Jim certainly did better than Joe").

• *Keep the classroom safe.* People take a chance when they participate. If you want to continue using this valuable process, you will have to continually affirm those students who dared to get involved.

• *Unless a student brings up a real situation, stay away from situations that too closely parallel those of the members in the group.* If a farmer is about to lose his farm, it's not the time to do a roleplay on bankruptcy. Also stay away from roleplays that are exact opposites of situations people in your classroom face. For instance, if you have a very fat boy in your class, you should think carefully about doing a roleplay about the self-image of a very skinny girl. This type of obvious pointing assumes students are too dumb to catch on. You may be trying to help that fat boy, but instead he may hear, "The teacher hates me, just like everyone else. I'm never coming back. I don't have to sit here and take this."

DEVELOP ORIGINAL ROLEPLAYS

Work alone or in a small group to compile a list of some general problems your class may have. For example:

Junior High	Senior High	Adult
Cliques	Peer pressure	Finances
Scholastic failure	Immorality	Fear of aging
Poor self-image	Earning money	Single parenting

Then brainstorm possible ways one of these problems could be put into lifelike situations. (Remember: avoid situations which too closely parallel those in which members of your class are involved.) Choose the brainstorm idea that best fits the aim of the lesson you will be teaching. Develop it enough so students will understand the problem when you present it to them, but not so much that you imply a solution. For a roleplay to be a learning experience, the content and solution must be supplied by the students. Usually it is best to end your prepared situation at a climax point. This forces students to answer the question, "What happens next?" Plan at least one discussion question on the roleplay and one personal application question.

It is unnecessary to write your original roleplays. Simply tell the class about the situation they will complete. This cuts preparation time.

Consider the junior high problem, scholastic failure. You might develop a roleplay like this:

SITUATION: Jon gets poor grades, but he has never cheated in an effort to improve them. His friend Gerry, although he is smarter than Jon, is not as honest.

On the day of the unit geography test, Jon prayed, "Please, Lord, help me get a 'C' so I'll pass this marking period." About midway through the test, he glanced over at Gerry, who was looking at a scrap of paper in his hand and copying something onto his paper.

When the grades came back, Jon had a "D." His friend who had cheated had a "B." Jon was frustrated, and told a Christian friend how he felt. "I'm not even sure I believe in prayer anymore," he said.

Roleplay the friend and Jon's conversation as the friend tries to help him with his problem by sharing Biblical principles and practical suggestions.

Discussion question: "In what ways might the friend's answers be helpful to Jon throughout his life?"

Application question: "Why is it important for us to discuss questions and doubts we might have about the way God works?"

An adult teacher may develop a roleplay on the fear of aging.

SITUATION: Mrs. Taylor's whole life has been her children, but now they are grown, married, and living in other cities. "I'm of little use to anyone," she tells a Christian friend. "I really don't know why the Lord doesn't take me home; I'm ready to go."

Roleplay the friend and Mrs. Taylor's conversation in which the friend tries to change Mrs. Taylor's attitude and give her reasons for living.

Discussion question: "What do you think was the most important thing Mrs. Taylor learned from this conversation? Explain your answer."

Application question: "In what practical ways can we help others find a place in which they can make valuable contributions to others and serve God?"

USE A ROLEPLAY TO WRITE A CLASS PLAY

Some classes are capable of writing and presenting their own original playlets. Although these are rarely of professional quality, they do have merit. Students participate in the creative process and this gives them a sense of achievement. Even more important, students learn to share with others the truth they have accepted.

The easiest way to write a playlet is to expand a roleplay. Begin by looking at the lesson in which you want to use the playlet. (Usually allow about three weeks for the creation.) Then develop a roleplay that you feel will help your students better understand the message of that lesson.

Now guide your students as they follow these steps:

1. *Become familiar with the roleplay situation.*

If the teen lesson is on salvation, you might write a roleplay like this one, and ask teens to begin their playlet preparation by studying it.

SITUATION: Tom admires the Christians he knows and would like to have Christ as his Friend, too. But when he was in junior high, he introduced his sixth-grade sister to drugs. He was able to stop using them when he realized what they could do to his body, but she wasn't so lucky. She's hooked, and he feels helpless to do anything for her. He feels that he killed his sister's future, and God would never be willing to be friends with him.

---

2. *Talk through the problems involved in the roleplay and the different ways those problems might be resolved.*

In the above roleplay, students might discuss what Biblical principles a Christian could share with Tom that would help him understand Christ's love, ways in which Tom might handle the guilt he feels, how a Christian teen and Tom could work together to help Tom's sister.

3. *Decide where the playlet should start, what scenes should be included, how many characters are needed.*

In Tom's story, a conversation between his sister and him would introduce the problems and get the class immediately involved in the situation. This playlet needs only three main characters—Tom, his sister, and a Christian teen.

4. *Roleplay and tape the situation. Then transcribe the tape and edit the transcription into playlet form. Duplicate copies for students who will be participating in the original class playlet.*

The final transcription of Tom's story might begin like this:

TOM: Listen, Cathy, it's bad news. I know, I was almost there. Please stop while you can.

CATHY: Not long ago your story was a lot different. *(Mimics Tom.)* "Try this, Cathy. Just one pill, Cathy. It will send you into orbit. A new world, Cathy."

TOM: I was wrong.

CATHY: No, you weren't. Why should I give up something I enjoy just because you changed your mind? Now will you give me the money or not?

TOM: No, I can't, Cathy. I feel like I'm paying to kill your future.

CATHY *(sarcastically)*: Let's get superdramatic about it, Tommy Boy. If you won't lend me the money, I know other ways to get it.

TOM: No! Here's what you need. *(She takes the money and leaves. William enters.)*

WILLIAM: Say, who's the cute girl? New girl friend?

TOM *(sadly)*: No, my sister. We just had a little argument, and I lost.

WILLIAM: Better luck next time. Maybe I can cheer you up with an invitation. A bunch of us kids are getting together for a Bible study every Tuesday after school. Since you and I have talked about God several times, I thought you'd like to come.

TOM: If I attended, God would probably strike the whole bunch with lightning. Your God wouldn't want me, William. No way!

This playlet could develop in any number of ways. Cathy could overdose, and William, Tom, and an adult counselor could work with her to help her understand that it is possible to break her habit. She agrees to try and forgives Tom for getting her started. When Tom experiences human forgiveness, he realizes how much greater God's forgiveness must be, and he accepts Christ.

Or, Tom could finally agree to attend the Bible study, and through the teens' witness, accept Christ. That same day, his sister is picked up for stealing a radio and trying to use it to buy drugs. Tom knows he may never be able to undo the damage he's caused in Cathy's life, but he tells her that, if necessary, he will continue praying for her for the rest of his life. Later William tells Tom about a fellow in his neighborhood who has just started popping pills. Tom realizes that this could be an opportunity to help someone else in a way he is unable to help his sister. He asks William to introduce them.

ROLEPLAYS PLUS . . .

Slide-and-Sound Roleplay

Have three or four different groups of students complete the same roleplay. The class should choose the one they consider best. Those chosen should participate in the same roleplay again. This time record both the roleplay situation and the group's solution. Each player should attempt to duplicate the feelings and facial expressions he or she thinks a person in this situation would have.

A photographer in the class should capture these expressions by taking close-up shots of each roleplayer.

Synchronize the slides and tape.

This recorded roleplay can be used in many ways. For example, a slide-and-sound roleplay on prejudice produced by the senior highs could be shown to the whole Sunday school. Then teens could divide the group and guide the different age levels in discussion.

An adult class might record a roleplay for use in the Sunday worship service. For example, a roleplay in which a Christian is an effective witness might be a creative way for a pastor to begin a Sunday sermon on the need for church members to get involved in evangelism.

Roleplay Outing

Suggest that your class plan an outing with another class or church that is also familiar with the principles of roleplay. Ask each person to bring one roleplay situation aimed at the theme for the outing.

For example, the teen and adult classes could use the theme, "Learning About Each Other." The roleplays would deal with areas such as establishing friendships and examining frustrations between the two age-groups.

Members of racially different churches might learn from an experimental outing built around the theme, "Let's Get Together."

At the end of the outing each person should share the insights he or she has gained from this experience. A list of projects that would continue interaction might also grow from this experience.

Share a Roleplay

Purchase a loose-leaf notebook for your Sunday school library and label it, "Roleplays That Work." Ask each teacher who develops a successful, original roleplay to write it in the book. Follow this format:

Age Level: _____

Topic: _____

(Roleplay itself written here.)

Discussion Questions: _____

Application Questions: ———————————————————————

Created by: ———————————————————————————

Used by: —————————————————————————————

Roleplay a Bible Story

Some young teen classes find roleplaying Bible stories they have studied a valuable experience. When they become involved in the situations, they are better able to understand some of the temptations, triumphs, and challenges Biblical people experienced. This understanding helps teens apply to their own lives the principles these stories illustrate.

One class had a videotape recorder available to them, so they decided to record the "Life of Joseph" and invite their families to see their movie.

It took three hours one Saturday afternoon to complete the half-hour tape. The students first talked through what they planned to do in each scene. Then they roleplayed each scene approximately the way they wanted to record it on tape. Students who were not involved in that scene would give their opinions about anything they felt was good or in need of change.

In one scene Joseph was in prison. The teen playing the part of Joseph knelt and prayed to God not only to help him but also to give him the strength to be a good witness to others around him. When the scene ended, his classmates didn't crowd around the video set to see the replay the way they usually did. Instead a friend of the player asked, "You were really praying, weren't you? I mean, you weren't just acting?"

The 13-year-old boy answered, "I guess God wants us to do things for real or others who watch this won't see much more than just a story."

The teens invited their parents to see and discuss their finished roleplay. Many came, some who had never been to the church before.

After the film, one father said, "It's not for me. I just can't seem to reach God, but my son has. I hope he never loses what he has found here in church."

1. A group of self-made millionaires was asked to list the qualities that had contributed to their success and the importance of each quality. The results: Enthusiasm—40%; attitude—40%; discipline—10%; knowledge—5%; ability—5%. How closely, do you suppose, would a successful teacher's percentages match these?

2. This excerpt and the situation surrounding it was taken from John Shaw's article, "Roleplays," in *Group Magazine*, September, 1979. Used by permission.

3. Richard Peace, "Giving Your Faith and Keeping It, Too," part of the **Christian Growth Elective** series. The three Focus roleplays are used as part of a review following in-depth study of the Scriptural basis for faith sharing.

4. For additional information on Maslow's pyramid and how it can be used in helping a Christian leader more effectively deal with others, see "Creative Leadership Communication," by Kent Stickler, part of the *Creative Leadership for Teacher Growth* kit, David C. Cook Publishing Co., © 1982.

5. Roleplay from the **Christian Growth Elective** series.

CHAPTER 6

Mime—
Miracle of Motion

The heart has reason which reason can never know.
Pascal

Mime, derived from the Greek word meaning "to imitate," is dramatic action in which players use motions rather than words to share experiences with the audience. One of the miracles of mime is that it enlarges the powers of imagination, not only for the participant, but also for the viewer.

The story is told of Demetrius who, during the reign of Nero, announced that mime was nonsense. If a person had something to say, that person should say it, and not just flap the arms and wag the head and hope that the audience came to some logical conclusion. The leading pantomime of the day accepted the challenge—to prove to Demetrius that he wasn't just hoodwinking the public. The mime performed, and Demetrius became a convert to the form. "Man!" he shouted in delight. "This is not seeing, but hearing and seeing, both. It's as if your hands were tongues."

Everyone in the world uses mime, but we seldom call it by name. It can be a universal language as people signal, gesture, and overemphasize their actions to let someone across the room "hear" what needs to be communicated.

Children can be great mimes. I was at a beach in Mexico one afternoon when three Mexican children came over to help me look for shells. They found some unusual ones I had missed because they knew where to look. With motions they described the fishy creature that had been in each shell. I learned from them that this was the spot where the fishermen bring in lobsters. The children lived in a little town about 30 minutes away from the beach, and this was their school holiday. They loved to swim, but not at that spot because the coral cut their feet. Would I like a piece of cake their mother had brought along? And, yes, they would love to taste the candy I had brought. All this without them knowing my language or me knowing theirs. Mime.

With the popularity of Marcel Marceau, mime has had a revival. It's not unusual in some areas of San Francisco or Toronto, for example, to find mimes on the street entertaining anyone willing to watch a silent story. "I first saw mime on a street corner," a senior high teacher said. "A woman performed and then collected the coins people were willing to put in her cap. I watched that mime go through the entire life cycle in only ten minutes. She was born, and I struggled with her as she arrived into the world. She grew and I pushed and strained with her. I saw her as an adolescent, a parent, an old person facing her own death. All I needed to participate was a healthy imagination; I lived a lifetime on that street corner. I wanted to take that woman back to my classroom, but you know, with the right suggestions my teens can participate without her professional help. No one throws money, of course, but the discussion is worth more than dollars."

Mimes are using their art to present their messages—political, social, environmental. Why not spiritual?

MIME AND DANCE—A CONTRAST

Mime and dance have similar origins, yet they are very different in focus. Mime expresses the movement of the soil—the earthbound creature who is aware of his or her earth roots. Within that person is the need to reach beyond self, and the Christian realizes that this need to reach is embedded in each person by the Creator. Mime, when used as "God talk," emphasizes our condition as earth people and our desire to be more than we are. Mime allows us to visualize the tremendous struggles of our lives. Mime is based on life.

Dance by contrast is not rooted to the earth.[1] It is more abstract, weightless and airy. The dancers leap and float through the air. Mimists walk with every muscle showing; every strain and burden is obvious.

Dance aims at pretense; mime aims at creating reality through illusions.

Mime deals with what is absolutely necessary to communicate—the symbolic movements that are common to all of us. Dance, on the other hand, elaborates and decorates for the sake of beauty. Were the mime to expand beyond the basic story line, especially in the unprofessional classroom setting, the class would be lost.

What's the difference between mime and pantomime? In our classroom settings, very little. But for the purists who are involved in presentation rather than teaching, there is a difference. Mime refers to a system of exercises, technical strategies, and dramatic movements. Pantomime is the use of these learned patterns to convey a story. Many of the current mimes, fathered by Marcel Marceau, combine mime and pantomime.

Mark Stolzenberg, in *Exploring Mime*[2], explains that mime deals with the hidden and underlying meanings and forces of the universe. Pantomime addresses itself to character and plot. Pantomime relies on the creation of imaginary objects and people to tell the story. Mime and pantomime both help us understand ourselves and our world better.

MIME—MESSAGE AND SYMBOL

This chapter will concentrate on mime for the nonprofessional—the type of mime that can be used by a teacher in a classroom situation, without whiteface, and without understanding the amazing movements of a trained mime. Classroom mime encourages people to use their bodies to give a reflection of life, using emotions rather than words.

So push back the chairs, and get involved in this ancient and new teaching method.

Once there was a church
that hired a toymaker for an architect.
He made church pews
so they were like crazy putty.
They could be bent
so people could see each other.
Once the people turned the pews
back to back and it worked.
There is hardly a Sunday
when they have them all
in long, straight rows.
People can make the pew
any shape they want
depending on
what they want to do.[3]

Our culture rewards the nonexpressive. Many people in this society are embarrassed by a show of emotions, even though it is often necessary and healthy for them to express what they are feeling, and compare and discuss these feelings with others. Mime gives teens and adults a secure vehicle for this comparison and discussion. Because there are no words, students are forced to draw their own conclusions. And as they consider the message of the mime, many will personally apply the truths it demonstrates.

Consider the following mime and how it could be used to teach lessons on friendship.

THE GIFT OF SELF

Characters: Everyman
         Friend Seeker (FS)
Props: Two paper stars. One star should be pinned to each player.

Everyman sits onstage and mimes reading. He turns the pages, and it is obvious from his expression that he is engrossed in his Book.

FS comes onstage. He seems to be looking for someone. Finally he spots Everyman. He is happy as he goes up to the reading man. He stands there a minute expecting Everyman to notice him. Nothing happens. He looks a bit puzzled. He walks around Everyman, reaches out and touches him, and finally gives Everyman a terrific shake.

Everyman looks up. He is obviously annoyed at being bothered.

FS mimes a suggestion that they shoot basketball together. Everyman shakes his head no and returns to his Book.

FS walks away, but suddenly he has an idea. He returns. Once again, after much effort, he gets Everyman's attention. Annoyed, Everyman puts his Book on the floor. FS smiles, takes off his star, and with a great flourish, he hands it to Everyman. Everyman looks at it casually, and then his eyes drift down to the floor where he has placed the Book. He resumes reading, and unconsciously, as he reads, he begins to tear the points from the star.

FS is horrified. With every point Everyman tears, FS moves farther away from him. Finally he sinks to the floor and puts his head on his knees.

Everyman finds something important in the Book. He picked it off the floor. With his finger, he underlines what he has just read. He looks embarrassed, ashamed. He sees the torn star on the floor and wipes a tear from his eyes. He sinks to his knees praying. Then he looks around for FS. When he sees him, he goes over and touches him. No response. He tries a second time. Finally FS looks up, but when he sees Everyman, he immediately puts his head down. Everyman tries again. Finally, although he is hesitant and afraid, FS responds. Everyman takes off his star and gives it to FS. FS looks surprised, happy. Everyman helps FS to his feet. Everyman suggests they shoot baskets, and the two walk offstage.

Like roleplay, mime should not be used without class discussion following it to help students clarify and apply what they have seen. Without this exchange mime is not a complete teaching tool.

Symbols play an important part in most teaching mimes. Begin the discussion by encouraging students to share what they feel each symbol represented.

The following discussion questions would help students analyze what took place in "The Gift of Self":

● "What did you feel the star represented?"

● "What part did the Book play in this mime?"

● "State what you feel the message of this mime was."

Since there are no words in the mime clarifying exactly what happened, different students may have different opinions. For example, an adult might say, "To me the star represented the gift of personhood. The play told me that unless I give myself to others, my Christianity isn't worth much." A senior high might point out, "The Book Everyman was reading had to be the Bible. The mime showed me that reading the Bible isn't enough. Unless we get involved with the world's people, we will never be able to win them to Christ."

WARM UP TO MIME

Twenty college-age students began to see the possibilities in mime, and to unbend a bit, when they participated in a silent skit. They were to pretend that they had all stopped at a roadside diner for lunch. They were part of different tour groups, and no group spoke any of the other groups' language. Each group was to communicate through actions exactly what it had seen on the morning tour. (The groups had been to the Grand Canyon, the ballet, a Japanese kimono showing, and a lecture on finance.) It took about three minutes for the first student to correctly identify all the tour groups. Everyone had a great time. Students who had been intimidated by the word *mime* saw just how versatile the 3000-year-old art form can be.

Consider some of these pre-mime activities. They can be used to quickly preview for students what mime is, or they can be part of an extended game approach to learning, like the one the college students participated in.

1. (*Adult Class*) Show the three facial expressions you think parents use most often on their children. (*Teen class*) Show the three facial expressions you think teens use most often on their parents.

Discuss: "How do you think the person on the receiving end of each of these expressions reacts to them? In what ways might they help or hinder your communication with that person?"

2. You have just shared your faith with five people, but none of them were ready to accept your Lord. However, all five had different attitudes toward your witness. Use facial expressions to show each of their attitudes. For example, one might be hesitant and another angry.

Discuss: "How does knowing a person's attitude help us witness to him? What should be our attitude when people reject our witness? Why?"

3. Sometimes we can tell that a person needs our friendship just by the way he or she walks or sits. First show how a person who is tired and discouraged might walk. Then show how that person might sit.

Discuss: "How can we initiate friendship toward someone who looks discouraged?"

4. Think of an attribute of God for which you seldom praise Him, for example, His love or His mercy. First tell the class what the attribute is and then ask a student to pantomime how he or she would describe that attribute to someone who doesn't speak the same language.

A student could pantomime mercy, God's total forgiveness to people even though they don't deserve it, by sinking fearfully to the ground. Hesitantly the mime glances up and the look of fear changes to one of joy. He or she raises hands and slowly rises as if God were doing the lifting.

Discuss: "Too often we forget to praise God for who He is. How can we incorporate more praise into our class period and into our own devotional lives?"

5. Encourage your students to think of three ways they are willing to help God within the church or community. Have several students pantomime these ways and allow their classmates to identify the service they are demonstrating.

Emphasize that these services do not have to be ones in which the students are already involved, but rather ones in which they are willing to become involved. Use only volunteers for this pre-mime activity, because as they participate, students will be testifying before God and their peers that they are willing to serve Him. This pantomime could lead into a praise and prayer service in which students thank God for the abilities He has given and ask Him for opportunities to put their talents and gifts to use.

Discuss: "What are some areas in our church where additional workers are needed? In what ways might members of our class help fill these needs?"

6. Divide the class into groups of four and ask each group to pantomime a Bible verse which says something important to the class.

Discuss: "What would you tell a new Christian who asks you to explain some methods of Bible study that he or she might use in personal devotions?"

AS YOU BEGIN

First, reduce anxiety levels. This can be done with activities like those mentioned above. Your attitude will play a part, too. If your students feel you're excited about using something different to communicate spiritual truth, they will catch your enthusiasm.

Consider sharing a bit of the history of sacred drama in the middle ages which had its roots in mime. People were generally illiterate and so the church communicated with the common folk through morality, mystery, and miracle plays. These were really sermons acted out in pantomime as the leader spoke to make certain the population understood what he was saying. Since television plays such an important role today in forming the way young people think (often in picture sequence), it may be the perfect time to return to the medieval concept of evangelism and training.

Professional mime is usually done in whiteface. In ancient Rome, the mime's face was covered with flour powder and outlined with charcoal. Today's whiteface starts with an even, thin layer of clown white, perhaps covered with white powder that sets the cream. The mime's objective is simplicity. Eyebrows are penciled in with black eyebrow pencil or liquid eyeliner. The eyes are outlined, enlarged, and accentuated. The mouth is red. A black line around the face completes the mask effect. The identity of the person is removed, and the player becomes anyone, anything. The mime character is Everyman, a character who is neither male nor female, but a representative of us all.

Whiteface is not practical in the classroom. Even if it were, it changes the teaching tool into a performance tool. The mime becomes more important than what the student can learn from it.

MOTION

A lot of pantomime moves will come naturally to students, especially those who have enjoyed charades. It might be helpful, though, to suggest that as students think of how they will act out their mimes they divide their bodies into three parts—their heads, arms/legs, and torsos. Each part can be used to express a primary action or emotion. The head is the intellectual part of the body. Cock your head slightly to one side and tap the top. You are saying, "I'm smart." The arms and legs are used to express physical actions. You clench your fist and wave it at someone. You are saying, "Watch it. I'm upset." The torso expresses emotions. Your shoulders droop and your back sways. "I'm so discouraged," you seem to say.

According to the Delicroix Theory of mime, it is also possible to divide each of those three parts of the body into three sections again.

The top of the head is the intellectual part. The mouth can express the physical. The eyes, of course, express emotions.

The shoulders are the intellectual part of the torso. The physical is the hips. The emotional is the rib cage—it heaves with sobs and sighs.

Consider the limbs. The hands and feet are used to express the intellectual. The hands, particularly, are important in mimes expressing Christian concepts. They bless, give comfort, praise God. The physical is the upper arms and legs. The emotional can be emphasized by the calf and the lower arms. This can be seen in the movements of a ballet dancer.

In each of these cases, the physical most often has sexual connotations—the slight smile, the push on the hip.

After the students have been introduced to what mime is and have had an opportunity to participate in several pre-mime activities, they will be ready to put mime to use. Actually, the steps to a successful mime experience in the classroom are much like those of a successful roleplay.

STEPS TO SUCCESSFUL MIME

• First, *examine the mime to make sure it will teach the students something about the lesson they are studying.* The mime must enhance the lesson aim.

• *Give students no more than five minutes to prepare for their mime.* If they spend too much time practicing, the spontaneity can be lost. During the preparation they should read the mime to get its general ideas. Then they should mime it once before they present it to the group—acting out the script the way they remember it, adding their own touches, and eliminating those which do not blend with their personalities. The script can serve as a jumping-off point. It gives suggestions for actions, but players should be encouraged to add any gestures, expressions, or additions to the story line which they feel would help the audience better understand what is taking place.

• *The sex of the players is usually of little importance to the mime's story line.* Often a character, such as Everyman in "The Gift of Self," is a microcosm of a larger group of people. Everyman represented all Christians who aren't aware of or don't accept their responsibilities to others. Friend Seeker could be anyone, man or woman, who has ever had an offer of friendship rebuffed.

• *Prepare the audience for later discussion by giving them suggestions about what to look for as they watch the mime.* The following general suggestions can help guide students as they watch almost every mime situation:

1. Identify with one of the characters throughout the mime. Ask yourself, "How does the character feel? Why does he or she feel this way?"
2. What symbols are being used, and what might they represent?
3. What message might the mime have for Christians?

Consider how these suggestions would help viewers understand the following mime, "Masks."

MASKS

Characters: Three people (A, B, and C).

Props: Three masks. Each player wears a mask made from a paper bag that has been painted black on one side and white on the other. A and B players have the left side painted white and C has the right side painted white. (See Figure 1.) When players face each other, the audience should be able to see only one color.

White A and B face white C and shake his hand (figure 2). Then they all switch places and face the opposite direction so only the black side is showing. The three shake hands again (figure 3). A turns around to face B causing the black and white masks to face each other. A holds out his hand, but B backs away. C comes up behind A and kicks him (figure 4). A falls over. As he turns around to see who kicked him, the black side shows. This pleases C, and he helps A to his feet and dusts him off. He shakes hands again (figure 5).

B walks over to A and stands facing him. This will put B's white face toward the audience. B places his hand on A's head and pushes down so hard that A is forced to fall in front of him (figure 6). A slowly comes to his feet again and turns away from B so the white side of his face shows. C walks around to face A and B and shakes their hands (see figure 7).

Quickly they change sides again, and black A and B shake hands with black C (see figure 8). All walk offstage.

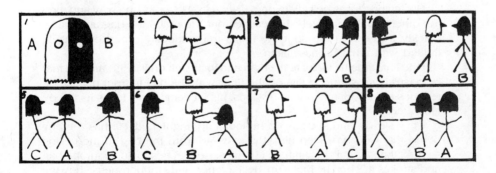

In "Masks" the discussion might begin with these questions:

- "The racial implications of this mime are obvious because of the black/white coloring of the masks. But what things other than color cause people to have unchristian reactions toward each other and keep them from becoming friends?"

- "What types of masks do Christians wear? What can we do first to rid ourselves of masks, and second, to help rid the world of them?"

As your students begin to feel at ease with mime, they may want to add musical accompaniment to their performances. Recorded selections must complement the emotional tone of the situation. When a live instrument, such as a guitar, is used, the musician should be familiar with the script so he or she will be able to anticipate what will happen and accentuate it.

Keep these steps in mind as you begin with some simple mimes, such as the following. I often give workshops on creative methods to Sunday school teachers and youth leaders, and I use the next mime, "The Guilt Bag," to demonstrate how mime can be used by almost anyone. The first person who walks through the door of the workshop is given a copy of the mime. Never once has the demonstration been unsuccessful. The mime is simple and is dependent on only one player. Of course, in the workshop situation, people who come to a session entitled "Creative Methods" are already open to new experiences and the challenge of pattern breaking.

THE GUILT BAG

Character: Everyman
Prop: Large bag tied at the top with string

Everyman enters the stage, obviously happy, carefree, nonchalant. He pretends to whistle, swings arms, skips.

Then he sees the bag. He stops, examines it closely without touching it. It's obvious that he's impressed.

His attitude turns quickly to one of secrecy. He looks one way and then the other. Slowly, furtively, he reaches out. He grabs the bag and walks quickly away from the spot. He looks tremendously proud of himself, thrilled with what he has taken.

One final time he looks to the right and to the left until he is satisfied that he hasn't been seen. He sits on the floor with the bag in front of him. He reaches out to open it, but as he does, his face suddenly loses its happy glow.

Very slowly and sheepishly, he looks up, frightened. He has remembered that God has seen him. His eyes go from the bag to the ceiling several times. Again his attitude changes. He reaches lovingly for the bag and strokes it. Then he looks up, belligerence and stubbornness showing on his face.

He stands and tries to hide the bag from God with his body, but he finds this an impossible, uncomfortable position to be in.

Suddenly he has an idea. He reaches upward with one hand, but keeps the other hand tightly gripped around the bag. But something is wrong. Evidently he can't find God. He shades his eyes with his hand and scans upward. He shakes his head in sadness because he can't find Him.

Finally, keeping just one finger on the bag, he moves his whole body as far away from it as possible. Again he looks upward, searching. Sad, frustrated, he wipes a tear from his eye.

He looks at the bag one last time. Then with a decisive movement, he jerks his hand from the bag, looks up, and shakes his head yes. He has made his decision to follow God.

His back toward the bag, he lifts his hands toward the sky. He smiles. He hugs himself and clicks his heels together. For the first time since he sighted the bag, he looks happy. Without ever looking at the bag again, he joyfully walks past it and off stage.

Students would find discussion questions like these valuable:
- "What emotions did you feel as you were watching this mime?"
- "The bag represents things that separate us from God. What specific sins might the bag represent to Everyman?"
- "How did your feelings toward Everyman change during the struggle between his or her desire for God and love for the bag?"
- "What feelings do you think Everyman was having at the very end of the mime? Have you ever had a similar victory in a struggle with a bag in your life? Share how you felt when you finally decided to ask God's forgiveness and follow Him."

You can add a Part 2 to "The Guilt Bag." You act it out after students have completed the discussion on the mime. Put the Guilt Bag in front of students again. Become Everyman. Walk around the bag. Eye it. Reach out to almost touch it. Jerk back. Look sheepish. Walk away, but glance back. Inch toward it again and reach out again. Jump away. A third approach, and this time you touch it just briefly, and pull away looking slightly pleased with yourself.

Now open the mime for further discussion:
- "What happens when we Christians ask God to remove our burden of sin? We're excited; He's done it. But we return to that sin and flirt with it. What are the dangers in this?"
- "What practical solutions to this problem can you suggest? Tie your suggestions directly to Scripture."

I've done this addition in a number of classrooms. Christian students who felt rather comfortable with the first mime often begin to squirm under this one. The implications are obvious.

As you read the following mime, consider what Scriptures might be used with it. What age levels might benefit? What questions might you use to stimulate discussion? What is the basic theme in it, and in what teaching situations might this mime most effectively help you reach your goal?

LIGHT TO THE BLIND

Characters: 2 people who are trapped in a totally dark room. For practical purposes, they are blind.

1 person (Christian) carrying a "light" (yellow piece of paper).

Two blind people are living their lives in a totally dark room. They have no sight, and they stumble around the room in fear and misery. Show this fear and panic by making use of some or all of the following mime actions:

- Stumbling, falling, bumping into things, and hurting yourselves in the process.
- Showing fear of anything or anyone you come in touch with. When you bump into each other, fight each other to get away. Show by your facial expression how afraid you are.

This should continue for about two minutes to set the feeling of hopelessness.

Suddenly a third person enters the dark room. He is carrying a yellow piece of paper that represents light. Unlike the other two, he can see where he is going.

When the blind people bump into him and start to fight to get away, he shows them the light. At first they are afraid of it and back away. But he goes after each of them individually and shows them his light. One is angered by it. He fights to get the light and it is obvious that he wants to tear it up. But he can't quite reach it.

The second person is scared but interested in finding out more about the light. After conquering his fear, he reaches out for the light and the third person shares it with him.

The mime ends with the two people holding onto the light and the person who rejected it crouched in the corner hiding, as far from the light as possible.

PREJUDICE MIME[4]

To present this mime, you will need:

3 students

4 identical red squares, used in sets of two, one square above the other, pinned to the backs of two students

2 identical green squares, one on top of the other, pinned to the back of one student.

PART 1

The three players approach each other from different directions. They meet and go through the motions of becoming acquainted. They should not see the back of the others. They smile, slap backs, perhaps mime playing ball.

Accidently, a red sees the green's back. He recoils; smile fades. He goes to the other red and points out the green. The two reds huddle together ignoring green.

Green is puzzled, sad, confused. He makes several attempts to establish friendship again. At first reds just ignore him; then they push him away.

Green moves slowly away from the reds, his anger growing. He stoops to pick up a stone. He mimes throwing it and hitting a red. The reds are furious. They start to throw stones, too. Finally all three are hit and hurt lying on the floor. They remain there perfectly still for a long pause.

PART 2

Slowly they rise and return to the point where they were at the beginning of the first scene. Again they go through the actions of becoming acquainted. They smile, slap backs, etc.

Accidently, a red sees the green's back. He points it out to the other red. They move away to discuss it. The green stands apart looking frightened, hopeful.

Then the reds return. They show him their reds. They feel each other's squares. Then they take the top ones off, and slowly tear them into pieces letting them fall to the floor. The second ones remain pinned to their backs.

They continue their friendship activities (smiling, slapping each other on the back, etc.). Occasionally, a red or green will look at the other color square on the back of another person, pat it, examine it, look proud of it, smile.

The three friends exit.

Note that the following dramatization mixes pantomime and words. It can be used in the classroom, but it can be more professionally developed for use in a worship service or all-church training session.

STRANGER IN THE CHURCH[4]

STRANGER enters the sanctuary, bizarrely dressed, and walks with obvious awe to the front of the church. (*Dress should include bare feet, loose unstylish dress (if a girl) or shirt and jeans, oddities such as ribbons around the ankles, Indian-style headband, garish rouge on the cheeks, etc.*)

The visitor pauses respectfully at the altar to pray, then takes his/her seat in the front row.

131

WORSHIPERS troop in a few seconds later, dressed in traditional Sunday best. Some titter and stare at the stranger; all sit in little groups apart from the oddball, whispering behind upraised hands, nudging each other, etc.

PASTOR enters finally and takes his place in the pulpit. Worshipers fall silent. Pastor announces his opening text as Hebrews 13:1, 2 (TEV) and reads, "Keep on loving one another as brothers in Christ. Remember to welcome strangers in your homes. There were some who did it and welcomed angels without knowing it."

PASTOR then calls upon his "congregation" to sing.

WORSHIPERS stand and cluster together sharing song books (the STRANGER stands alone) and pretend to sing by chanting in unison: "Sing, sing, sing."

PASTOR now announces it is time to "Welcome Neighbors" (or use whatever phrase is used in your church). He comes down from the pulpit, shakes a few hands of the conventionally-dressed worshipers, and returns to platform.

WORSHIPERS meanwhile enthusiastically pump each other's hands, chat together, and in general ignore the STRANGER who is patiently reaching out his/her hand across the aisle or toward this or that person. All finally quiet down and sit in the pews.

PASTOR delivers his sermon by chanting: "Preach, preach, preach." He then closes with the benediction, chanting again: "Benediction, benediction, benediction."

WORSHIPERS file out of the sanctuary, still staring at or ignoring the visitor, shaking hands with the pastor, chatting.

STRANGER turns again to the altar, looking wistfully at the stained-glass windows (or whatever symbolic decorations are used in your church—cross, Christian flag, etc.), stands thoughtfully for a few moments, finally shrugs, and walks out.

YOUR STUDENTS CAN CREATE MIMES

After they have participated in several mimes, your students may want to work with you to construct and act out an original mime.

The group should choose a subject that lends itself to mime—for example, new life in Christ or service to Christ. Students then discuss what situations could be mimed that would help the class understand the lesson better. From these suggestions, they choose the best one and develop it. You may want to use a symbol in your original mime.

Symbols should not be so obscure that their meaning is lost to most of the students. For example, an obvious yet effective symbol to use in mime about salvation could be tree branches. Those who are satisfied with the old life, life without Christ, could carry dead branches, while those who have made Christ Lord of their lives could exchange their dead branches for ones with leaves. (A "Light of the World" mime used a yellow piece of paper to symbolize the new sight a Christian has.)

A group of teens and adults from Circle Church, Chicago, worked for several months on an hour-long original mime called "Norman Newcreature." In the mime, a modern *Pilgrim's Progress*, Norman struggled with the forces of evil, reacted to interpersonal relationships, and grew in his Christian life. Symbols were obvious and effective. For example, whenever Norman became more interested in the things of the world than he was in spiritual things, he was given a burden (Styrofoam block) to carry. Only through trust in God could he lighten his life's load. The mime made such an impact on the congregation that several other Christian groups in the area heard about it and asked the cast to present "Norman Newcreature" for them.

Usually original mimes need not be written. Students can simply talk through their ideas and practice the action once before they present it to the class.

Idea starter: "New Life in Christ"

Non-Christian Everyman mimes a number of negative activities he is involved in. Then he meets Christ. (What symbol could be used to show the class that Everyman has accepted the Savior?) Finally he mimes some positive Christian disciplines that are part of his new life.

Idea starter: "Serving Christ"

Use a ladder as a symbol of spiritual growth through service. Everyman climbs a few steps and then comes down and does something for Christ or his acquaintances. A second student could play the character of the acquaintances. After each service he performs for Christ, the first student returns to the ladder and climbs a rung or two higher. Occasionally, he might do something to disappoint God and this would cause him to slip back a step.

MIME A PRODUCTION

It is effective to use aspects of mime and reader's theater to create an entire production.

The following scripts, "Joy to the World" and "Light in the Caves of the Lost," will get your students started. However, the success of the project will depend on what the students bring to the presentation. Before students take on assignments like these, they should have participated in mime in the classroom. They need not be professional, or even excellent.

But they must be excited about the process of acting out feelings. The scripts suggest motion, but only real people can bring those actions to life.

"Joy to the World" can use junior high, senior high, and adult students. The teachers of each group should practice with their students, so that only one or two rehearsals with the three combined groups would be necessary. An excellent reader should be chosen as Reader.

JOY TO THE WORLD[5]
Mime Drama for Christmas

Characters:
Reader
Red All-Man
White All-Man
Black All-Man
Yellow All-Man
4 Scarlet Hat People
4 Blue Hat People

Props:
Several large world maps
Reader's lectern
Red paper circle
White paper circle
Black paper circle
Yellow paper circle
4 scarlet hats
12 blue hats (keep 5 near Reader)*
Balloon
Basket of fruit*
Sign: "For Sale 10¢"*
Ball
Coin
Baby doll in manger (box)*
Bible
Many paper circles (red, yellow, black, and white)

*All starred props are placed onstage by the Reader and should be within easy reach. Hats can be made by turning construction paper or lightweight poster board into a cone shape. Circles should be about 5 inches in diameter and fastened to the players' clothes with a straight pin. Generally, players may be either male or female.

(Scene opens with Reader standing on stage left with script on a stand in front of him. The four All-Men stand in middle of stage. Each wears a circle of red, white, black, or yellow. Large world maps are on stage walls.)

READER: In our world, we have people of different colors, but basically they are much the same. For this reason, we've chosen four people to represent all the people in the world. We call them All-Men and identify them by the color circle they wear. Our mime uses two other symbols. The first is a scarlet hat. When a person is wearing a scarlet hat, he or she represents evil and sin. When a person is wearing a blue hat, he or she represents a Christian sharing joy.

(All the All-Men, except Red All-Man, leave stage.)

SCENE I

(Red All-Man wanders around the stage looking lonely as Reader reads.)

READER: Now let's go to a small town near a (Canadian/western) reservation where Red All-Man has just moved with her Indian family. She is the only Indian in her school class, and she wants desperately to make friends with the rest of the kids, but they only make fun of her.

(Scarlet Hat enters, and suddenly Red All-Man sees him. She brightens and rushes up to him to say hello. Scarlet Hat turns his back and pretends she isn't there. She runs offstage and returns immediately with a balloon. She offers to share it with him, but he breaks it. She begins to cry. Scarlet Hat teases her, pointing to the color of her skin and hair. As Scarlet Hat teases, Red All-Man gets angry. Finally she runs to far corner of stage and stoops to pick up some stones. She pretends to throw them at Scarlet Hat. He ducks and runs offstage laughing. She looks very sad and walks slowly offstage.)

READER: When will the message of the angel reach lonely Red All-Man? "Fear not: for, behold I bring you good tidings of great joy, which shall be to all people."

SCENE II

(As Red All-Man leaves the stage, White All-Man enters.)

READER: In Europe and North America, the White All-Man also misses the message.

(White All-Man rubs his stomach. He is obviously hungry. When his back is turned to the Reader, Reader places a basket of fruit and the sign, "For Sale 10¢," on the floor near his stand. Scarlet Hat enters and spots the fruit and the hungry man. He points out the fruit to White All-Man. For a minute, All-Man is excited, but then he sees the sign. He shakes his head sadly and pulls out his empty pockets.

(Scarlet Hat, smiling slyly, sneaks up to the basket, looks around to make sure no one is watching, and steals a piece of fruit. He indicates to White All-Man that he should steal one, too. When he shakes his head no, Scarlet Hat teases him until finally he agrees and steals. Both walk offstage in opposite directions. Scarlet Hat is skipping, clapping his hands. White All-Man is sad, obviously disappointed in himself.)

135

READER: White All-Man feels guilty. Deep inside, he knows there must be another way to live. When will he hear, "Fear not: for, behold, I bring you good tidings"?

(Reader removes fruit and sign.)

SCENE III

READER: Now we join Black All-Man in a large city of the world. School is out for Christmas vacation, and he must earn some money if he is to buy his family presents. We see him knocking on doors trying to find a job.

(Black All-Man enters stage. He walks to an imaginary door and knocks. He acts out his request to shovel snow. From his dejected look it is obvious that he's been turned away. At the next door, he indicates that he would like to wash the car or do the dishes, but again he is turned away. He sadly looks at his black circle and walks away. When he is at stage right, Scarlet Hat comes and walks a short distance behind him laughing and pointing at the sad Black All-Man. Black All-Man isn't aware of Scarlet Hat until he catches up with him, about center stage.

(Black All-Man is glad to see Scarlet Hat. He acts out what has just happened, and Scarlet Hat looks sympathetic. Suddenly Scarlet Hat snaps his fingers. He has an idea. He rolls up his sleeve and pretends to pull a needle from his pocket. He pretends to inject himself. Then he offers the same thing to Black All-Man. He shrugs as if he doesn't care one way or the other. The two walk offstage with Scarlet Hat's arm over Black All-Man's shoulder.)

READER: Is there no one to repeat the message? Can no one share the angel's song?

SCENE IV

Reader: In Asia, Yellow All-Man plants rice in the hot sun as her ancestors have always done.

(Yellow All-Man comes onstage. She sits on the floor and takes off her shoes. Then she steps into the wet rice bed. She bends almost double as she sticks imaginary plants into the wet soil. She goes across the stage planting row after row, stopping occasionally to wipe her face and rub her back. Scarlet Hat comes onstage and walks quietly to stage right. He stands there with his hands above his head and his legs turned out as if he were an idol. Yellow All-Man sees the idol and gets a look of hope on her face. She goes over to it and bows low praying. Then she gets up and shakes her head sadly. Nothing has happened. She slowly goes back to her rice fields and continues planting one more row. Then both she and Scarlet Hat leave the stage.)

SCENE V

(The stage is empty except for Reader. He places a baby doll in a manger (box) in center of stage. He then goes to lectern and begins to read his next paragraph. As he reads, all players come onstage in groups of

twos and threes. None are wearing hats or circles. They stand—or sit—in semicircle around manger. Some look excited, others afraid. They point at the baby and nudge each other. Some pretend to talk, deciding among themselves what the baby means.)

READER: Have no fear, for behold I announce to you good news of great joy that will be for all people; for today there was born for you in the city of David a Savior, who is Christ the Lord. And this is a token for you: you will find a baby wrapped in swaddling clothes and lying in a manger.

(Suddenly the group is happy. They hug each other and clap. Some kneel by the baby. Some begin to say a word, JOY. This is the only time in the play that anyone other than the Reader speaks. The group all begin saying the word, louder and louder until the Reader raises his hand. Then all is quiet again as those around the baby turn to face the Reader to listen to what he has to say.)

READER: The angel's message is heard by a few who accept Christ, the Son of God, as their Lord and Savior. They also accept the responsibility to carry this message to all men of the world. Who now will tell others that joy has come to the world?

(Those who will play the parts of Blue Hats come forward and the Reader gives each of them a blue hat. As they accept them all the others around the manger walk offstage.)

READER *(To those standing beside him in the blue hats):*

Go into all the world, to your country and city, to the person next door, and share the Christmas message. Jesus was born to save us from our sins. Joy to the world.

(Blue Hats nod. Then all leave stage except one Blue Hat.)

SCENE VI

(Red All-Man wanders onstage, still crying. Blue Hat goes over to her. He holds out his hand, but she looks scared, untrusting, and backs away. Then he reaches into his pocket and pulls out a ball. He bounces it and indicates that he wants to play ball with her. They throw it back and forth. Slowly Red All-Man's fear disappears, and she begins to have a good time. After they have played a short time, Blue Hat indicates that she should sit beside him. Then he begins to share the story of Jesus' birth, gesturing and pretending to talk as the Reader reads.)

READER: Joy to the world, the Lord is come; Let earth receive her King: Let every heart prepare him room, And Heaven and nature sing.

(Blue Hat points to Red All-Man. She nods yes, and the two of them bow their heads as if they are praying. Then they stand up smiling. They throw the ball back and forth as they leave the stage.)

SCENE VII

(Reader places fruit basket and sign onstage again. White All-Man enters. He is still rubbing his stomach and looking hungry. He sneaks up to the basket and is just about ready to grab a piece of fruit when Blue Hat

runs onstage, grabs his hand, and shakes his head no. White All-Man looks scared because he has been caught. Blue Hat smiles at him and gives Reader a coin to pay for two apples. Then they go to center stage to eat. As they eat, Blue Hat shares the message of Christ with White All-Man by gesturing as Reader speaks.)

READER: And she shall bring forth a son, and thou shalt call his name JESUS: for he shall save his people from their sins.

The wages of sin is death, but the gift of God is eternal life through Jesus Christ our Lord.

The choice is up to you.

(White All-Man nods his head yes, and the two of them pray together. As Blue Hat and White All-Man walk offstage, White All-Man's arm is around Blue Hat's shoulder.)

SCENE VIII

(Black All-Man and Blue Hat enter from opposite sides of stage. Blue Hat goes to center of stage and stands perfectly still facing stage left. Black All-Man walks up to an imaginary door in front of Blue Hat. He starts to knock, but hesitates. It's obvious that he's afraid to try again to get a job after so many failures. But finally he knocks. Blue Hat opens the door. Black All-Man acts out his request to baby-sit to earn some Christmas money. Blue Hat nods and hands Black All-Man an imaginary baby. He sits down and rocks it while Blue Hat watches smiling. Then Blue Hat brings out her Bible. As they look at the Bible together, Reader speaks.)

READER: And suddenly there was with the angel a multitude of the heavenly host praising God, and saying, Glory to God in the highest, and on earth peace, good will toward men. And hastily they went, found both Mary and Joseph, and saw the baby lying in the manger. And the shepherds went back, sharing with others what they had discovered. They had found the Christ who will save anyone from his sins. They had discovered the joy of the world.

(The Black All-Man points to himself and Blue Hat nods. They pray together. Then Black All-Man gives the baby back to Blue Hat and receives his pay. He starts walking away. They wave. Then suddenly Black All-Man comes running back and points to Blue Hat's hat. He indicates that he wants one, too, so he can witness to others. Blue Hat gives him hers and immediately gets another one from the Reader. Blue Hat and Black All-Man exit.)

SCENE IX

(Yellow All-Man and Scarlet Hat enter. Scarlet Hat resumes his idol position on stage right. Yellow All-Man resumes planting in the hot sun. Blue Hat walks onstage and sadly shakes his head when he sees the idol. Then he sees Yellow All-Man planting, and takes off his shoes and enters the rice field. The two of them plant together. As they plant, it is obvious that they are talking to each other.)

138

READER: The gods who did not make the heavens and the earth shall perish from the earth. They are worthless, a work of mockery; they will perish. But Mary will give birth to a Son, and you will call His name Jesus, for He will save His people from their sins. And His name shall be Immanuel, which means God with us.

(Yellow All-Man shakes her head no and runs to the idol. She throws herself in front of it. Blue Hat goes to the opposite corner of the stage and prays. Then he comes back to talk to the woman again. She looks sadly at the idol, and listens to Blue Hat as the Reader repeats the message of Christmas.)

READER: And His name shall be Immanuel, which means God with us. Joy to the world!

(Yellow All-Man nods, and the two of them pray together. As they pray, Scarlet Hat looks disgusted, puts his hands on his hips, and shakes his head. Finally, he sneaks offstage. Blue Hat and Yellow All-Man rise, and turn to greet the others who are forming onstage.)

SCENE X

(All players return to the stage. Each is wearing a blue hat and carrying a number of colored circles cut from red, yellow, black, and white construction paper. One player should give Yellow All-Man a blue hat and circles for her and Blue Hat. The players should then walk from the stage to different parts of the auditorium as the Reader speaks.)

READER: We know the joyful meaning of Christmas and are part of the wonderful celebration of Christ's birth. We must share what we know with all men. If you are willing to join us in sharing this message with those around you who may not know the message that can change their lives, raise your hand. One of the players will give you a circle. This will serve as a reminder of your promise to God to bring His joy to the world.

(As the players hand out circles, the Reader concludes by leading everyone in singing "Joy to the World.")

"Light in the Caves of the Lost," an Easter drama, is a combination of reader's theater and mime. The words are presented by a narrator and a speech chorus who hold their scripts in folders in front of them. The action is interpreted by players who speak no words, but pantomime emotions, feelings, and deeds.

LIGHT IN THE CAVES OF THE LOST[6]

by Karen Burton Mains

Characters:

NARRATOR—must be able to read with expression. The narration should

not be hurried, but deliberate in order that the players will have time
to interpret the full meaning of the words.

SPEECH CHORUS—*uses the spoken word as a musical choir uses song.*
READERS *(1, 2, and 3) have solo parts for dramatic emphasis.*
READER 1 *reads the Man's (Christ's) words.*

PLAYERS—*these are the actors who interpret the drama. Seven or nine*
would be a good group.

THE MAN—*dressed as ordinary player but actions show He is not blind.*

Stage Directions: The action takes place in the CAVES OF THE LOST. The
CAVES will be allotted to half of the stage (Stage Left—SL) and half to
the LAND OF LIGHT (Stage Right—SR). Action for PLAYERS *will be sug-*
gested in italics. Expand these suggestions to fit the personality and
ability of PLAYERS.

Props: Black blindfolds for players positioned so players can see enough
to carry out stage directions. Folders to hold scripts for NARRATOR,
SPEECH CHORUS, READERS. *Everything else is pantomimed.*

CHORUS: The true Light has come into the world! And this is the judgment:
people loved darkness rather than light, because their deeds were evil.

NARRATOR: These are the Caves of the Lost. They stretch for endless
miles—a series of subterranean caverns inhabited by men who have
never seen light. It is always night in the Caves.

(Enter PLAYERS *wearing blindfolds. They grope, stumble, make way to*
SL. *Each* PLAYER *is alone in the darkness, fearful of being touched. If*
touched, he pulls back or pushes frantically.)

NARRATOR: The Cave Dwellers wonder what eyes are for. They feel their
way with hands which are often wounded on the granite walls and
with feet that often stumble over unseen rocks.

In the darkness, all men are enemies. It is impossible to distinguish
between friend or foe. The Cave Dwellers do not touch each other,
except to fight. They are filled with fear.

PLAYERS *have assumed various positions. Some search for a way*
along an unseen wall with their hands; some crawl on knees; some
huddle in darkness; some bury heads in arms on knees in despair.)

CHORUS: All we like sheep have gone astray, we have turned every one to
his own way.

NARRATOR: Through the middle of the caverns surges a great and terrifying
river. *(All* PLAYERS *look toward Stage Center—SC.)* A legend exists
among the Cave Dwellers that it flows from another world, a world
completely different from anything they have ever known. But there
has been no one to lead them to that world, and they know they can't
find it on their own.

*(*PLAYERS *now mime activities of the Cave existence: searching for food,*
drinking water, soothing baby in arms, sleeping, inching by on a narrow
ledge as the NARRATOR *continues reading. Two can bump, become angry,*
and threaten. PLAYERS *can change actions. Someone else can sleep or*
look for food. Whatever is mimed must be done in a manner which also

140

portrays aloneness, fear, blindness. PLAYERS are representing spiritual souls lost in the darkness of sin.)

NARRATOR *(Continues)*: So the Cave Dwellers go on in the darkness, in the eternal night. They search the granite walls to find food, leeches, and slugs which cling in the seeping crevices. They drink brackish water from stagnant pools because they fear the treacherous river. Above all else, they do not reach out to each other. They do not share the food they have found, or guide one another along the narrow cavern ledges. They do not pull a fallen Cave Dweller from a hole or call out, "Be careful! The going is rough here."

Some love the darkness because there are no eyes to see the evil deeds that they do. But others long for someone to find the outlet in the great river that leads from the Caves of the Lost to a different and new world. They long for a day when someone will show them a way out of the captivity of this eternal night.

CHORUS *(The first phrase is read in three-part round and is repeated twice)*:
> In the fullness of time,
>> In the fullness of time,
>>> In the fullness of time,

READER 2: God sent forth His Son, born of a woman, born under the law . . .

CHORUS: To lead them that were in darkness.

READER 1: The Spirit of the Lord is upon Me, because He has anointed Me to preach the Gospel to the poor, to heal the brokenhearted, to preach deliverance to the captives, and the recovering of sight to the blind.

NARRATOR: A rumor has been sweeping through the Caves of the Lost. Men are creeping down from their ledges, crawling out of their holes. They stumble along the footpaths. They grope blindly in the darkness. "A man has come into the Caves of the Lost," the rumor whispers throughout the caverns. "He does not stumble in the darkness or feel His way along the walls! He is talking about a Land of Light."

(PLAYERS mime listening to rumor. They stop activities and begin to grope toward SC.)

READER 2: The people were astonished at His doctrines.

READER 3: And the fame of Him went into every place in the Caves of the Lost.

CHORUS *(Each member repeats one phrase five times at the same time as the other chorus members are talking; the noise will sound like a crowd)*:
> Come see the Man.
> He is over there.
> He told me all I ever did.
> Hurry!
> Don't be afraid.
> Who is the Man!
> Why is He here?

READER 1 *(Breaks into the noise of Chorus. They stop. PLAYERS wander to*

SC one by one, sit and listen. The MAN *enters and acts out the motions of teaching while* READER *says):* You must not push your brother off the path, but make way for him. In fact, lead him back where you have been. Yes, take his hand on the narrow ledge, and go before him so he will not fall.

If you have found food on the cavern walls and your fellow Cave Dweller has none, share with him what you have.

If someone has fallen into a hole, reach down and pull him out. Then, comfort him.

The land of My Father is a Land of Light. It is filled with color and brightness, full of beauty and warmth. All who dwell in that place can see Me, and I can see them.

CHORUS *(Again like a crowd, but this time repeating the same words):* Where is the way?

READER 1: I am the Way. I have come that you might know this Land of Light, that you might not stumble in the darkness. I am the Way, the Truth, and the Life. I am the Light.

CHORUS: In Him was life, and the life was the light of men.

READER 2: The Light shines in the darkness, and the darkness has not overcome it.

NARRATOR: The Cave Dwellers were amazed by the words of the Man. They were amazed at the things that He did. He walked upright, not crouching lest He strike His head in the darkness. He was not afraid of the river and dipped fresh water from it for those sick with fever. He went into the narrow, dark passageways seeking those in hiding and telling them about His Father's Land.

*(*PLAYERS *have divided into two groups during this narration. Some sit at SC learning at the feet of the* MAN. *The mime must show an attitude of response—some with hands outstretched reaching for more truth. They begin to sit straighter, hold heads high.*

(The other PLAYERS *obviously hate the* MAN. *They withdraw to SL. They plot, hunching in a group. They draw their garments about them, indicating stealth and hiding. One shakes a fist in direction of SC.)*

NARRATOR *(Continues):* A strange glow seemed to surround Him; it illumined the darkness. For the first time, the Cave Dwellers knew light, and they hardly understood what it was.

Some hated the Man. They despised His loving, gentle deeds. They abhorred the light which surrounded Him. They were jealous that He never groped with His hands or stumbled on the paths or fell in the darkness.

ALL: Men loved darkness rather than light . . .

READER 3 *(Read each word deliberately):* Because . . . their . . . deeds . . . were . . . evil.

ALL *(Whispered echo):* Evil, evil, evil.

READER 1: Come, follow Me! I will give you eternal light. If you trust and believe in Me, you will dwell in the Land of Light. See! Light is here now!

First I will go into the river. I will go through the outlet to the world outside. Then, I will come back for you.

(PLAYERS SC mime horror, surprise, dread. Plotters SL take note of the MAN's words, mime pleasure, move closer to SC, listening. The MAN goes to the middle of SR, and while NARRATOR reads He sinks to His knees, then head touches the floor. He remains perfectly still in this crouched position.)

NARRATOR: The Man stood on the banks of the great subterranean river. He stepped from the shore. He plunged into the waters. Great boulders flew at Him. The current tore at His clothes. His head disappeared under the surface. The river was certain death.

Suddenly the Caves of the Lost were in utter darkness again.

(PLAYERS at SC put hands and arms over heads which are bent in mourning.)

NARRATOR *(Continues)*: The eternal night had come, descending again upon the Caves.

(PLAYERS at SL begin to grope in the darkness, bumping, pushing, falling to knees.)

NARRATOR *(Continues)*: The Man was gone!

(Everyone freezes. PLAYERS SL become statues. Count slowly to 15 before continuing.)

READER 1 *(Softly)*: Come, follow Me.

READER 2 *(Echo)*: Come, follow Me.

READER 3: Come, follow Me.

(READERS repeat, calling a little louder second time.)

READER 1 *(Louder)*: Come, follow Me!

(PLAYER SC—one head starts up, listening.)

CHORUS *(Breaking into three groups)*: Come, follow Me. Come, follow Me.

(More PLAYERS SC look up.)

CHORUS *(Continues)*: Come, follow Me!

ALL: Come, follow Me!

(PLAYERS SC all looking up. PLAYERS SL still statues.)

READER 1 *(Quietly)*: Come, follow Me.

(The MAN suddenly stands.)

NARRATOR: Suddenly! The Caves were filled with light! The Man had come again! He was standing on the shore of the river! "Come, follow Me," He called, and some of the Cave Dwellers stepped into the waters and followed Him.

(NARRATOR reads, as PLAYERS SC stand up, one by one. They mime walking to shore; some hurry; some are timid. They step into the waters. The MAN helps them. Blindfolded still, they extend hands, find each other, hold hands. PLAYERS SL stand still at attention in whatever direction they have been facing, hands at sides, feet together.)

NARRATOR: The waters engulfed them. A whirlpool pulled them down, down, down, and then cast them up and out of the water.

(PLAYERS SC whirl around, hands clasped to chest. As NARRATOR

continues, MAN *removes their blindfolds. They look around, then in joy toss blindfolds in air!* PLAYERS SC *now act as though they are seeing for the first time in their lives.*

(They look at the beautiful Land of Light at SR, eyes wide open in amazement. They look at the blue sky, stretch hands up to it. Look at the ground below, turn around. They see their hands, hold them in front of eyes, turn them around. Look down at their bodies, lift a foot, look at it. They see each other, touch a cheek.)

NARRATOR: Their heads jerk back; their eyes open. Light! Light everywhere! Color—beauty—the Land of Light! The Man had led them out of the Caves of the Lost through the waters to the Land of His Father, the Land of Light!

*(*PLAYERS SC *now move to SR. They join hands, make a circle around the* MAN, *then turn 'round and 'round, gaily, like children at games. No narration is read for a short time. After a while* READER 1 *begins.)*

READER 1: He who loves his life loses it, and he who hates his life in this world will keep it for eternal life. If anyone serves Me, he must follow Me; and where I am, there shall My servant be also; if anyone serves Me, the Father will honor him.

*(*PLAYERS SR *have begun to sit, facing the Man without blocking the audience's view of Him.)*

CHORUS: God is light, and in Him is no darkness at all. If we walk in the light . . .

READER 2: We love one another, and the blood of Jesus Christ cleanses us from all sin.

READER 3: The light shines in the darkness, and the darkness has not overcome it.

*(*PLAYERS SL *mime meaningless activities such as putting stones into a container and taking them out again. One by one they get disgusted and leave the stage.)*

READER 1 *(No pause between this portion and previous* READER*)*: Be of good cheer, I have overcome the world.

READER 2: And to all who received Him, He gave power to become children of God.

NARRATOR: And so those who were once Cave Dwellers, but now dwell in the Land of Light, became children of the Father of Light. They eat at His table.

READER 1: I have meat to eat that you know not of. I am the Living Water; he that drinks of Me will never thirst.

(All SL PLAYERS *are now offstage.)*

*(*PLAYERS SR, *still seated, pantomime opening books, reading, and showing others what they have found.*

NARRATOR: And after so many years in darkness, they are learning how to walk.

*(*PLAYERS SR—*one pretends to walk on imaginary line, holding arms out to balance. Others applaud his efforts. The* MAN *helps when he stumbles.)*

NARRATOR (*Continues*): They are learning which paths to choose, who to walk beside, how to run.

CHORUS: They that wait upon the Lord shall renew their strength.

READER 2: They shall mount up with wings as eagles.

READER 3: They shall run, and not be weary.

CHORUS: They shall walk, and not faint.

(*PLAYERS SR form a straight line facing audience. Slowly, as the MAN shows them how, they copy His example of the disciplines of the Christian faith. He lifts hands to Heaven in a wide circle—praise. They copy Him. He folds hands and bows head—prayer. He bends knee to group—obedience. He pours water and gives to another—service. At the end of this mime action all who participated in the production come onstage and join hands symbolizing unity. The MAN is in the center of the line.*)

ALL: Though once your heart was full of darkness, now it is full of light from the Lord.

READER 1: Share the Light.

READER 2: Share the Light.

ALL (*Softly, growing louder*): We will share what we have found. We will share the Light.

STAGING

Staging in most classrooms is more a case of creative adaptation than an attempt at real staging. We just move the chairs back a bit and in the little cleared spot, the students do the mime or roleplay or any dramatic action.

Hopefully, your students will want to expand their dramatic ministry from time to time, sharing what they have prepared with the whole congregation on Wednesday evening or perhaps presenting a dramatic illustration as part of the worship service. Remember, no matter how good the material you'll present is, unless people can see and hear it, the impact will be lost and time wasted. In a classroom a lot of action might take place on the floor (remember the "Guilt Bag"?), but that low action won't work in a sanctuary.

"I took a course in drama and worship," an adult teacher said. "The assignment that was the most difficult and the most helpful to me was the construction of an original mime that had to be adapted to three different church locations. The success of the project depended on the mime working in a large church with a raised chancel, a house church where people sat in the round, and a church that had a podium at the same level as the congregation's seats. Flexibility was the key factor. I actually had to restructure my mime slightly for each situation."

A stage can be divided into nine areas. Action in some of these areas comes across stronger than in others. We can actually communicate messages about our content based on the place on the stage from which we present our lines.

Stage directions can sometimes be confusing. We still talk about upstage and downstage because during Shakespeare's time the stage was actually built on a slant down toward the audience. So when you place a person upstage, he or she is as far away from the audience as the stage will allow that person to get. Downstage puts the person right in front of the audience.

Divide the stage area into a large tic-tac-toe board.

upstage right	upstage center	upstage left
	center stage	
downstage right	downstage center	downstage left

audience

The weakest part of the stage is upstage left. This is the place where the eye goes last. So if you want someone to come sneaking onto the stage, you might want that person to enter from upstage left. This would be appropriate in the mime "Light in the Caves of the Lost." While the people in blindness grope around the stage, the person with the light approaches almost unnoticed from upstage left. (Along with Shakespeare's upstage and downstage terms, the terms right and left can be confusing. Right and left are used with reference to the *players'* right and left as they face the audience.)

Downstage center is a strong stage point. A reader or a mime can stand there and give the audience a sense of being one with him or her. It's as if the player is saying, "I'm with you. I'm your friend."

Downstage right is also a strong point. Action that takes place in this block and in the center block will catch the attention of the congregation much faster than action on any other block of the stage.

The position of the player's body is another communication tool. When someone faces the audience with his or her full front toward the audience, the player comes across as a very open person. But this is also a shallow position for the player; it allows only one dimension.

When a person turns a bit to the left or the right, he or she can change the mood of the scene. These are very freeing positions. They allow for shades of meaning to be communicated.

Quite often in the classroom, and perhaps in a more formal presentation as well, students will place their full backs to the audience. This may be appropriate for the player who wishes to portray total dejection. In the friendship mime, for example, this might be a good position with the back bent, the shoulders rounded, the head slightly down, the feet spread apart just a few inches. But usually the back position is not helpful. We usually communicate best with our faces, so when we play with our backs turned, we lose our most useful communication tool. When a player does this, you'll need to correct it. I usually mention the problem before players begin. Then if the class is missing most of the action because all the members can see is the player's back, I can whisper, "Back," and the person will immediately correct the problem. My quiet hint should not ruin the mime or roleplay, and teaching time won't be lost because we had to redo the whole activity.

1. Neta Jackson, a Sunday school teacher at Reba Place Church in urban Evanston, Illinois, tells how dance was used by one Sunday school class:

"Every other Sunday one of our children's classes does a presentation for the whole congregation to share what they have been learning in Sunday school. When it was the seventh grade boys' turn, their teacher prefaced their presentation in this way: 'What you will see today is totally the boys' own idea. They wanted to use *break dancing* (a dance form common in urban black culture which resembles high-energy tumbling) as their form for presenting the choice they face as adolescents between good and evil, between God and the world. I mentioned their idea to someone else in the church, who said, "What an excellent choice for that concept! Because break dancing *originated* for urban street kids as that kind of choice. Anyone who is involved in break dancing at Y's or neighborhood centers cannot be involved in a gang, or use drugs. That's the rule. So those who choose break dancing are making a choice to stay off the streets and do something creative with their energy." '

"Two boys represented the world and evil choices; two others represented the choice for God. A fifth boy 'break danced' between the two choices, and finally with the help of the 'godly friends,' focused his dancing on the side of God. The congregation gave them a standing ovation."

2. Mark Stolzenberg, *Exploring Mime* (New York: Sterling Publishing Co., 1979).

3. Herbert Brokering, *I Opener*, © 1974 Concordia Publishing House, p. 6. Used by permission.

4. Barbara Kuehn wrote "Prejudice Mime." "Stranger in the Church" was written by Carol Amen and dramatized by Neta Jackson. Both were part of a *Senior High Creative Teaching Aids* packet for use in the Sunday school classroom.

5. Marlene LeFever, "Joy to the World," *Junior High* and *Senior High Creative Teaching Aids*, © David C. Cook Publishing Co., 1979.

6. Karen Burton Mains, "Light in the Caves of the Lost," *Junior High Creative Teaching Aids*, © David C. Cook Publishing Co., 1973.

CHAPTER 7

Simulation Games

How can we sing the Lord's song in such a familiar
land?

—Lois Wilson in *Like a Mighty River*

A Christian magazine did a review of my 1973 book, *Turnabout Teaching,* commenting that there was an interesting chapter on *stimulation* games. A fun misprint, but there is some truth in it. Simulation games *can* shoot adrenalin into the veins of a sluggish Sunday school class.

Very broadly, there are two types of games. First, there are competitive games. Participants follow the rules and work toward a specified goal. Second, there are games known by the interchangeable terms "socio-drama," "simulation," and "gaming." These games try to reproduce some aspect of reality—poverty situations, power struggles in government, ecological problems, etc.—so the people participating will be better able to understand that one life area, and perhaps through understanding they will make better, wiser decisions within that area.[1]

DEVELOP AN ORIGINAL COMPETITIVE GAME

Let's look first at the more traditional types of games in which people work individually or in teams to win. Obviously there are lots of games on the market, but junior high and senior high teens will enjoy developing and playing their own competitive Bible games. (Often adults do not. Many feel threatened by the value placed on content knowledge.)

Read the directions to the game, Bible Basketball, to your class after you have completed a unit of study. Have each student help complete the game by writing three content questions about the Bible lessons the class has just studied. Then play the game as a review.

Or the class could use the ideas in Bible Basketball as an idea starter and develop its own original review game. For instance, ask students what rules might be needed to make a game of Bible Hockey, Bible Soccer, or Bible Checkers. The students' imaginations will be the only limitations on these original game possibilities.

Bible Basketball

Each student should write three or more review questions. The teacher shuffles these and picks questions at random.

The class divides into two teams. The teacher asks a tip-off question, and the first team to answer correctly gets the first chance to sink a basket.

The teacher then reads the first game question to the team that answered the tip-off. If the team players answer without being blocked by the other team, they score two points. If they give no answer, they neither score nor lose points.

After the tip-off question the teams alternate opportunities to make baskets.

Blocking: After each answer, the teacher gives the opposing team an opportunity to say whether the answer just given is incorrect. If students say that it was incorrect, they have blocked the answer. If their accusation is correct, the other team does not score and the blocking team gets one point and an opportunity to correctly answer the question. If they give the right answer, they earn another point. If they give an incorrect answer, they neither gain nor lose a point. However, if they have incorrectly blocked and the answer given by the other team was correct, the blocking team fouls and loses two points.

If the original answer was incorrect but the opposing team does not block it, the teacher gives the correct answer and the team giving the incorrect answer is allowed to keep the two points it scored.

(Additional rule for advanced players: each team member must take his turn answering a question. No member may answer a second time until each player has answered once.)

A winning team is declared at the end of a designated time or when one team obtains a certain number of points.

SIMULATION GAMES: DESIGNED FOR EXPLORATION

Basically, all games which fit into this category try to simulate reality, make it simpler than what it is, reduce its size so players will better understand the aspect of reality covered in the game.

For example, World Vision has developed a simulation for teenagers that allows them to experience just a bit of what it's like to be hungry. The simulation, called "Let It Growl," asks young people to eat nothing except a bit of juice for 30 hours.

Nancy Kelly told about her experience with 30 teenagers in a downtown Los Angeles church. "I entered the program expecting to learn more about world hunger as I discovered what it was like to go without food." During the first evening discussion centered around the needs of Third World nations. Morning without eating wasn't as bad as she thought it would be. Here she tells about her experience:

I feel buoyant. I smile as I hear a stomach growling in the sleeping bag next to mine, but I'm not hungry at all.

My mouth tastes awful—dry and stale. I can't wait to brush my teeth. In the girls' rest room, someone says, "Enjoy the Colgate. It's the best thing you're gonna taste all day."

We're all dressed and ready for breakfast. But there is no breakfast. Instead we play some more games to pass the time.

Saturday, midmorning.

As an appetizer, we play a game with the names of foods. Peas on earth. Turnip your nose. The Apple-achin Mountains.

I'm yawning. It's probably lunchtime. It's funny how I pace my day by the meals I eat. It's hard for me not to think in terms of breakfast time, lunchtime, and dinnertime.

Without meals, time goes slowly. We're getting restless with all this talk, so we sing some action songs.

Then I have a conversation with some of the older kids. Daniel, a high school senior, tells me about his relationship with the Lord. He is eager to share, and he's obviously growing.

"We're not fasting because we have to," he says to me. "We're fasting because we want to." There's the matter of choice again. We all recognize that fasting is our choice.

Saturday afternoon.

I'm relaxed and mellow. The group is slowing down, too. I feel like I'm moving in slow motion.

Am I hungry? I keep asking myself that question and the answer is always no. I've gone for 24 hours without a bite to eat. I think I'll take a nap.

My nap is restless. The noise around me never seems to let up. I keep hearing bouncing balls, giggles, and piano music. The noise is beginning to irritate me.

It's time for a simulation game. (*This is a simulation within the hunger simulation.*) Charmi divides us into groups of rich and poor nations. Each group gets some dried beans to represent its food supply and some money to represent its wealth. In the next hour the group lives through several months of buying, selling, giving, and stealing. We see what a fragile balance there is between life and starvation.

I'm in the United States group. Our bowl is filled with twice as many beans as we need. Many of the other countries come to us for food, but we don't have to give any away if we don't want to.

In a sudden act of aggression, China steals most of our beans and for a few minutes we panic. The fragile balance is tipped. But soon we reap another harvest and have plenty; it seems we can't lose.

The 29th hour of our fast is here. Larry asks us how we feel.

"I'm hungry, and I want a pizza."

"I'm too tired to feel hungry."

"I'm tired, and I have no energy."

Most of us agree that our fast has only scratched the surface of real hunger. It's been a symbolic experience that's opened our eyes to how much we take for granted.

After this 30 hours without food, I'm face-to-face with my own blessings. As a response, I have lots of questions to ask myself about how I will use the resources the Lord has given me.[2]

Many different groups, Christian, Jewish, and secular, are using simulation to teach experientially. Paula E. Hyman, professor of Jewish history at Columbia, wrote about simulations used by junior high and senior high teachers to turn their classrooms into concentration camps.[3] Max Nadel of the American Association for Jewish Education specializes in the preparation of Holocaust curriculums. A number of Jewish summer camps also promote roleplaying and simulation. "Creative camping personalizes the Holocaust" reads one slogan.

One simulation, called "Gestapo," attempts to convey what happened during the Holocaust by involving its players in life-and-death decisions as victims of Nazi persecution. Most people do not "survive" the game.

There are, of course, mixed reactions to some simulation games, including those that bring people face-to-face with the Holocaust. But if I were a Jewish teen and my grandparents had gone through this experience, what would I learn by reliving in a simulation some of the things they faced in reality? I would certainly understand myself and my family and my heritage better. As a Christian or a Messianic Jew going through this simulation, I would be forced to ask myself important questions about Christ's work through me, had I been part of that world. How much is my life worth? What would I do in order to survive? How willing am I to be my brother's and sister's keeper? Yes, I can ask myself these questions while reading a book on the Holocaust or by watching a television program. But the questions become more real when I have "lived" the panic and the death threats—real in ways I can experience in no other form.

A student, through simulation games, experiments with life. For example, he or she might play a politician who must please both conscience and constituency, or a scientist who must deal with pollution problems. Simulations, like roleplay, are one step removed from reality. This minimizes the sense of risk. A student feels free to participate and learn through involvement because he or she realizes the situation isn't real life.

Simulations can lead a student to think deeply about issues that were previously only words. It's easy for an adult to yell, "I made it by myself. Why can't they?" until that person has participated in an inner-city poverty simulation and realized some of the pressures and frustrations of being manipulated by those with money and influence. When students learn to examine issues rather than yell slogans, they are beginning to develop skills in decision making, communicating, and understanding people.

For example, try "The Lifeboat" simulation. Here students are forced to ask life-and-death questions. Although they will probably never be placed in an identical situation, they can certainly learn a lot about themselves and the way people respond to truly difficult choices by participating in this simulation.

The basic premise is that a group of people are adrift in a lifeboat out of the regular shipping lanes. This boat can only support five (adjust the number to your group) people and there are six in the boat. Give an identity to each person in the boat. Everyone is convinced that the lifeboat will sink in half an hour. The group talks over this Jonah-like situation, but no Jonah agrees to be thrown overboard.

Identities of the people in the lifeboat might include a doctor, a 16-year-old, a mother with a small baby, a sailor, a criminal, a famous female composer. (You can adjust the identities to your group's size. One thing I have noticed in Christian groups is that if any of the characters is identified as a minister, that person feels responsible to jump overboard. So I have stopped including that role in order to help people grapple with the situation.)

After the half hour, you will want to debrief "The Lifeboat." Some questions I have used include:

153

- "What Biblical principles come into play in a situation like this? How are those principles implemented? In what kind of situations might principles like these come into play?"
- "Is it possible to say that one person's life is worth more than others? Prove your point by using Scripture."
- "What did you learn about yourself from the simulation?"

(A group of full-time Christian workers participated in the lifeboat simulation. In the debriefing, the doctor, the painter, and the sailor, all who were in reality pastors, explained how they had survived. "We weren't going to let anyone throw us out of the boat, so we made a pact with the criminal. We figured he would know how to take care of himself, and if we were his friends, he would protect us, too.")

Simulation is a potential attitude changer. If after playing a game a student better understands how government works, he or she may want to participate in its functions. Or when a student takes part in a Christian simulation, such as the game of "Guidance" included in this chapter, that person may gain the confidence needed to begin to help others. Simulation leads to personal growth when students begin to practice positive things they've learned in the game, or work to eliminate the negative things such as prejudice and misused power they saw demonstrated.

There are, however, several problems associated with using simulation in a Sunday school situation:

- Most simulations require at least an hour's playing time with additional time following the game for discussion.
- Most games require a lot of space and a large number of people.
- Many simulation games are priced beyond the church budget.
- Although many of the secular simulation games have a lot to teach Christians, students and teacher will have to structure their own discussion to include the Christian implications of the game, since guidelines for this type of investigation are not given. For descriptions of many simulations now available, see *The Guide to Simulation/Games for Education and Training,* compiled by David W. Zuckerman and Robert E. Horn and published by Information Resources, Inc., P.O. Box 417, Lexington, Massachusetts 02173.

Quite often, however, the teacher will find that the benefits students gain from a simulation experience far outweigh the problems that must be overcome.

'CULTURE SHOCK'—A SIMULATION TO TRY

Just to get you started, consider using the "Culture Shock"[4] simulation to help people understand what new missionaries go through when they enter a new culture.

What happens to a missionary when that person goes to a new and unfamiliar culture? "Culture Shock" is a fun and silly game, but it's designed to help participants empathize with those God calls to serve Him in this unique, difficult way. One thing is for sure! If your people take this simulation game seriously, the new missionaries from your church will be upheld in prayer like never before.

In this simulation game, a new cultural experience is reduced in size so that people can participate in it for a few minutes and gain some understanding of what culture shock is. In this mission simulation, you won't make people feel all the frustration of learning a new language and new customs, but you can let them feel for a few minutes some of the frustrations of being different, of not belonging and fitting in, of being lonely and ineffective.

This simulation could turn people on to missions in a new way because for a half hour or so, they were there!

I've chosen to develop a simulation about cultural differences because this is an area in which I have faced frustration. And I think others who have lived in different cultures would agree.

I remember being in Venezuela as a short-term missionary. I thought it would be dandy if I organized the little boys at the Vacation Bible School into baseball teams. We used our arms as bats and hard lemons as balls. It was great fun until the mission leader explained that baseball was a no-no! In Venezuela people bet on baseball games in the same way Americans do on the horses. So as a testimony to nonbelievers, Christians don't play baseball.

The same thing happens, of course, to people who come into our Western culture. One missionary kid who had spent all his teen years in Japan came back to the States for college. He was thrown out of a shoe store the first week back when he told the manager that he wore size twenty-eight. The manager thought he was just another rude kid, smarting off. The boy had a terrible time getting up enough nerve to go to another store.

CULTURE SHOCK
A Missionary Simulation Experience

Explanation

When missionaries go into a new culture, they try to conform to the habits and customs of the people, as long as they don't violate the principles taught in the Bible.

That can be terribly hard, because we are so used to our old cultural habits. Add the pressures of learning a new language, new living and eating situations, and removal from close friends and familiar places. It's only through God's help that missionaries survive the first year.

Today we're going to go through a culture shock as we pretend to be missionaries entering the unusual country of Flockland. In this simulation, our language will remain English, of course, but we will make the experience difficult by setting up a crazy series of cultural imperatives. These are things newcomers must do if they expect to communicate effectively with the people in Flockland.

The list is silly, of course, but then who's to say that the cultural rules are any stranger than our own—we're just more used to our own.

Cultural Rules

(Here you can make your own list or use mine. Or combine yours and mine. You might want to place these on a chalkboard or large sheet of paper so they remain in front of everyone during this first part of the simulation.)

- In Flockland, a cultured person never uses pronouns—only complete names.
- In Flockland, when people meet, they jump up and down twice and clap once. When they part, they rub noses.
- In conversation, it is considered very poor manners to laugh or show your teeth. Pleasure is shown by rubbing the tongue quickly back and forth across the lower lip.
- Conversations in Flockland are limited to two minutes. Longer conversations indicate the person is lazy, making poor use of time and vocabulary.
- No one sits with legs touching.
- People snap their fingers in a regular rhythm when they are talking with someone of the opposite sex, even a spouse, if they're in public.
- A refined person never covers more than ten inches with each step.
- A sign of friendship is to pull a hair from your head and present it to the person to whom you're talking. This can also be a sign that you're telling the truth.
- Upon leaving a person, you should bestow a wish upon him or her. For example, "I wish you rain for your potatoes."
- When a Flockland person sits, it is improper to lean back. Usually a person perches on the edge of the chair.

Spend five minutes getting used to the rules. Interact as people of Flockland. At the end of this time, the list of cultural rules will be taken down and you will be asked to act on them without seeing them.

Note mistakes others make and correct them. This is not the main part of the simulation; it's more a practice for it.

It will be impossible for most people to get through the five minutes without making many errors in the etiquette of Flockland. Of course, the rules are ridiculous, but in many lands—Japan, Zaire, France, etc.—if a missionary disobeys cultural rules, credibility is lessened, the people who will listen to the message are fewer, and in some primitive cultures, his or her very life may be in danger.

At the end of the five minutes, allow time for people to share some of their feelings and their experiences. If necessary, get conversation going with a few questions:

"How did you feel after the five minutes? Silly? Tired? A failure?"

"To us these things are silly. But consider a foreign student coming to our country. What things in our culture might he consider funny, strange?"

The Simulation

Divide the participants into two equal groups. One group will be the native Flockland people. They are 100 percent at ease with themselves and their culture.

In order to illustrate this, they should act normally. We will all assume that they are doing the list of things that are culturally right in Flockland.

The burden lies with the second group. They will be the missionaries, and they must remember all the rules of Flockland. (Take the posted rules down.)

It is the responsibility of the second group of people to try to build friendships with Flockland people while remembering all the cultural rules and trying to obey them.

Whenever the missionary makes a mistake, the national should simply walk away from him. Nationals and missionaries interact for about five to eight minutes.

Remember, the one group acts perfectly normal and we assume it is obeying all the rules. The other group represents the culturally struggling missionary.

If you have time, you might want to switch groups.

After the end of the simulation, debrief. These questions will help:

- "How many of you feel you laid a friendship base? Did you concentrate more on making friends or on your cultural correctness?"
- "How realistic do you think it is to assume that nationals will turn off the message of Christ if the missionary violates their cultural rules?"
- "What part does the Holy Spirit play in the communication of Christ in a real cross-cultural experience?"
- "What have you learned from this experience?"

'GUIDANCE'—A ROLEPLAY SIMULATION

"Guidance" combines roleplay and simulation. It can be played in a few minutes, using only a few of the roleplay situations, or it can become the basis for a half-hour life response section of a Sunday school or club meeting.

"Guidance" is developed around roleplay situations. In each, a person with a problem asks a Christian for help. The way in which the Christian helper deals with both the person and the problem is evaluated and rated by each student in class.

Incorporate this game into your teaching plans when lessons deal with how Christians can put Biblical principles to work in today's life situations.

"Guidance" is designed to help your students:

- Analyze the opportunities they have to help others and react correctly to these opportunities.
- Develop sensitivity to others.
- Discover more about how God works through Christians to accomplish His purposes.
- Develop their knowledge of the Bible so they can use it effectively in everyday situations.

Guidance

Playing Data

Age Level: Junior high through adult. (Before the game is played, the teacher should read all Situation Cards and delete any that do not apply to the age level.)

Number of Players: Two roleplayers and any number of evaluators.

Playing Time: Minimum, 15 minutes; no maximum.

Preparation

Cut out the Situation and Attitude Cards printed on pages 162 through 182.

Reproduce a large number of Guidance Score Cards from the sample printed on page 159. Each evaluator will need one Guidance Score Card for every roleplaying situation he or she witnesses.

Be thoroughly familiar with how the game is played before your students play it. If necessary, review the principles of effective roleplay with your students. (See chapter 3.)

Playing Directions

Although the whole class participates in playing "Guidance," the burden of each roleplay situation falls on two students. One will play the Christian helper and the other the problem student. The problem student chooses a Situation Card and reads it to the helper and the group. Then the problem student takes an Attitude Card. Without revealing the information on this card until the roleplay is over, the person assumes the attitude suggested on the card.

Each roleplay situation asks or implies a question. The session should begin with the Christian helper asking the problem student two or three questions to gain a greater understanding of the problem and to get an idea of the attitude of the problem student. After he or she has this basic information, the person is ready to deal with the problem situation.

Although the problem student has the stronger acting part, it is the ability of the Christian helper to aid the problem student in working out a Christian solution that is being judged by the class.

Each class member should be given a Guidance Score Card on which to rate the helper from one to five points in four categories. Five are the most points a helper can earn in any category with the exception of two bonus points for using a relevant Scripture verse in the roleplay.

Guidance Score Cards

Points are scored
in the following areas:
Effective use of Bible
—5 points or less
    (bonus 2 points for
effective use of reference)
Personality understanding
—5 points or less
Biblical carry-over
—5 points or less
Practical suggestions
—5 points or less
A perfect score is 20.

GUIDANCE SCORE CARD

☐ Effective use of Bible

☐ Bonus reference

☐ Personality understanding

☐ Biblical carry-over

☐ Practical suggestions

☐ TOTAL

Before the game begins, explain the significance of each scoring category:

Effective use of Bible—In "Guidance," the helper must use Biblical principles correctly. Often the helper will not be able to quote the verse verbatim, but the game assumes that if the helper knows what the Bible says on the subject, he or she would in a real-life situation be able to use a concordance to find the specific verse. However, if a helper is able to use any relevant verse, explain the message it contains, and give the reference, the helper scores an extra two bonus points.

At least one Biblical reference is given on each Situation Card; however, these verses do not contain the total answers to the problems. They may be used as a starting basis if any student would like to study a situation more completely. The principles found in the Bible, when applied to any life situation, offer a sound base from which Christian decisions can be made and problems solved.

Personality understanding—This category demands that the helper understand the attitude of the student. It keeps the helper from being more interested in the problem than in the person being helped. It is an exercise in awareness.

Often the problem student will accept or reject advice on the basis of how the helper approaches the problem. The attitude of the problem student determines the helper's approach.

Biblical carry-over—This simply means putting the Bible into life today. It is the application part of the roleplay. The helper must show first what the Biblical principle is and then show how this principle fits the problem of the other student.

Practical suggestions—In this area the helper gives the problem student some positive steps for action. For instance, if the problem is devotional life, the helper might suggest the two of them have partner devotions for a few weeks to share what they have learned in some specific part of the Scripture.

After the roleplay is concluded—the average roleplay runs from three to four minutes—observers fill out their sheets. These are given to the helper, and from them, the player will be able to tell the greatest areas of strength and weakness.

Score Evaluation

20-22—Too good to be true.

18-19—Excellent.

16-17—Good.

14-15—Average. Work on lowest areas.

12-13—Fair. Practice a few more roleplays to bring up your score.

11 or below—Poor. Work hard to improve your score so that when an opportunity arises, you'll be able to give God your best.

Discussion

For students to get the maximum benefit from playing "Guidance," discussion must follow every situation. The value of the situation to the group and what happened in the roleplay should determine the amount of time spent on discussion—usually from three to ten minutes.

Discussion should include questions like these:

- *(To the Christian helper)* What clues did you pick up from the problem student that told you how to deal with him? *(To the total class)* What additional clues did you see?
- In what ways did the helper show understanding of the problem?
- What was the most effective thing the helper did in this situation? Why?
- What would you have done differently? Why?
- If you had been the problem student, how would you have reacted to the helper? Why? How do you think a person with this problem in real life might have reacted? Why?
- What principle(s) for helping others did you see demonstrated in this roleplay? *(If you will be doing a number of "Guidance" situations, list these principles on a chalkboard.)*
- What additional Scripture could you suggest? Explain your choice. *(Consider writing these suggestions on the Situation Card.)*

Adding to the game

When your students are familiar with this roleplay simulation, they may want to add additional Situation and Attitude Cards to help them gain roleplay practice in other areas of their Christian lives.

For example, "Guidance" doesn't deal directly with witness situations and touches only briefly on interpersonal relationship situations. These would be excellent areas in which your students could expand their game. Suggest they write each original situation on one side of a 3 x 5-inch card and each attitude on one-half of a 3 x 5-inch card. This will limit the size of the situations and keep the new game cards uniform.

Challenge your students to write situations which are complex enough to simulate real-life situations. No Situation Card should be included in the game until at least one relevant Scripture reference has been included on it. This will force students to get into Biblical research and at least begin to find answers to their own roleplay problems.

Cut apart the following Attitude Cards for use in the "Guidance" roleplay simulation.

Guidance

A Roleplay Game

ATTITUDE	ATTITUDE
ATTITUDE	ATTITUDE
ATTITUDE	ATTITUDE
ATTITUDE	ATTITUDE
ATTITUDE	ATTITUDE
ATTITUDE	ATTITUDE

Ready for change in life. Anxious to ask questions	Impressed with own Bible knowledge. Inattentive.
Desperate for an answer. Anxious to listen.	Anxious to find easy solution. Lazy, not willing to work at it.
Discouraged. Doubting salvation because of problem. (Lead helper to this deeper problem.)	Argumentative. Want to argue more than find solution.
Disinterested in finding solution. Merely talkative.	Resentful. Fighting changes in your life you know God wants.
Amazed to find someone who really cares.	Tired of struggling. Hoping for solution.
Happy to find someone who cares. Anxious to listen.	Sarcastic. Determined to counter all helper's suggestions with biting remarks.

ATTITUDE	ATTITUDE
ATTITUDE	ATTITUDE
ATTITUDE	ATTITUDE
ATTITUDE	ATTITUDE
ATTITUDE	ATTITUDE
ATTITUDE	ATTITUDE

Worried. Anxious for someone to help you change this attitude.	Joking. Just kidding the helper about the problem. Whole thing is a put-on.
Argumentative. Unable to believe an answer is available.	Angry. Blaming God for problem.
Scared the helper will reject you as a person because of your problem.	Unhappy. Too tied up in self to see God's way out.
Pessimistic about life. Certain any solution will fail.	Excited by the possibility of a solution.
Worried that any solution will just lead to another failure.	Determined not to be influenced by Christian helper.
Polite, but not overly interested in finding a solution.	Upset with self for sharing. Resentful of helper.

ATTITUDE	ATTITUDE
ATTITUDE	ATTITUDE
ATTITUDE	ATTITUDE
ATTITUDE	ATTITUDE
ATTITUDE	ATTITUDE
ATTITUDE	ATTITUDE

Embarrassed. Feeling foolish for not being able to solve own problems.	Physically, emotionally tired. Not concentrating.
Embarrassed by religious talk. Try to change subject.	Hesitant. Unable to believe God guides life.
Fearful of exposing too much of self. Anxious to change subject.	Unhappy with self and life in general.
Frightened. Afraid you will fail.	Afraid. Want God to rule life but scared to try.
Embarrassed. Joking to hide importance of issue from helper.	Busy, hurried, anxious to hear simplest solution in shortest amount of time.
Doubtful if suggestion will work. Willing to try.	Resentful of anyone who tries to help.

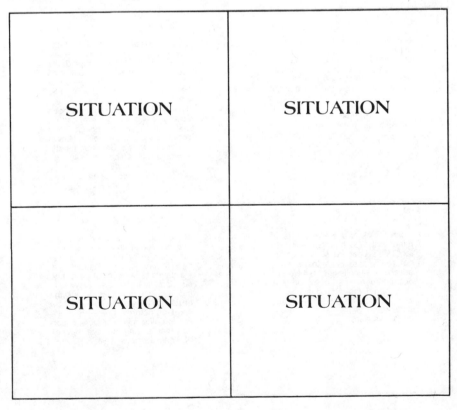

| ATTITUDE | ATTITUDE |

Cut apart the following Situation Cards for use in the "Guidance" roleplay simulation.

| SITUATION | SITUATION |
| SITUATION | SITUATION |

Optimistic. Looking for a workable solution to problem.	Doubtful if any solution will work in this difficult situation.

I've always thought God was guiding me to be a medical missionary, but today I discovered that I'm flunking biology. No nursing school would take a chance on me now. What happened to what I thought was God's will? I feel like God failed me, and I wish you could prove to me that I'm wrong. (James 1:5; I Peter 4:10)	Before I became a Christian, I had the habit of shoplifting small items. Since I met Christ, I repaid the merchants from whom I stole. But I know a number of my non-Christian friends are still playing the shoplifting game. If I report them, I lose the opportunities I have been having to witness to them; and if I don't, I'm living as though I approve of what they're doing. How in the world does a Christian handle a problem in which any way I go seems half wrong? (Ephesians 4:28; I John 5:4)
I can't think of a single prayer of mine that God has answered. In fact, He's been so silent that I'm not really sure He's there. Well, deep down I believe it, but He just doesn't seem a part of my life now. How can I make God speak up loud enough for me to hear and understand Him? (Hebrews 11:6)	My kid brother is into drugs, and our folks don't know. I hate to be responsible for my brother's life, even though I know he is ruining it. He claims to be a Christian, but he sure isn't living like one. I love him, but if I tell the folks about the drugs, he'll hate me forever. How can God help me guide my brother? Is doing my duty more important than saving his love for me? (II Thessalonians 3:14, 15)

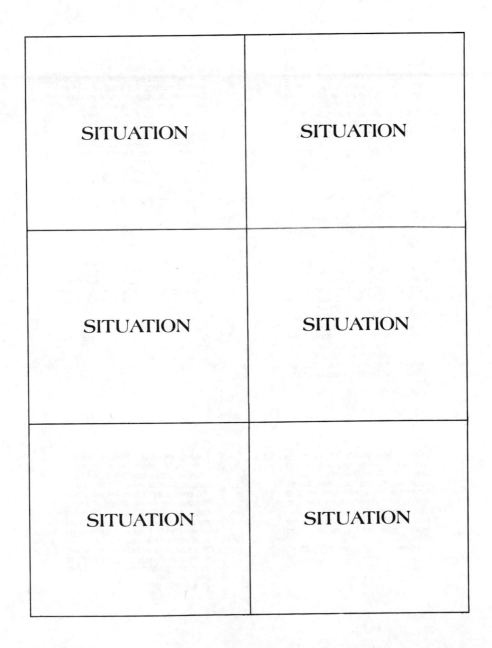

SITUATION
SITUATION

SITUATION
SITUATION

SITUATION
SITUATION

I promised the Lord I would have devotions every morning if it killed me, and to be honest, it just about has. I spend the whole time being bored. Sure, I want to know God's will for my life, but how can I get to know Him well enough to find out what it is without falling asleep in the process?
(Psalm 71:23)

Cheating has become a way of life for me, and even though I know it's wrong, I don't see how I can stop without hurting my testimony. You see, people respect me because I always succeed. They listen when I talk about God, and if they find out my whole life has been a lie, they would never trust another Christian. My life would be a less effective witness if I were honest. I know this is wrong reasoning, but what can I do to keep my sin from damaging how non-Christians feel about God?
(Ephesians 4:28; Romans 2:21, 24)

There is no way I can get to college. My folks can't send me; I'm not smart enough to get a merit scholarship or poor enough to get a help scholarship. Grades come hard for me, so I couldn't work and study at the same time and expect to graduate. This might limit what I can do for God, but I figure if He can't get me an education, it lowers my obligation to Him. If life is unfair to me, why should I cooperate with the God who allows it to be that way?
(Matthew 25:14-30)

I avoid and even fear people who are different than I am in race, color, or even the part of town they come from. I know God doesn't like my attitude. But all my friends feel the same way, and I don't see how I can break a pattern I've lived in ever since I was kid. I know being a Christian should help me, but exactly how does it?
(Luke 18:9-14)

I can't believe that all the things my Christian friends say are wrong really are. Does God expect me to think exactly the way they think? Does He just speak to them and not to me? Sometimes I am sure God wouldn't mind if I did a certain thing and they are just as sure He would. How can I know what God thinks?
(I Peter 2:21; I John 3:20, 21)

I have two non-Christian friends who have been living together. They've finally decided to get married and have asked me to be in the ceremony. If I accept I'm afraid the teens in my neighborhood who know I'm a Christian will think I'm condoning premarital sex. On the other hand, I have had several opportunities to share Christ with this couple. I wouldn't want to destroy our friendship by refusing to be part of their wedding. What should I do?
(Titus 2:7, 8)

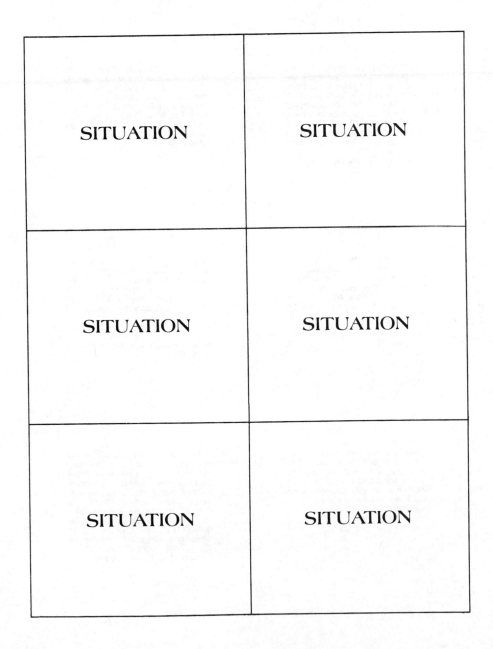

I'm seriously interested in going into politics. I know there are few people who can live a Christian testimony in the political world. Do you think that might be an indication that this occupation is outside the will of God? If so, why would God have given me the abilities and desires I have? How can I know God's will?
(Romans 12:2; Psalm 18:4-9)

I blow my stack over the least little thing. People make one wrong move, and I explode and make enemies for life. Unless I can control my temper, I am of little use to God. But it will mean a complete personality change, and how in the world can I do that?
(Proverbs 10:14, 31, 32)

Most of my school friends aren't popular. I know God has given me the ability to fit in with all kinds of people, including the leaders of the class. But if I work at joining the "in" group, my old friends will be hurt. How can I widen my circle of friends without hurting or losing my old friends?
(Matthew 25:40)

Right now it's very important for me to be a part of my group. I've read that this need for group identity lessens as a person gets older. I know if I lived completely for Christ now, I would lose my friends and be awfully lonely. Why can't I just be a Christian inside now and save the out-and-out dedication until I'm older and it will be easier to make a stand?
(Proverbs 1:10)

It seems to me that the most dynamic Christians I know are either good looking or very outgoing. I'm neither, but I really want to serve God. How do you suppose God would use a person like me?
(Romans 12:4, 5)

I don't think I have a single friend who doesn't know I'm a Christian. But even though I talk a lot about God and what I believe, I've never led one person to Christ. My witnessing never turns out the way it does in most of the Christian stories I read. Is it possible that God doesn't want me to witness? If He does, why doesn't He make my efforts more successful?
(Galatians 2:20; Acts 4:20)

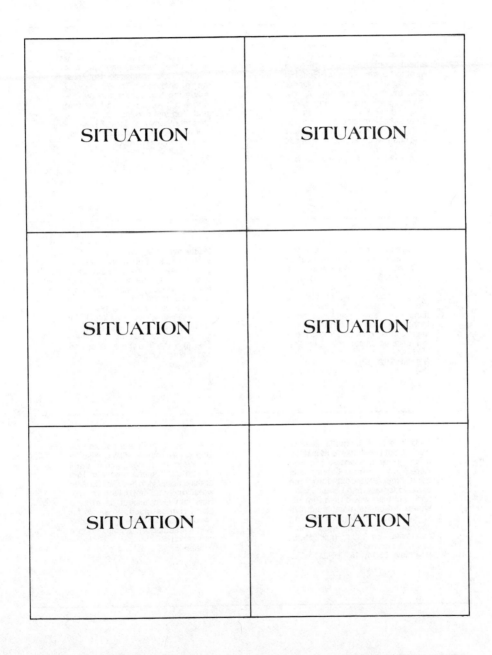

SITUATION	SITUATION
SITUATION	SITUATION
SITUATION	SITUATION

I have a bad heart and the least amount of exercise wears me out. I want to do what I can for God, but because of my handicap, I wonder how much He expects of me. When I think of the energy some people can devote to the Lord, I'm defeated before I begin. How much use can I be to God, who can use any healthy Christian He pleases to get the job done faster?
(Psalm 94:17, 18; I Peter 4:10)

Years ago we promised to love each other forever, and we were sure of our decision. But now we've divorced. This has really made me think about the permanence of love. How can I be sure that God will continue to love me throughout my life? Maybe His love will end like my partner's love did when things got rough?
(Jeremiah 31:3)

I've been a Christian for years, and it's a little hard to take God as seriously as the people who have recently met God. Their lives were pretty messed up, and Christ brought about a big change for them. God works in new Christians' lives, and my life just plods along in the same humdrum way it always has. How can I get more enthusiastic about my Christian life?
(Psalm 51:8, 12)

Inside my head, I'm a great conversationalist. But when I have to get the words out where someone else can hear them, I turn quiet and even mousy. I wish God would make me more like what I am on the inside so I could use the opportunities He gives me. Now, for instance, instead of witnessing, I turn clammy. What can I do to help God turn me into the type of person I want to be?
(Psalm 28:7)

I don't believe I should live for money, but I do think it's stupid not to try to be a financial success. Here's my problem. On the one hand, I feel God wouldn't want me to settle for less than I could make, and from this I would give Him His share. But on the other hand, I've always felt there was something spiritual about being poor. How can I keep from feeling guilty about being a success?
(Matthew 25:14, 15, 19-21)

I've heard it said that I should love God more than anything else in life. When I'm honest, I know that I don't. I don't spend time with Him or think about Him like I would if He were really all-important to me. How can God expect us to care about Him as much as we do for people we can see and touch? Isn't He setting a standard no one can reach?
(I John 5:1-3)

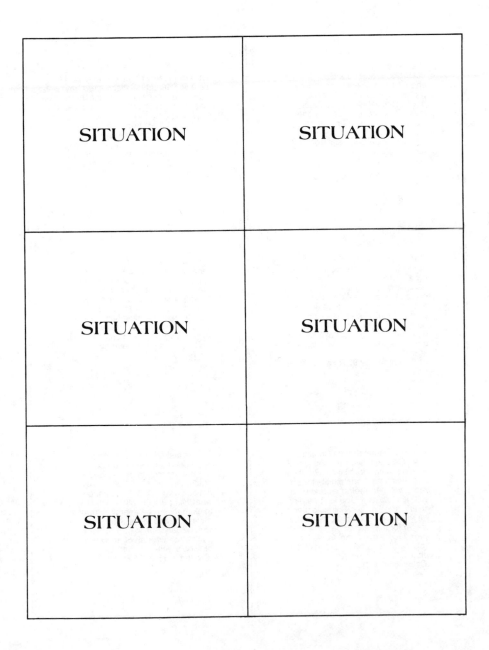

SITUATION	SITUATION
SITUATION	SITUATION
SITUATION	SITUATION

I've never said I hate my parents but inside I know I do. God says we should honor them, and He even promises long life if we do. I've asked Him to help me see them as lovable people, but whenever we're together, we blow up at each other. So what am I supposed to do to change both our attitudes? (John 13:34)

I've always heard that God takes care of those who love Him. And I believed it until I discovered my father/husband/wife (choose one) has cancer. Short of a miracle, he/she is going to die. And I need him/her. What good is being a Christian if I can't depend on God to pave my way? How is God any better to me than He is to people who consider His name nothing more than a swear word? (I Peter 5:8-10)

One of the men in our group figured God was important in every area of his life except the sexual part. Now he's contracted venereal disease and is sick with shame and worry. He thinks God will never forgive him, and he's sure the people he loves won't. What can I do to help him and get him back to the place where God can use him again? (II Chronicles 30:9; Romans 6:19)

The sections I read in the Bible never seem to have anything to do with the life I lead after devotions are finished. I feel as if I'm being hypocritical to have devotions at all—they just aren't as great as people tell me devotions should be. But I feel guilty if I miss them. What are real devotions anyway, and how can I have them? (II Timothy 2:15)

Since my parents aren't Christians, I feel God has given me the job of winning them for Him. But I've been living the Christian life for two years without seeing a single result. It's just as if God isn't helping at all, and I'm beginning to think He's unfair not to answer my prayer for their salvation. How long does God expect me to wait and how can I keep being a consistent witness? (Colossians 4:2)

For the last few years of school I've been dating the same person, and we are planning to be married after graduation. But my folks feel we haven't given God time to show us what His perfect will is. Don't you think that in three years God would have had time to show us if we are wrong? Isn't the fact that we love each other enough of an indication of God's will? (Proverbs 15:21, 22)

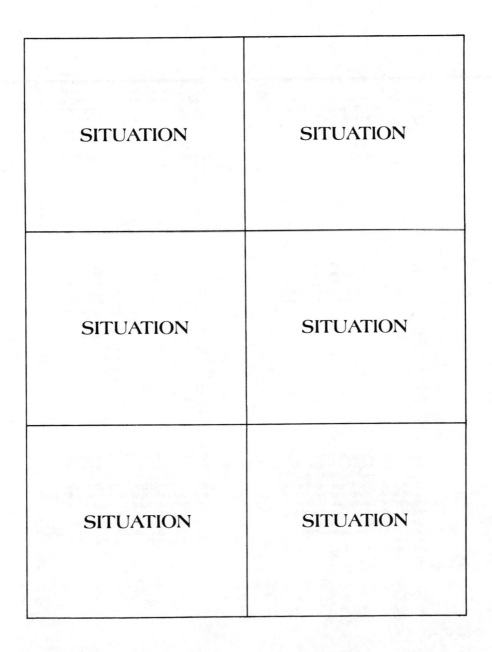

SITUATION	SITUATION
SITUATION	SITUATION
SITUATION	SITUATION

I want God to rule my life, and I think I'm fair when I say He does rule my actions. But how can I let Him rule my thought life? I spend so much time thinking about sex that there is little time left over for other thoughts. Is there something sinful about the sex drive? Should I try to control what I think about, or doesn't it matter?
(Philippians 4:8)

I'm the type of person who always plays second fiddle. If I get invited to a party, it's because someone else canceled out. I get to sing in the school chorus if someone comes down with a sore throat. I don't have a single quality I can use for Christ that someone else doesn't have more of. I'm discouraged. How does a second fiddle fit into God's plan?
(Luke 22:27)

Before I can really let God rule my life, do I have to go back and correct all the wrong things I've ever done? What is my association with my past now that I'm a new person?
(Psalm 32:5)

I dislike myself. In fact, there isn't one thing about me I admire. I hear people say God loves me and can lead me in a successful, useful life of service. But I can't believe He really cares. If He did, He would help me like myself better. I wish you could prove to me that I'm worth liking.
(Mark 3:35)

Last week I ruined my testimony so badly that people I didn't even know made snide remarks like, "If you're a Christian, I wouldn't want to be one." God's cause would have gone ahead a lot faster without me. How can I ever be of any use to God again? Will God ever forgive me for failing Him so completely?
(Psalm 25:7, 11, 18; I John 2:1, 2, 12)

It seems to me God has picked favorites just like everyone else in the world. Take money, for instance. I don't have enough to buy a complete lunch tomorrow, and yet I'm supposed to accept this with a smile. Well, how can God expect a hungry Christian to really love and follow Him?
(Philippians 4:19; Acts 2:44, 45)

SITUATION	SITUATION
SITUATION	SITUATION

It's great to be in control of a speeding car. I know I often break speed limits, but I rarely do anything really dangerous. A friend told me last night that since I didn't obey my country's laws, I probably didn't really obey God's laws either. How can he relate speeding to Christianity? Isn't he being overly religious? (John 12:26)	I have no desire whatsoever to go into full-time Christian work, and sometimes I get the feeling that this makes me less of a Christian than the people who do feel this calling. Is full-time work always God's best for a person? If so, I want it, but how can I get the desire to do it? If it isn't, how can I get rid of my guilt feelings? (Galatians 6:4)
If God gave us love, how can any expression of love be wrong? What harm is there in sleeping with someone I love, especially now that unwanted pregnancies are no longer the problem they used to be? Why can't I satisfy my needs and live a completely useful Christian life at the same time? (Hebrews 13:4)	Most Christians at my church are hypocrites, and I am less than excited about associating with them. I think it would be more of a worship experience for me to stay away from church and pray at home. Isn't it possible that once I got away from these people who are such pains God would be better able to speak to me? What value is there in my continuing to come to church? (I John 4:20; Romans 14:10)

Idea: Instead of using the Attitude Cards, collect pictures from magazines and newspapers of people's expressions. You may want to back these pictures on 3 x 5-inch cards. If you have a photographer in your group, you may want him to take a number of pictures of people with different expressions on their faces—or even of the same person with different expressions on his or her face. The Christian with a problem would assume the mental attitude suggested on the photograph. It would be up to the Christian helper to discover the attitude and deal appropriately with that person.

Consider these examples:

182

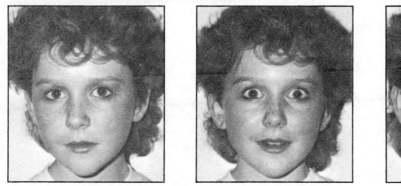

'TROUBLE DOWN AT THE CHURCH'
—SIMULATION AND LESSON PLAN[5]

Simulation games must be used as part of a teaching plan if they are to be most effective. The teacher's goal is to use the games to help students learn something new, or to gain practice in an important area of Christian life. "Trouble Down at the Church" is a simulation to help students understand the principle, "God commands all who share His fellowship to love one another." It can be used in teen and adult Sunday school classes. It might also be used by church leaders to demonstrate in an unthreatening situation how to love when the situation gets difficult.

The simulation begins with the leader reading the following situation aloud to the participants.

TROUBLE DOWN AT THE CHURCH

To build or not build a gym. That was the thing that started the trouble.

Some of the congregation were for it. A gym would be a great youth center for Christian kids. It would be a perfect place to bring non-Christian friends. Now they had no supervised place where they could meet. The gym could also have a stage at one end that could be used for special musical programs and Christ-centered plays.

Other members of the church were against it. Some felt it was too much money. The church couldn't afford it. Many felt that it was poor use of the Lord's money to build an expensive building. This group, including members of the Missions Outreach, felt that any new money raised should be given to poor people who didn't have enough to meet daily needs. Or the money could be donated to mission programs for building churches overseas or buying Christian literature to give to non-Christians.

183

The sides were drawn. Some kids threatened to stop coming to church if adult members didn't care enough to see the value of the gym. Some adults threatened to cut off all their church giving if such an extravagant plan were accepted. If they carried out this threat, there would not be enough money to support existing church programs.

Joe Lemon, the youth director, thought the gym plan was a good one, and for a while it seemed that on the weight of his support the program would carry. The kids loved him, and under his leadership the youth group had tripled in size. He was even working with the public school on his own time as a part-time coach. Through his invitation, many kids on his team came to church for the first time.

Now suddenly things have begun to happen that are causing some people to doubt if Joe is a competent youth leader. Some who had supported the program are beginning to back down, and a few are even quietly hinting that Joe should be asked to leave.

Joe made some bad business investments and is heavily in debt. Phil Parker, chairperson of the Mission Outreach at the church, lent him money to keep him from defaulting on his payments. Phil told Joe he thought it would be a bad testimony for the church to have a leader who couldn't pay his bills.

Then Sherry McFarling, a member of the youth group since ninth grade, rejected Christ after only one semester at college. She wrote explaining that she still believed in God but she could no longer accept Jesus as the Son of God.

To add to Joe's problem, his ninth-grade son had been in a car when the driver was stopped on drunken driving charges. Joe had to go to the police station to pick up his son. The boy, Robert, has refused to come to church ever since.

The big meeting to make the final decision on the gym is this evening. Most of the church will be there.

Following the reading, discuss questions like these:
- "What are the key issues?"
- "At this point, what possible choices do you see available to the church?"

Ask the group to work together to study inductively I John 3:10—4:21. As part of this study, students could chart facts about people who follow God's command to love in these verses and facts about people who don't. These verses aren't difficult to understand, just difficult to live. The objective of the simulation is to give students practice in the difficult life area. How do they live Christ's command in a complex situation where obedience is difficult?

In this simulation, give seven students special identities. The others take parts of people who are either for or against the building and Joe Lemon. Each student who assumes these special roles should be given only his or her part of the following information.

Joe Lemon—Youth Director

You are dedicated to your youth group. You believe this gym could be used to the glory of God. You also believe that the group needs your strong leadership.

You are upset because of your poor business dealings, and you are grateful to Phil Parker for his financial help. Without him, you couldn't have paid your bills. You know he is against the gym, and you hate going against him.

You don't understand your son's choice of friends. You love your boy and refuse to believe anything bad about him, even though he's recently been in trouble. He was in a car when the driver was arrested for drunken driving.

Phil Parker—Chairperson of Mission Outreach

You are extremely concerned about putting the Lord's money to good use. You feel that Christians are commanded to give to the poor and those in need. You are very interested in missionary work and give heavily to missions in foreign lands and at home.

You have strong opinions. You believe that the Lord would be more pleased by money for missions than money for gyms. You are determined to use every method available to you to get the gym vetoed. You doubt Joe's leadership and his value as a Christian example to teens. You had to loan him money to pay his bills. Eventually call for a vote to find out how many others feel he should be asked to leave.

Sandra Farraway

You have been saved under Joe Lemon's ministry. He is your spiritual father. You are determined that the youth group is not going to lose Joe. You speak up in his defense.

Karen Holdings

An excellent athlete, you are thrilled at the possibility of having a gym. You are certain that most of the kids you're friends with at school will come to the church if a gym is built. You look forward to many non-Christians meeting Jesus. You are extremely outspoken.

Kenneth Fitz

You're a reporter from the village paper, and, although you are not a Christian, you are interested in improving the community with a gym that would provide a good healthy entertainment and fun for a generation which, in your opinion, has so many ugly influences. Speak hotly for your issue. You do not have a vote at the meeting but work hard to persuade people to vote for the gym.

185

Linda Williams

You are a social worker and spend much of your life trying to help families who are just barely surviving. You think it's a crying shame that the spoiled teens of this church need a gym when they have the whole outdoors and safe streets and Christian homes to meet in. You threaten to pull out of the church if the vote swings for the gym. Work hotly against it.

Mary McFarling—Mother of Sherry

You want Joe Lemon out. You figure that your daughter must have received poor training from him to have fallen away from Christianity so quickly. You feel too much time is being spent on sports and special programs and not enough on Bible study. The gym will add to this problem.

Steps in the Simulation

1. *Get all major parties to state their positions.* Then allow eight to ten minutes of open discussion. Call for a straw vote to allow students to see who is voting in what way.

If in the straw vote everyone votes for the gym, add the extra point that migrant workers' children on nearby farms are dropping out of school because they don't have the special help they need. Mr. Parker points out that it would cost about the same amount to hire tutors for these children for the next five years as it will to build a gym. He asks the group to vote to save the futures of these young people—and against the gym.

If in the straw vote everyone votes against the gym, add that due to a cutback in public school funds, all athletic activities have been stopped. The school gym is being used as a day-care center. The vote to make these changes passed only because people were convinced that the church would build a gym. Mr. Lemon points out how valuable athletics are in developing leadership qualities.

2. *After the straw vote, allow free lobbying.* Students talk among themselves for a few minutes. There are no rules. They should use this time to talk to anyone who might change positions. They are trying to win votes to their side.

3. *Then call for a final vote.*

4. *Debriefing.* Students should share their feelings and opinions about the simulation. People assigned specific parts should share how they felt about their character. Did they remain in character? In a real situation, how might this person behave?

Identify times when the Biblical principles the group studied were practiced. Violated.

If students were placed in a real situation similar to this, what would they do? Why?

Discuss the value of a simulation like this. To close the session, ask students to express love to God and thank Him for one Christian who has demonstrated the love of Christ in action. For example, "Lord, thank You for Raymond. He spent hours helping me with biology so I could keep my grades up for college."

1. There are a few games that do not fit in either category. One of the most valuable for teachers and parents is The Ungame, developed by Thea Zackac (© 1975, The Ungame Co., Garden Grove, Calif.). In The Ungame, people move around a never-ending board. As they move, they have opportunities to answer questions that give the other players information about themselves. The group also has the opportunity of directing original questions to other players. No one wins in the traditional sense, but everyone wins in reality. Friendships are built, and people become more effective at communicating their feelings.

2. Nancy Kelly, "Let It Growl," reprinted in part from *World Vision* magazine, February, 1979. Used by permission.

3. Paula E. Hyman, "New Debate on the Holocaust," in the *New York Times Magazine*, September 14, 1980.

4. Marlene LeFever, "Project: Mission Awareness," in *Creative Hospitality* (Wheaton, Ill.: Tyndale House Publishers, Inc., 1980), pp. 120-122. Used by permission.

5. Marlene LeFever, "Trouble Down at the Church," from *Friendship Like You've Never Known* by Ruth Senter and David R. Mains, part of the **Christian Growth Electives** series, 1978.

CHAPTER 8

Never Too Old for "Tell Me a Story"

Jesus was not a theologian. He was God who told stories.

—Madeleine L'Engle

Who has not had the experience of listening to a sermon or lecture and tuning out? The words drone and our minds drift in other directions . . . drift, until we pick up phrases like, "Now, let me illustrate that," or "I found out how true this point is the other day as I was . . ." We tune back in for the anecdote, the story.

Story continues to be a teaching tool throughout our lives, yet all too often, if we are not teaching children, we don't use it effectively.

My first contact with living story was Miss Bennett. I was in my early teens, a product of Sunday-after-Sunday Sunday school. I knew all the stories and even practiced telling them to the preschool class in our little church. I don't remember when the words *flannelgraph* and *flash cards* were not part of my vocabulary. But Miss Bennett didn't just tell stories; she became stories. She was ancient and wrinkled, with her slip hanging out, a funny little hat and veil on top of her head. I knew the minute I saw her that there was no way I was going to listen to her—and then she began to talk. Without any aids, she talked me up the long road to Calvary and made me participate in the pain and dust and flies and smells of that awful Jerusalem day. This adolescent, sophisticated Sunday school snob was captured by the reality of a story.

Stories—personal illustrations, life experiences of others, sections from books, short stories, parables, myths—no matter what the form (and often no matter if the writer is Christian or non-Christian), story helps us participate in the reality of the Christian experience.[1] The primary goals of this chapter are (1) to sensitize teachers to the importance of using story with teens and adults, (2) to encourage teachers to start a file of stories that can be used in their classes, and (3) to provide some practice in cutting a long story down to size so it can be used in a limited time slot.

"My own experience has taught me how important story can be," an adult teacher said. "My mother used to read books to me when I was a child and she continued the practice until I went away to college. It wasn't that I couldn't read myself, but the shared experience made a big impression on me and was one of the factors that held us together during my turbulent adolescent years. *The Robe* was the first adult book I was exposed to. Mother read each evening until her voice started cracking, and then I'd go off to bed. What I didn't discover until years later was that after I was asleep, she would return to the book and read more for herself. Then the next night she would quickly summarize what she had read until we came to the new part, and off she'd go again."

A pastor shared his experience with story. "We gather an hour before the evening worship service to read the *Narnia Chronicles* together. Old and young alike are delighted with the reading. There is no discussion or dissection of the books, just the simple, glorious story. All of us from third grade to past retirement bemoan the shortness of the hour."

Story—what an important tool for Christian teachers.

GUIDELINES: HOW TO READ AND TELL STORIES

● *First, begin to read yourself.* Read the stories of the Bible again, perhaps aloud and from a modern language translation or paraphrase. Read books that others have labeled excellent. "One of the things I missed most when I was away from a college setting," said a Christian school-teacher, "was the hints on good books to read. I finally contacted a few teachers and asked them for the book lists they were giving their students. I enjoy wandering through college bookstores, because I find cutting-edge books there. I was in one when the salesperson came up to me with *Ridley Walker*[2], an experimental book in which the author plays with the degeneration of language. 'Buy this,' the salesperson said. 'If you don't like it, I'll take it back with a full refund.' People who read will almost pay you to read books they have loved!"

"I recently discovered science fiction,"[3] an adult teacher said. "I'm a reader, but I always considered science fiction below me. Then I read *Dune*[4] and a whole new world opened. I rushed for more science fiction, but the ones I chose were trash. I went to my bookstore and asked the salesperson for some of his favorites. I left with eight books, every one of them excellent. I've even used portions of several in my Sunday school class, and encouraged my students to grapple with the issues they raised."[5]

A junior high teacher pointed out that some of the best things she finds in stories never get shared with her students. "Often I'll find something that serves as a warning to me as a teacher. I don't read that warning to my students, but it does make a difference in how I teach. I read *The Diviners*,[6] a Canadian fiction best-seller that contains a negative example of a Sunday school teacher who failed to affirm her student's struggle to find herself and feel positive about what she had discovered.

"The author, Margaret Laurence, creates a strong and lonely character, Morag Gunn. Raised by the town garbage collector, Morag has little in life except her keen awareness and determination to overcome problems. Morag loves Jesus and she respects the pastor's wife, Mrs. McKee, who 'doesn't bawl people out, nor look at clothes.' After some thought she decides to risk showing the teacher a poem she had written. It began:

> Despite the cold and wintry blast,
> To Bethlehem they came at last.

"The teacher is surprised, and then corrects the poem by saying, 'It was a middle east desert country, dear, so they wouldn't have a wintry blast, would they?'

> Morag's face—flames of shame. She snatches the paper back.
> "Wait—I'll fix it."

"She does and gives it back to Mrs. McKee. During class Mrs. McKee says, 'I want to read you a poem today.'

> Morag's heart quits beating. Hers? She will faint. A talented poem written by one of our members, class. The others will stare. Who'd have thought it. Old Morag.

"The poem, however, is by the English poet, Hilaire Belloc.

At home, Morag takes off her galoshes and coat. Goes to the stove.
"What's that you're burning, Morag?"
"Nothing. Just nothing."
Morag goes to her room. Sits thinking. Wants to cry.
She has shown 'The Wise Men' to Mrs. McKee, and there is no way she
can unshow it.

"The little section from the novel has often flashed through my mind as I teach. I don't want to miss an opportunity to affirm and challenge a young person to be even more than she dreamed. After that Sunday, Morag's interest in church diminishes and eventually she leaves the church. It's a novel—Morag and Mrs. McKee are characters of fiction. But the message from that small segment came through to this Sunday school teacher."

In the *Autobiography of Malcolm X,* an English writer asked him what his alma mater was. He answered, "Books . . . . Every time I catch a plane, I have a book with me that I want to read . . . . I could spend the rest of my life reading, just satisfying my curiosity."

● *Record your voice as you read or tell a story.* Start with a children's story, for example, *Yertle the Turtle* by Dr. Seuss.[7] Listen to yourself a day after you've recorded. Rate yourself by deciding how true the following statements are of you. Use a scale from 10 (totally true, describes me perfectly) to 1 (oops! I think I'm terrible here).

___ 1. I captured the feeling of the story. When things were funny, my voice sparkled with fun. When things were sad, my voice reflected that as well.

___ 2. I varied the speed of my reading. Everything didn't move along at an even pace. I sped up and slowed down, just as I do in normal conversation.

___ 3. I varied my expression so listeners could tell which character was speaking.

___ 4. I used pauses to build suspense.

___ 5. I enjoyed reading the story. (When a person is committed to a story, his or her enthusiasm shows in the reading.)

___ 6. If I read this story again, I know what I would do to make my reading more effective. (Try reading the story again. Record and evaluate a second time. If you're really daring, ask an honest friend to rate you on the first four points.)

● *Remember eye contact.* If you're telling a story, eye contact may come more naturally than it does when you're reading one. Either way, eye contact is important. You need to be familiar enough with the story and at ease enough with the presentation to look at your students.

● *Let your facial expression convey part of the message.* For example, if something terrible has just happened, you should not be smiling. No, you are not acting out the story with your face as you might in a roleplay or drama. Instead you are reflecting seriousness or happiness or sadness—some of the larger categories of emotions—rather than the nuances of the emotions an actor or actress would try to capture.

● *Let your voice reflect the emotions in the story.* Try reading the following excerpt from *The Wounded Land.*[8] As you read, let your voice feel the pain of the giant who has been trying to get Thomas Covenant to tell the story of how giants have been murdered. Covenant doesn't know how to share that the giants allowed themselves to be killed because some of their number had violated the truth they stood for. The others could not live as lies. In happier times, the giants had made power and beauty and laughter through story, and they often complained about short stories that had to be squeezed into only three days!

The giant begs Covenant to tell the story.

"Such tales must be shared to be borne. An untold tale withers the heart. But I do not ask that you ease your heart. I ask for myself. Your tale concerns my kindred . . . .

"Thomas Covenant, I ask for your tale because I must choose. Only in stories may the truth to guide me be found. Lacking the knowledge that moves your heart, I lack means to judge your path and your desires. You must speak."

Descending toward the trees, Pitchwife Giant began to sing. His voice was hoarse, as if he had spent too much of his life singing threnodies, yet his song was as heart-lifting as trumpets. His melody was full of wind and waves, of salt and strain, and of triumph over pain. As clearly as the new day, he sang: . . . "We are the Giants,
      born to sail,
      and bold to going wherever dreaming goes."

Change your tone as you practice this reading from *The Manticore.*[9] Try to capture a bit of the humor and sarcasm the writer intends. End with a challenge.

"But just because you are not a roaring egotist, you needn't fall for the fashionable modern twaddle of the anti-hero and the mini-soul. That is what we might call the shadow of democracy; it makes it so laudable, so cozy and right and easy to be a spiritual runt and lean on all the other runts for support and applause in a splendid apotheosis of runtdom. Thinking runts—of course—oh, yes, thinking away as hard as a runt can without

---

getting into danger. But there are heroes still. The modern man is the man who conquests the inner struggle. How do you know you aren't that kind of hero?"

STORY FILE

If you're a reader you will often come across something that rings a bell. "If I had only had that illustration last Sunday, it would have been a perfect addition to the lesson." Last Sunday's gone, but there will be another. But if you don't start a file of those illustrations, when the second chance comes, you'll be unable to find it.

It's time to start a file. Develop your own file topics. Here are some suggestions, but you'll have others that fit your age level's specific needs. For each topic have two files—one for specifically Christian stories, and one for secular.

Death—Secular/Christian	Holidays—Secular/Christian
Sex—Secular/Christian	Life-Style—Secular/Christian
Marriage—Secular/Christian	Life Issues—Secular/Christian
Fear—Secular/Christian	Futurism—Secular/Christian

EDITING FOR CLASS TIME

It's hard to know exactly how much time a story should be given. The final decision is the teacher's. Always consider the aim of your class hour. That aim will never be "To tell a good story." The story is an effective way to help students examine truth and learn to apply it to their lives.

Even the telling of a Bible story should not take the whole teaching time. It easily could. What a dramatic story Ananias and Sapphira make! Throw in conversation; include background on the early church; add some probable comments of the Christians who viewed this display of God's power—and 45 minutes will be gone. Your students will know the Bible story, but wouldn't you rather have them go beyond that? Did they understand the lesson God was teaching the early church? Do they have questions about the attributes of God that would allow Him to kill people for a half lie? What does this story say about the way we live for God today? We're never interested in just the story for the story's sake in a teaching situation.

Often teacher's guides will include stories that can be read or told in class. They are exactly the right size, usually edited to from three to five minutes.

You'll think of your own illustrations, too, as you're preparing your lesson—something that happened at work, or something your grandson said that perfectly illustrates a point. These usually take from three to five minutes to share. But is anything longer ruled out? No, but it will have to be cut.

One of the primary problems for the storyteller or reader will be cutting an illustration or story down to size. "Christbirth"[10] perfectly illustrates an attitude toward living, but we certainly can't read the 11-page story to the class. We can summarize it (but much of the excellent writing will be lost). We cannot use it at all (so much for the perfect illustration). Or, we can cut it down to time size. This is editing. It allows us to keep the flavor of the writing, and yet we can still use the story or even excerpts from a novel in class.

You, too, can edit. Follow this pattern:

1. *Begin by reading the story or section aloud.* Time yourself. How many minutes need to be cut to make the reading effective in the time you have?

2. *Look for sections you could delete.* Start with whole paragraphs. Yes, these sections are good, and you'll want to encourage your students to go back and read the whole story, but for your teaching goal, these sections aren't totally necessary. Hint: paragraphs can more often be cut from the middle of a story than from the beginning or the end.

3. *Maintain the tone of the story.* The writer usually sets this at the beginning of the story. If you cut out all the flair and color that are the writer's signature, you'll be losing the very thing that drew you to the story in the first place.

4. *Right before you cut a section, reread the last thing you will read aloud before the cut.* Do sections 1 and 3 work together if you cut out section 2? Quite often it is necessary to add the transitional words: "Three weeks later . . ." "He said . . ." "Meanwhile back at the ranch . . ."

5. *Practice your edited version.* Is it still worth reading in class? An effective edit should read smoothly, making its point without the listeners feeling the absence of the deleted portions.

"How Shall We Remember John?"[11] is a short story designed to help young people and adults better understand communion. The story takes about six minutes to read. Your assignment is to edit the copy to about four minutes. When you've finished, check your edited copy against the copy that follows. Yours will not be exactly the same.

HOW SHALL WE REMEMBER JOHN?

By Joseph Bayly

My big brother John and I were great pals. In fact, our whole family was close, including Mom and Dad, my sister, the brother I'm telling you about, and me. We were close in a way that you find few families today.

Breakfast was always a special time. We sat around this round oak table with a red-checked cloth on it. Mom almost always served the same thing: steaming hot oatmeal with brown sugar cooked in it (we piled a lot more on top of it, too), and milk.

We'd talk about what we were going to do that day, and maybe we'd joke some. Not that we had a lot of time—we didn't, but we had enough to talk some before Dad went off to work and us kids went to school.

John and I were two grades apart in school. That was sort of hard on me, because the teachers who had him were always comparing us when I got into their class. And the comparison wasn't too flattering to me.

Don't get me wrong. John wasn't a teacher's pet or bookworm. He was a regular guy, and the kids all liked him, including the girls. Maybe one guy who was sort of a bully didn't, but everyone else did.

Life went on like that—breakfast of oatmeal and milk, walk to school, classes, walk home, chores, supper, study around the kitchen table—and you never thought about anything else. Except vacation. Vacation was always stuck in your mind.

You know the kind of life, day after day, when it's so great you hope it never ends. Maybe you cry at night sometimes if you ever think of your mom or dad dying—you know they will someday. But then you go to sleep, next to John, who's already sawing wood.

It was Christmas vacation, when I was in sixth grade and John was in eighth, that it all suddenly came to an end. Actually, it was two days after Christmas.

John and I had gone to ice-skate on Big Pond. It was a real cold day, cold enough so that your scarf got ice on it from your breath. I put on my skates in a hurry and sailed out to the middle of the pond. I noticed a slight cracking sound from the ice, but it wasn't much and I wasn't worried. It had been pretty cold for about a week. So I showed off some for John, who was still lacing up his skates, sitting on a log, and then I headed for the opposite shore.

John stood up and went real fast, right out to the middle, too. Just as he got there, I heard this sickening cracking noise, the ice broke up, and John fell through.

I got a long branch and went out as far as I could on the ice. But I couldn't see John anywhere. He had just disappeared. I yelled for him, and I went even farther out, but he wasn't there.

I must have panicked, because first thing I knew I was running into the house shouting for Mom, crying my eyes out, yelling that John was in the pond. It was awful.

They found his body later that afternoon.

A few days after the funeral, we were sitting at the table, eating breakfast one morning. Nobody was saying anything; all of us were thinking about that empty chair over against the wall.

You could tell Mom was trying to talk. Finally she just sort of blurted out, "Look, we all miss John, terribly. We loved—love him, and we'll always miss him. Now I have a suggestion to make. Do you remember how he liked oatmeal and milk?"

"Do I!" I said. "I sure do. He used to pile on the brown sugar until—"

"That's enough. He liked his oatmeal sweet and so do you. What I want to suggest is this. Let's think about John every time we eat breakfast. Let's remember him whenever we eat oatmeal and drink milk. Let's talk about him—"

"Yeh, like the time he and I went swimming in Big Pond and . . ." I knew before Sis spoke that I had said something I shouldn't have. Everyone sort of choked up.

"Time for school," she said.

And Dad said, as we all left the table, "We can continue this later."

Well, we did. And we agreed with Mom's suggestion.

So each morning, when that big pitcher of cold milk went on the table, and our bowls of steaming oatmeal were set in front of us, we'd talk about John.

It wasn't sad talk, but happy. Remembering. I don't mean we never said anything that made us choke up—other people besides me did. But mainly it was happy talk. And we still talked about what we were going to do that day, and even—after a while—joked some.

One day, some months later, Mom said, "You know, I don't think what we're doing is quite respectful enough for John's memory."

"Respectful?" I said. "Why, it's fun. Sometimes it's almost like John is here with us. I like it."

"So do I," Mom said. "But I think we're too casual about it. So I think we ought to set aside a time when we're not rushed like we are at breakfast. Let's say Saturday morning. And we'll remember John in a more fitting place than the kitchen. We'll sit in the parlor, and we'll have a special time worthy of John's memory."

"Aw, Mom," I said, "John always liked breakfast in the kitchen. Lots of oatmeal with plenty of brown sugar on it. And milk. Why make a big deal of it?"

"That's enough, Son," Dad said. "We'll do as your mother says."

So every Saturday morning, after we had eaten our regular breakfast in the kitchen, we went into the parlor and remembered John. Mom had gotten some little silver cups for the milk, and some tiny plates for the oatmeal.

Later we only went into the parlor once a month, instead of every week, and now we only do it every three months. It doesn't seem right to me, but I'll soon be leaving home, so it doesn't matter.

I still wish we had never begun that "fitting" remembrance, and had just kept on remembering John every time we ate breakfast.

Here is one way in which the editing could be done.

197

HOW SHALL WE REMEMBER JOHN?

By Joseph Bayly

My big brother John and I were great pals. In fact, our whole family was close, including Mom and Dad, my sister, the brother I'm telling you about, and me. We were close in a way that you find few families today.

Breakfast was always a special time. We sat around this round oak table with a red-checked cloth on it. Mom almost always served the same thing: steaming hot oatmeal with brown sugar cooked in it (we piled a lot more on top of it, too), and milk.

We'd talk about what we were going to do that day, and maybe we'd joke some. ~~Not that we had a lot of time—we didn't, but we had enough to talk some before Dad went off to work and us kids went to school.~~

~~John and I were two grades apart in school. That was sort of hard on me, because the teachers who had him were always comparing us when I got into their class. And the comparison wasn't too flattering to me.~~

~~Don't get me wrong. John wasn't a teacher's pet or bookworm. He was a regular guy, and the kids all liked him, including the girls. Maybe one guy who was sort of a bully didn't, but everyone else did.~~

~~Life went on like that—breakfast of oatmeal and milk, walk to school, classes, walk home, chores, supper, study around the kitchen table—and you never thought about anything else. Except vacation. Vacation was always stuck in your mind.~~

~~You know the kind of life, day after day, when it's so great you hope it never ends. Maybe you cry at night sometimes if you ever think of your mom or dad dying—you know they will someday. But then you go to sleep, next to John, who's already sawing wood.~~

It was Christmas vacation, when I was in sixth grade and John was in eighth, that it all suddenly came to an end. Actually, it was two days after Christmas.

John and I had gone to ice-skate on Big Pond. ~~It was a real cold day, cold enough so that your scarf got ice on it from your breath.~~ I put on my skates in a hurry and sailed out to the middle of the pond. ~~I noticed a slight cracking sound from the ice, but it wasn't much and I wasn't worried. It had been pretty cold for about a week. So I showed off some for John, who was still lacing up his skates, sitting on a log, and~~ then I headed for the opposite shore.

John stood up and went real fast, right out to the middle, too. Just as he got there, I heard this sickening cracking noise, the ice broke up, and John fell through.

~~I got a long branch and went out as far as I could on the ice. But I couldn't see John anywhere. He had just disappeared. I yelled for him, and went even farther out, but he wasn't there.~~

~~I must have panicked, because first thing I knew I was running into the~~

house shouting for Mom, crying my eyes out, yelling that John was in the pond. It was awful.

They found his body later that afternoon.

A few days after the funeral, we were sitting at the table, eating breakfast one morning. Nobody was saying anything; all of us were thinking about that empty chair over against the wall.

You could tell Mom was trying to talk. Finally she just sort of blurted out, "Look, we all miss John, terribly. We loved—love him, and we'll always miss him. Now I have a suggestion to make. Do you remember how he liked oatmeal and milk?"

"Do I!" I said. "I sure do. He used to pile on the brown sugar until—"

"That's enough. He liked his oatmeal sweet and so do you. What I want to suggest is this. Let's think about John every time we eat breakfast. Let's remember him whenever we eat oatmeal and drink milk. Let's talk about him—"

"Yeh, like the time he and I went swimming in Big Pond and . . ." I knew before Sis spoke that I had said something I shouldn't have. Everyone sort of choked up.

"Time for school," she said.

And Dad said, as we all left the table, "We can continue this later."

Well, we did. And we agreed with Mom's suggestion.

So each morning, when that big pitcher of cold milk went on the table, and our bowls of steaming oatmeal were set in front of us, we'd talk about John.

It wasn't sad talk, but happy. Remembering. I don't mean we never said anything that made us choke up—other people besides me did. But mainly it was happy talk. And we still talked about what we were going to do that day, and even—after a while—joked some.

One day, some months later, Mom said, "You know, I don't think what we're doing is quite respectful enough for John's memory."

"Respectful?" I said. "Why, it's fun. Sometimes it's almost like John is here with us. I like it."

"So do I," Mom said. "But I think we're too casual about it. So I think we ought to set aside a time when we're not rushed like we are at breakfast. Let's say Saturday morning. And we'll remember John in a more fitting place than the kitchen. We'll sit in the parlor, and we'll have a special time worthy of John's memory."

"Aw, Mom," I said, "John always liked breakfast in the kitchen. Lots of oatmeal with plenty of brown sugar on it. And milk. Why make a big deal of it?"

"That's enough, Son," Dad said. "We'll do as your mother says."

So every Saturday morning, after we had eaten our regular breakfast in the kitchen, we went into the parlor and remembered John. Mom had gotten some little silver cups for the milk, and some tiny plates for the oatmeal.

Later we only went into the parlor once a month, instead of every week, and now we only do it every three months. It doesn't seem right to me, but I'll soon be leaving home, so it doesn't matter.

I still wish we had never begun that "fitting" remembrance, and had just kept on remembering John every time we ate breakfast.

WHAT ABOUT SECULAR STORIES?

When I was teaching contemporary literature to juniors and seniors in a Christian high school, I began to realize how much they and I could learn from secular fiction. "There is nothing so secular that it cannot be sacred," says Madeleine L'Engle in *Walking on Water.* "And that is one of the deepest messages of the incarnation."

One assignment was built around William Golding's *Lord of the Flies.*[12] Assignment: "As you read, make a list of all the questions about life and a list of all the assumptions about life that this book makes." In the story a group of choirboys survive an airplane crash on a deserted island. They form societies that pattern all the pain, evil, and superstition of adult societies. The weak become weaker; the strong either protect or destroy.

The students in my class were MK's (missionary kids whose parents were serving in Japan). They brought a lot of Biblical knowledge to the literature class. The secular fiction forced them to use that knowledge to structure and answer some difficult questions. "What if there had been a Christian kid in the group?" "How could that writer see how sinful even children are and not be drawn to Christianity?" "How do you think some of the boys dealt with their fear and hatred after the island experience ended?" "What would salvation mean to kids like these? How are they different from us? Are they different?"

The young people were challenged to make use of their knowledge because they knew they were studying a secular book. They knew the writer wasn't going to insert the right answers in the last chapter.

It is often easier to find excellent secular stories than excellent Christian stories. "You know, I read the stories in my Sunday school papers, right up to the point where the kids get saved," a junior high boy told me. "After that it's boring. Nothing exciting ever happens."

A sad fact which nevertheless needs to be faced is that a deeply committed Christian who wants to write stories or paint pictures or compose music to the glory of God simply may not have been given the talent, the gift, which a non-Christian, or even an atheist, may have in abundance. God is no respecter of persons, and this is something we are reluctant to face.

We would like God's ways to be like our ways, his judgments to be like our judgments. It is hard for us to understand that he lavishly gives enormous talents to people we would consider unworthy, that he chooses his saints.[13]

Bruce Lockerbie elaborates:

There will always be artists whose experience is not necessarily Christian but whose gifts, through common grace, enables them to tell as much truth as they know. There are also artists whose vision is distorted, whose purposes may even be debased, whose art is thereby twisted and maimed. Yet from them too, in spite of decadence and corruption, we may obtain momentary vestiges of truth . . . We can't tell God where he can or can't be seen.[14]

"I was raised in a Christian home, and I had never been exposed to a really intelligent person who rejected Christianity," said a college junior. "But I met such a person through the book, *Old Man and the Sea*.[15] In it, Ernest Hemingway has an old fisherman struggle to bring a big fish back to his village. But the man had gone too far out into the sea for the fish, and by the time he got it back to shore the sharks had eaten it. There was nothing but the carcass left. I know that Hemingway rejected the notion that his book was really a parable of what happens when people search for truth in Christianity. The fish (Christianity (?)) is wonderful, but not practical. By the time the seeker has landed the fish and brought it back to shore where it can feed hungry people, there is nothing left but the cleaned bones. Whether Hemingway was making a statement or not, the story illustrates for me why some people reject Christianity. I wish I had a mind that could structure the Christian answer as skillfully as I felt Hemingway was forming the question. I wish I could have talked to him about my practical Christianity. I wish I could have answered his, 'Yes, but . . .' "

Novelist Anthony Burgess, in his discussion of "Modern Novels: The 99 Best," gives Christians an interesting perspective on the novel as a moral tool:

A novel ought to leave in the reader's mind a sort of philosophical residue. A view of life has been indirectly propounded that seems new, even surprising. The novelist has not preached. The didactic has no place in good fiction. But he has clarified some aspect of private or public morality that was never so clear before. As novels are about the ways in which human beings behave, they tend to imply a judgment of behavior, which means that the novel is what the symphony or painting or sculpture is not—namely, a form steeped in morality.[16]

John Calvin cautioned Christians against ignoring truth, even partial truth, as it is found in the secular world: "All truth is from God; and consequently if wicked men have said anything that is true and just we ought not to reject it, for it has come from God."

Whenever we come upon these matters in secular writers, let that admirable light of truth shining in them teach us that the mind of man, though fallen and perverted from its wholeness, is nevertheless clothed and ornamented with God's excellent gifts. If we regard the Spirit of God as the sole foundation of truth, we shall neither reject the truth itself, nor despise it wherever it shall appear, unless we wish to dishonor the Spirit of God. For by holding the gifts of the Spirit in slight esteem, we condemn and reproach the Spirit himself.[17]

However, there is the other side, as well. We must carefully choose what we will use as part of our teaching plans. What the teacher is mature enough to handle may be very damaging to an immature student. Consider Lionel Trilling's caution:

Any historian of the literature of the modern age will take virtually for granted the adversary intention, the actual subversive intention, that characterizes modern writing—he will perceive its clear purpose of detaching the reader from the habits of thought and feeling that the larger culture imposes, of giving him a ground . . . from which to judge and condemn, and perhaps revise, the culture that has produced him.[18]

Pick secular stories carefully. Delete what is inappropriate for discussion. Edit out problems for your age level or for the spiritual maturity level of your students. (If you are a teacher of teens, you may want to disqualify from your teaching material any excerpt from secular fiction that you would not recommend to your students in its entirety.)

The next two excerpts deal with Biblical themes: Creation and the Crucifixion. Both can help students deal with overly familiar material in new ways. As you read this edited section from J. R. R. Tolkien's *Silmarillion* (a secular myth with religious overtones), consider what questions you might use to encourage discussion among college students.

There was . . . Iluvatar; and he made first the Ainur, the Holy Ones, what were the offspring of his thought, and they were with him before aught else was made. And he spoke to them, propounding to them themes of music; and they sang before him, and he was glad. . . .
• And it came to pass that Iluvatar called together all the Ainur and declared to them a mighty theme, unfolding to them things greater and more wonderful than he had yet revealed; and the glory of its beginning and the splendour of its end amazed the Ainur, so that they bowed before Iluvatar and were silent. . . .
Then the voices of the Ainur, like unto harps and lutes, and pipes and trumpets, and viols and organs, and like unto countless choirs singing with words, began to fashion the theme of Iluvatar to a great music; and a

sound arose of endless interchanging melodies woven in harmony that passed beyond hearing into the depths and into the heights, and the places of the dwelling of Iluvatar were filled to overflowing, and the music and the echo of the music went out into the Void, and it was not void. . . .

But now Iluvatar sat and harkened, and for a great while it seemed good to him, for in the music there were no flaws. But as the theme progressed, it came into the heart of Melkor to interweave matters of his own imagining that were not in accord with the theme of Iluvatar; for he sought therein to increase the power and glory of the part assigned to himself. . . .

Some of these thoughts he now wove into his music, and straightway discord arose about him, and many that sang nigh him grew despondent, and their thought was disturbed and their music faltered; but some began to attune their music to his rather than to the thought which they had at first. Then the discord of Melkor spread ever wider, and the melodies which had been heard before foundered in a sea of turbulent sound. . . .

In the midst of this strife . . . Iluvatar arose . . . and his face was terrible to behold. Then he raised up both his hands, and in one chord, deeper than the Abyss, higher than the Firmament, piercing as the light of the eye of Iluvatar, the Music ceased.[19]

This edited section takes approximately 2½ minutes to read aloud. The original section takes approximately 7½ mintues.

An excerpt like this could be used to introduce a study from Scripture of Satan and his interaction in creation, this world, and in our own spiritual songs. Where else could it be used? (*Silmarillion* is most effectively used with college students. Practice it carefully before you use it in class; it's difficult to read.)

Questions that might spark discussion on "The Music of the Ainur" include:

- "In what ways is this story similar to the Biblical ideas of the fall of Satan? In what ways is it different?"
- "How does 'Melkor' influence the songs of people in the non-Christian world? How, if at all, does he influence our Christian songs?" (If students have read Calvin Miller's book, *The Singer* (see page 66), students may want to compare songs of the Singer and World Hater to the songs of Iluvatar and Melkor.)
- "After the music ceased, Iluvatar spoke. What do you think he said? What do you think God says about the 'music' our church is producing in our immediate community?"

The Jesus Incident is a secular science fiction book that is worked into a complex plot from which the story never gets extradited. However, in one section, Hali is sent back from the future to the Crucifixion. This is not a

Christian story, yet from the "You Are There" sequence high school students and adults may begin to feel the reality of what Christ did for them as they never have before. People who grow up in Sunday school can hear the horrors of what our Savior went through so often that our mental picture loses the blood and pain and becomes a pretty sunset on which three crosses are silhouetted.

This excerpt is less than half the length of the original story section.

Abruptly, she felt herself tumbling slowly in darkness. And at the front of her awareness was Ship's promise to give her another body for this experience. An old woman's body.

How will that feel?

There was no answer except the tunnel. . . .

Now, there was a pulsebeat, though. It was in her breast. She put a hand there, felt rough fabric and looked down. The hand was dark, old, and wrinkled.

That's not my hand!

. . . She could feel her awareness creeping through halting linkages. Sandals covered her feet; she felt the straps. Rough ground underfoot when she tried two shuffling steps. Fabric swished against her ankles—a coarsely woven sack of a garment. . . . There was a piece of cloth wound around her hair. She reached up and touched it, turning as she did this to face downhill.

A crowd of several hundred people could be seen down there—perhaps as many as three hundred. She was not sure.

She felt that this body might have been running before she assumed her place in it. Breathing was difficult. A stink of old perspiration assaulted her nostrils.

She could hear the crowd now: a murmurous animal noise. They were moving slowly uphill toward her. The people in it surrounded a man who dragged what appeared to be part of a tree over his shoulder. As he drew nearer, she saw blood on his face, an odd circlet at his brow . . . it looked like a spiney sweat band. The man appeared to have been beaten; bruises and cuts could be discerned through his shredded robe.

[He fell.] . . .

The crowd was milling around now, concealing the fallen figure from her. There was a great screaming and crying from them—a conflict which she did not understand.

Some called out: "Let him up! Please let him up!"

And there was one shrill voice heard about all the others: "Stone him here! He won't make it to the top."

A line of the armored men pushed the crowd back, leaving a tall dark man beside the fallen one. . . .

One of the soldiers shook the pointed tip of his spear at the dark one, shouted something which Hali could not make out. But the dark one stooped and picked up the tree, lifting it off the fallen one.

What is happening here?

Observe and do not interfere.

. . . Why had Ship insisted she witness this scene?

They drew nearer. The beaten man lurched along and, presently, stopped near the wailing women. Hali saw that he was barely able to stand. One of the women slipped through the ring of soldiers and mopped the injured man's bloody face with a gray cloth. He coughed in long, hard spasms, holding his left side and grimacing with each cough.

Hali's med-tech training dominated her awareness. The man was badly injured—broken ribs at least, and perhaps a punctured lung. There was blood at the corner of his mouth. She wanted to run to him, use her sophisticated skills to ease his suffering. . . .

She gripped her hands into fists, took several deep gasping breaths. This brought the smell of the crowd into focus. It was the most disgusting sensory experience she had ever known. They were rank with an unwashed festering. How could they survive the things which her nostrils reported? . . .

Turning back, the injured one looked full at Hali. He still clutched his side and she saw the characteristic red froth of a lung puncture at his lips.

Ship! What are they doing to him?

Observe.

The injured one said: "You have traveled far to see this." . . .

The dust of the crowd welled up around her and she choked on it before being able to speak, then: "How . . . how do you know how far I've come?"

It was an old woman's cracked voice she heard issuing from her mouth. . . .

A hand touched her arm and she jerked away in fright, whirling to see a young man in a long brown robe at her side. His breath smelled of sewage. And his voice was an unctuous whine.

. . . The foul-breathed one said, "Do you know him?"

The look in Foul-breath's eyes made her acutely aware of the vulnerable old flesh which housed her consciousness. This was a dangerous man . . . very dangerous. The look in his eyes reminded her (that he) could cause great pain.

"You had better answer me," he said, and there was poison in his voice.[20]

Questions that could be used after this reading:
- "How do you think a secular teen would feel reading this account?"
- "What new ideas came to you as I read? What things do you think you would have felt or seen or understood if you had been an elderly person at the scene of Jesus' death?"
- "If this story had been written for the Christian readership, what things do you think the writers might have included? Deleted?"

Not every response to the reading of a story or story segment must be in the question/answer format. Here are two other ways students could interact with the excerpt:

- Roleplay what Hali shared with a friend when she returned to Ship.
- Work in pairs to put yourselves into any segment in the story of Jesus' life. Discuss in pairs what you hear, see, and feel. Plan a two-minute conversational skit to share with the other students.

Both *The Jesus Incident* and *Silmarillion* have direct parallels to Biblical stories. When you use excerpts like these in class, make certain students realize that what you are sharing is fiction, not the true Biblical story. The younger the students the more important this caution becomes. "I was amazed," a junior high Sunday school teacher said after many of her students saw the Hollywood version of The Ten Commandments. "My students were not able to separate fact from fiction. They asked me questions about important characters in the movie who had not been part of the Biblical story at all. There was one benefit to their seeing the movie. It got them into Bible reading for themselves. Some were quite upset that the writers had dared to make so many changes in the real story."

The following short conversation is from Hermann Hesse's *Steppenwolf*. There will be no doubt in any college or adult class that this is a totally secular situation, and therein lies its teaching value. Assignment: If you were a Christian adult friend, how would you step into this conversation and help the main character understand his feelings and how he might deal with them if Christ were his center?

"What I have got is very beautiful and delightful, a great pleasure, a great consolation. I'm really happy—"

"Well then, what more do you want?"

"I do want more. I am not content with being happy. I was not made for it. It is not my destiny. My destiny is the opposite."

"To be unhappy in fact? Well, you've had that and to spare, that time when you couldn't go home because of the razor."

"No, Hermine, it is something else. That time, I grant you, I was very unhappy. But it was a stupid unhappiness that led to nothing."

"Why?"

"Because I should not have had that fear of death when I wished for it all the same. The unhappiness that I need and long for is different. It is the kind that will let me suffer with eagerness and lust after death. That is the unhappiness, or happiness, that I am waiting for."[21]

WHAT ABOUT CHRISTIAN STORIES?

It's in vogue to talk about how awful Christian writing is. "Holy shoddy is still shoddy," quips Elton Trueblood. Lockerbie points out that Christians sometimes forget that easy-does-it-not.

> The cost of being a writer is this commitment to excellence and integrity. But for the writer who professes to be a Christian, there is a surcharge to be paid. This is the call to sacrifice, service, and sacrament—a recognition that in using the medium of language, we are in fact employing symbolic representations of the Living Word.[22]

The creative writing of many Christians defeats itself because the authors have a great message to get across. The message becomes their whole reason for telling the story, and the results are preachy, artless tales. You know the type. The authors begin with the problem, often a safe one that most Christians aren't grappling with. The solution comes near the end of the story when the characters discover a Bible verse or finally remember to pray about the problem. The formula is often used. I know, because I read it over and over again in the free-lance pieces that Christians submitted to the Sunday school youth papers I edited. The message never becomes part of the story itself. It's tacked to the end, or obviously squeezed into a dull, little paragraph between action scenes.

A truly Christ-centered story is first of all a good story. It is also first of all a work designed to bring readers to a deeper or clearer understanding of some aspect of life. Putting those two first-of-alls together is difficult. Our fiction, illustrations, and poems must have Christian values woven throughout them. They do not spoon-feed intelligent readers what the writer thinks those readers ought to know, but rather, they present them with ideas and possibilities that they can expand and imaginatively act upon.

So what about Christian writing? Let's not be overly pessimistic. Many Christian writers, like many secular writers, are masters. Their works can add to our personal understanding of the world and our ability to prepare Christians to live in that world. Perhaps the biggest challenge doesn't have to go to the Christian writers: "Hey, you people, how about getting your art polished!" Instead it goes to Christians who aren't taking the time to read what is excellent. Dorothy Sayers, C. S. Lewis, Flannery O'Connor, and the newcomers, Harold Fickett, Joseph Bayly, Calvin Miller, Madeleine L'Engle—you add your favorite storytellers to the list.

Just for fun, and because Robert Farrar Capon calls his story of Creation a crass analogy ("I give you the central truth that creation is the result of a Trinitarian bash, and leave the details of the analogy to sort themselves out as best they can"), consider this excerpt from *The Third Peacock*, a book on God and the problem of evil:

> Let me tell you why God made the world.
> One afternoon, before anything was made, God the Father, God the Son and God the Holy Ghost sat around in the unity of their Godhead

207

discussing one of the Father's fixations. From all eternity, it seems he had had this *thing* about being. He would keep thinking up all kinds of unnecessary things—new ways of being and new kinds of beings to be. And as they talked, God the Son suddenly said, "Really, this is absolutely great stuff. Why don't I go out and mix us up a batch?" And God the Holy Ghost said, "Terrific, I'll help you." So they all pitched in and after supper that night, the Son and the Holy Ghost put on this tremendous show of being for the Father. It was full of water and light and frogs; pine cones kept dropping all over the place . . . There were mushrooms and grapes, horseradishes and tigers—and men and women everywhere to taste them, to juggle them, to join them and to love them. And God the Father looked at the whole wild party and he said, "Wonderful! Just what I had in mind! *Tov! Tov! Tov!* And . . . they laughed for ages and ages, saying things like how great it was for things to be, and how clever of the Father to think of the idea, and how kind of the Son to go to all that trouble putting it together, and how considerate of the Spirit to spend so much time directing and choreographing.[23]

Questions like these might help draw your senior high and adult students into a discussion:

- "How to you think the real Creation took place? How do you feel about this analogy?"
- "What's your favorite part of God's Creation? Why?"
- "You are part of God's Creation. What thing about you do you think He is most pleased with? What quality do you think He would like you to work on during this coming week?"
- "Some people teach that God just created us and left us alone to work out our own lives. What do you think about this idea? How have you personally seen God's work in your own life?"

This last question is a perfect lead into another paragraph in Capon's clever story:

What happens is not that the Trinity manufactures the first duck and then the ducks take over the duck business as a kind of cottage industry. It is that every duck, down at the roots of its being, at the level where what is needed is not the ability to fertilize duck eggs, but the moxie to stand outside of nothing—to *be* when there is no necessity of being—every duck, at that level, is a response to the creative act of God. In terms of the analogy, it means that God the Father *thinks up* duck #47307 for the month of May, A.D. 1970, that God the Spirit rushes over to the edge of the formless void and, with unutterable groanings, broods duck #47307, and that over his brooding God the Son, the eternal Word, triumphantly *shouts,* "Duck #47307!" And presto! you have a duck. Not one, you will note, tossed off in response to some mindless decree that there may as well be ducks as alligators, but each one neatly fielded up in a game of delight. . . . The world is not God's surplus inventory of artifacts; it is a whole barrelful of the apples of his eye, constantly juggled, relished and exchanged by the persons of the Trinity. No wonder we love circuses, games and magic; they prove we are in the image of God.[24]

What a wonderful smidgen of story to remind people of the wonder of their own creation. We are loved enough individually to be called into being by God.

Story is such a broad term. It can mean analogy, as in the two illustrations from *The Third Peacock*; it can mean fiction, as in *The Jesus Incident*; it can mean life lifted directly from those who lived it. And these can be among the most poignant of all teaching tools. Aleksandr I. Solzhenitzen is difficult to use in class because his stories are often long. If excerpts are taken from his text, as shown here, these sections still have a strong impact on the reader.

Solzhenitzen shares from his personal observations in *The Gulag Archipelago, Two* what happens when children are thrown into Russian prison camps:

So early and so strangely did their adulthood begin—with this step across the prison threshold!

And upon the twelve- and fourteen-year-old heads burst a lifestyle that was too much for brave men who were experienced and mature. But the young people, by the laws of their young life, were not about to be flattened by this lifestyle but, instead, grew into it and adapted to it. . . .

From this life they took for themselves all its most inhuman essence, all its poisonous rotten juice. . . .

They grew into camp life so swiftly—not in weeks even, but in days!—as if they were not in the least surprised by it, as if that life were not completely new to them, but a natural continuation of their free life of yesterday. . . .

Children accepted the Archipelago with the divine impressionability of childhood. And in a few *days* children became beasts there! . . . The kids master the truth: If other teeth are weaker than your own, then tear the piece away from them. It belongs to you! . . .

The weaker their victim, the more merciless were the kids. They openly tore the bread ration from the hands of a very weak old man. The old man wept and implored them to give it back to him. "I am dying of starvation." "So you're going to kick the bucket soon anyway—what's the difference?" And the kids once decided to attack the invalids in the cold, empty building in front of the kitchen where there was always a mob of people. The gang would hurl their victim to the ground, sit on his hands and his legs, and his head, search his pockets, take his makhorka and his money, and then disappear.[25]

Interaction with this piece would vary with the age level, but these excerpts could be used with all ages, junior high through adult.

● Junior high: "Pretend our whole class had been taken to a prison camp

209

because we are Christians. What are some of the things we would and would not do in order to survive?"

- Senior high: "How far do you think a Christian ought to go in order to survive? How important is life? Based on what you know about the lives of Christians in other countries, how do you suspect their life views differ from yours? What things do you think a Soviet Christian living in a situation like the one described could teach us?"
- Adult: "What do you think would happen to the children in our church if they were to suddenly find themselves in a situation like the one we read about? What specific types of training do we have to give them in order to strengthen them in their faith?"

Short fiction, especially the stories that are published in weekly Sunday school papers, are extremely difficult to write. They must be short, perfectly age-graded, and easily used in a lesson plan. The following piece is condensed from a fiction for senior highs.

REV. ALGEBRA B. COONS WAS A LOVER[26]

Mrs. Schmale, who was so old that living was a habit with her, was the first one of them to get suspicious. She stayed in the church after the line of handshaking people had broke for the cars, after the hatted and windblown women had finished inviting each other's family over after the evening service. She stayed in the church to put away the Communion set. Then as she crept up the back stairs, she saw him ripping the plastic ivy out of its plastic pot by its plastic roots. She told others, and they told others. That Sunday was his eighth Sunday in our church.

Algebra B. Coons had come tall and raging into our pulpit in June, and his blue eyes had a life of their own. His skin was stretched haphazardly over his bones as though he were camping in his body.

"Jesus was a lover," he said from the pulpit. With his crooked mouth and hot eyes he said it every day.

He used to hang out at the jail. I went there once with him to see broken men whap him on the back and joke until I pretty nearly couldn't tell which one was the free man and which were the convicts. On the way out a guy in a uniform stuck his thumb into my stomach and said, "Hey, fella, you a friend of his?"

I said, "Yes, he's my preacher."

"He's crazy, is what he is," the man in the uniform said, making elaborate circles with his finger in the air to his ear. "We gotta let him in here," he said. "Me—I wouldn't myself, but we gotta let him in since he's a preacher." He talked out of the side of his mouth. "He asked me to lock him up once. Can ya beat that? He wanted me to lock him up with these other jerks."

I looked at Rev. Coons to see if he would do that, and he stood with one

210

foot ahead of the other, straining his body to wave at a man in the end cell. Yes, I could see he would.

When we were in the sunshine again I said, "Why did you want to be locked up?"

"It's the only way to spend time with them," he said. "They give me 30 minutes," he said, and he laughed. "You can't be natural."

And that got around, too. Mrs. Schmale stood in front of the church the next Sunday and spoke to my mother about the Reverend Algebra Coons. "He goes to that jail," she said. "He has not been to our ladies' aid once. What's the minister's job if it's not to help his own?" She clutched her purse and leaned down to scratch her leg. "I'm just afraid he might be crazy, and it'll come off on our young ones." She stared at me, her eyes hard and reddish as prune pits. "This one here, you can already see it on his face; it'll come off."

Two months later, in September, Rev. Coons announced that his brother was coming. He said that his brother was also a peacher and would give the sermon next Sunday.

That week was September-hot and school had started; anything could have distracted us from studying—an ant on an anthill or a kid on a merry-go-round. So when Lenny came in one day and had told us some crazy guy was standing on a downtown corner in an engineer's uniform hollering about hell, we took off to see him. We ran most of the mile and a half downtown, and there he was, staring sadly at something far away, bent over as if the suspenders of his engineer's uniform had been too tight for many years. He was saying, "Jesus can save you from the wickedness of the world. He can bring your hearts rest. Jesus can bring you peace. He's the lover of the world."

Across the street in a knot of people, Mrs. Schmale stood, her face wrinkled around her eyes like an apple doll. She knew, as I knew when I heard him preaching, that he was Rev. Algebra B. Coons' brother.

I could not stay on the corner. My feet pulled me down the road towards Rev. Coons' house.

On his screen porch he sat on the edge of his chair writing.

"It's your brother," I said to those bony shoulders, tattered pants and dirty sneakers.

He looked up and said, "Down there telling them Jesus is a lover?"

"In an engineer's uniform," I screamed.

"He's an engineer," he said.

"You said a preacher."

"And an engineer," he said. "What are you doing here during school?"

"I don't know," is what I thought, but I said, "And he's crazy, isn't he?"

"You do crazy things for what you believe in," he said, sitting on the edge of his low chair with his knees in the air.

Rev. Coons was dismissed from our church. He was dismissed before his brother could preach on Sunday morning, before anybody learned that everyone does crazy things for what he believes.

PARABLE—TEACHING TOOL

There are a number of literary styles used in the Gospels. Perhaps the most obvious is the *narrative*, both the simple outline of events and the detailed stories of what took place. We often use this style to renew our faith by sharing the narratives of our lives, the testimony of moments when we allowed Christ to be part of our days.

Another form used in the Gospels is the *dialogue*, for example, the complex dialogue in Mark 9:14-29.

There are also the *speeches* such as the Sermon on the Mount in Matthew 5 or the Olivet Discourse in Matthew 24.

But perhaps the most prominent literary device in the Gospels is the *parable*. Parables fall into two basic categories. In the first, the parable is a short story which illustrates just one important point. None of the other details have any special meaning: they are simply window dressing for the one main point. The Parable of the Yeast in Matthew 13:33 is an example. In the second category, the parables are short stories that illustrate a main point, but they also have details with specific meaning. See Matthew 13. This parable form with its extended meanings can also be called an allegory.

The parable is meant to shock or surprise—a Samaritan violates a social code; a coin that represents fidelity is lost in a land where adulteresses are stoned. It uses what William A. Beardslee calls a deformation of language. In other words, parables stretch language so that they show the hearer or reader new or greater insight. When a parable becomes too familiar, the readers are no longer shocked by it.

Perhaps, along with the familiar Biblical parables, we need to shock with contemporary parables that contain spiritual truth. We can stretch people's thinking by using the same literary style Jesus was so fond of. Perhaps parables can help us stop our students' yawns and replace them with delighted understanding.

At a Christian school, a teacher assigned her eighth-grade Bible students to write a parable that would help their friends see a spiritual truth in a new way. Thriteen-year-old Dawn Berg handed in this parable:

One day while riding across a large cattle range, Ben found Marvin, a small blind turtle who was starving because he was unable to find food. Ben found Marvin, so he belonged to him.

It was Ben's job to supply his needs by directing and controlling him. Day after day, Ben would place Marvin's food where he could locate it by his sense of smell. Sometimes Marvin succeeded but at times he would ignore his sense of smell and go astray.

One day Marvin got tired of being under Ben's direction. "I can get along fine without Ben," he thought. He didn't realize that as he walked away, Ben continued to watch him.

All morning Marvin walked. "I've come a great way without Ben," he thought proudly. But Ben could see Marvin had been walking in circles.

As time passed, Marvin got hungry; his pride began to waver. The air got cooler, and Marvin could tell it was almost night. Finally he admitted his mistake. "Help, Ben," he called.

Ben's voice came from very near him. "Right over here."

And when Marvin returned, he found Ben had kept his supper there waiting for him.

"I'm sorry, Ben," Marvin said. "Thank you."

What is the message of this junior high's parable? What internal clues can you find that show the young writer understood the concept she was explaining?

How very important it is to present the Gospel message in ways that people will understand. Our message is forever new, yet sometimes we can forget, become dulled to the wonder of our position in Christ.

By settling unduly on legitimate, worthy phrases that once had enormous impact in their original use, we may become secondhand in the expression of our faith—which we cannot afford to do. The world desperately needs to be stopped in its tracks by our new stretching of language, our juxtaposition of the divine and human to distract, to point and make others look. We may have to risk misunderstanding by the masses at times so that a few true seekers can be struck dumb and find life. By our imaginative participation in Scripture and our own continual use of creative language to talk about the spiritual life, we fulfill the spirit of Christ's ministry.[27]

As you read this next parable, identify its primary message and your own reaction to the message.

PALM MONDAY[28]

The donkey awakened, his mind savoring something pleasant. He arched his neck, walked around with mincing steps.

"That group of people by the well," he said. "I'll go and show myself to them."

They took no notice.

"Throw your garments down," he said crossly. "Don't you know who I am?"

They stared at him in amazement. Someone threw a stone.

"Miserable infidels!" he muttered as he turned away in rage. "I'll go down to the market. Some good people are sure to be there."

213

But it was the same.

"The palm branches! Where are the palm branches?" he shouted. "Have you forgotten?"

Dazed he returned to his mother.

"Foolish child," she said gently. "Without Him you can do nothing."

A good parable is like a bad case of whiplash, according to Gloria Durka and Joanmarie Smith. "The function of the parable is to unnerve us, to create a contradiction to shatter our world view. . . ."

ROWAN: What would you like to do with your life?

MARTIN: Well, I'd like to feed all the hungry, eliminate poverty, and keep peace in the world and find a cure for cancer.

ROWAN: And if you don't do that, what will you do?

MARTIN: Then I'd like to learn to tap dance.

". . . It seems almost obscene to place side by side some of the great miseries of the world and tap dance lessons. But the root of the parable means to place beside or, more precisely, to throw beside."[29]

Do you feel the whiplash in the following parable by Naomi Yunker, daughter of missionaries to Japan, who wrote her parable when she was in eighth grade?

THE TREES AND THE STORM

The King of all the lands was an excellent tree planter. In fact, He spent many hours training His trees to grow strong and straight.

Then one day He noticed a barren spot along the banks of a great river. The King immediately transplanted five of His trees to one side of the river and five to the other. He knew they would have problems getting adjusted to the new situation, but the King was sure they were strong enough to handle the difficulties.

The King told the trees to grow and spread their seeds all around so new trees would begin to grow. For a few weeks, the trees were happy with their new job. They even started a contest to see which side could get the most new trees first.

Then suddenly a storm arose. The wind beat against the trunks of the trees until it practically bent them double. Some of the trees fought the wind, but many of them thought the struggle was too difficult. They gave up, and the wind snapped their trunks.

After the storm, it was discovered that only two trees had fallen on the west side of the river, and all but one had fallen on the east.

"This is terrible," thought the lonely tree on the east bank. "Surely the great King wouldn't expect me to stay here and spread seeds all by myself." So he packed his trunk and left. "The great King can do without new trees on this one little riverbank," he said.

Where do you find parables to use in your classes? First, look for them in your teacher's guides and in the student material. Look for them in magazines and newspapers. Usually the source will be a Christian one. Begin to file those you find.

You may want to try your hand at writing one, or asking your students to write one. Sometimes all it takes is the challenge, your personal enthusiasm, and a few examples. Before you decide that your students could never do something this creative, remember that "Marvin, a Blind Turtle" and "The Trees and the Storm" were both written by eighth graders.

When you write, follow these four steps:

1. Start by deciding what spiritual truth your parable will communicate. For example: witnessing, loving neighbors, trusting the King of Kings, living as Kingdom people, handling criticism, helping our church grow, learning to study the Bible. Robert Ludlum advised writers in *The Chancellor Manuscript:* "Know where you're going, give yourself a direction so you're not floundering, but don't restrict the natural inclination to wander."

2. Decide on a problem situation around which to build your parable. Parables are usually about ordinary people doing ordinary things. They are usually true to life, even if the characters are personified animals or plants. I suspect Jesus taught in parables because they are down to earth, concrete, and heavy on application to contemporary life.

3. Limit your characters. One or two are often enough.

4. Talk your parable before you write it. You might want to make a few notes and talk it through with a friend. Especially if you don't consider yourself a writer, this can be an effective way of sharpening whatever message you want to give.

Writing the parable may not be the hardest part of parable development. Sharing it with your class may be—that's where you'll open yourself up for evaluation. If your parable is good, you might want to share it with other class teachers, or even with the whole church. Unlike most creative writing, parables stretch across age levels. With just a few word changes, for example, I published the following parable in a young teen magazine, *Trails,* and a woman's magazine, *Today's Christian Woman.*

POTENTIAL PARABLE

Once upon a time, there was Gregory who collected potentials—big ones, shiny brass ones, miniatures, and even one with a music box attached.

It was his mother who got the whole thing started. "You've got a great potential in math," she said one day when he figured out how to cut an egg yolk into seventeen equal portions.

Gregory wiped the egg off his fingers and put the potential on a shelf. He was eight.

Then there was his doting uncle. "You've got a great potential for helping others," he cooed when Gregory offered to do dishes for his mother. Twelve-year-old Gregory took the potential out of the suds, dried and polished it, and added it to the growing collection.

By the time he was thirty, he had one of the best collections in his church—potential for writing, public speaking, playing musical instruments—and even teaching potential. He would spend hours meditating on his collection, dusting it, counting it. He was finding more and more time for looking at his potentials, because lately not too many people were interested in doing much with him.

And he would notice with a certain amount of queasiness that other people were given more opportunities to speak, write, teach, than he was—people who didn't have half his potential. Boy, did they have to work at it! But he had to admit they got better each time they did anything.

Enter villain. She had a mini-potential collection, in Gregory's opinion. So he decided to impress her by showing her his collection.

She yawned.

"But I've got great potential." Gregory wasn't used to being on the defensive.

"Gotta run," she said without a second look at the collection. "Every night after work I read to an old lady who used to teach at Community College. She's losing her sight, and reading is what she misses most."

"But you don't have the potential for good reading," he sputtered. "No expression."

"Not yet," she agreed wisely. "But soon."

PARABLE STARTERS

Choose one of these parable starters that deals with a subject you will be teaching, and ask students to develop it as a homework assignment. The Sunday the assignment is due, give opportunity for each student to share what he or she has written and for the class to discuss the message found in each parable.

Encourage students who have ability in this area to continue writing original parables. Consider compiling their creative work into a class booklet of parables.

1. *Aim: To help students grasp how important it is to follow God.*

A young Canadian goose refuses to follow the leader and decides that instead of flying south, he will stay in northern Canada for the winter. Write what happens to the foolish goose and how he learns that even though it involves work to follow the leader, it is also very important.

2. *Aim: To help students understand that in order for God's Church to move forward, each Christian must do his or her share.*

Write about a lazy team horse who comes into a farmyard. He pulls only half his share of a load and often plays sick. Tell how the actions of the horse affect life in the barnyard. Include how the farmer eventually deals with the problem.[30]

3. *Aim: To help students recognize how important it is to keep witnessing even when there seem to be no positive results.*

Write about a garden in which all the plants are drooping, except one. That one has discovered that if she lifts her leaves up, she catches the sun, and if she digs her roots down, she finds water. These discoveries are saving her life. What happens when she tries to share what she has found with the other plants?

As you read the following parables verbalize the message(s) you find in each. With which Biblical texts could you most appropriately use each?

YOU'LL NEVER GUESS WHAT HAPPENED IN CHURCH THIS MORNING[31]

Behold, the preacher climbed up to his pulpit and one hundred faces looked up at him. And the preacher placed a cough drop on his tongue so that his voice would be both sweet and smooth. And smiling, he said, "Let us give thanks." And one hundred voices murmured, "Amen." But there was no joy.

"Let us give thanks," said the preacher, "for the wholeness of our bodies."

And sadly, without a word, there arose blind men and crippled women, and behold, ten people made their way out of the church.

But the preacher continued on and said, "Let us give thanks that all of our lungs breathe in fresh air and that we all experience the enjoyment of food and drink."

And there arose and departed those with lung cancer, and those who were starving, and behold, ten people left the congregation.

But the preacher continued and said, "Let us give thanks that all the people in our church enjoy the comforts of this world."

And there departed ten more—the poor who had seen their children die of malnutrition.

But the preacher, his eyes raised in contemplation of comfortable thoughts, saw none of this and said, "Let us give thanks that we all have homes and families."

And there departed the refugees, the old man from the convalescent home, the young girl who had alcoholic parents.

And the preacher persisted, "Let us give thanks that we all have friends!"

And then from the congregation there arose all the lonely people, the painfully shy who ate every night in cheap restaurants, those who had been rejected because they were from a different race.

But the preacher, sucking on his cough drop, said, "Let us give thanks that we are all beautiful."

And Sally, who knew her chin receded, and George, whose eyes were crossed, arose and departed that place.

Yet still the preacher spoke. "Let us give thanks for our wonderful minds!"

And several people of below-average intelligence blushed and a mentally retarded child stared blankly, and they arose and walked to the door.

But the preacher, without a glance downward, almost sang as he said, "Let us give thanks for our virtues!"

And there were those who were tortured by bad tempers, wracked by jealousy, flooded with conceit, and behold, they left the congregation.

"Let us be thankful that we all experience justice!" the preacher went on.

And all those who had been deprived of good lawyers and money to pay bail and others who had never had medicine or education arose and departed.

"Let us give thanks that we have all worked for peace!"

And there departed ten more, victims of war.

And the preacher looked out upon his congregation.

And there was no one there.

The preacher's cough drop had melted. And there was no more smoothness to his voice.

And he cried out, and his voice cracked, "O Lord, my Lord, where have they gone?"

And behold, a voice spoke from Heaven and said, "You know what you have been doing? You have been patting yourself on the back! When have I ever told you that I love only the wealthy, only the beautiful, only the intelligent? When have I ever told you that justice and peace and healing would come all by themselves? The people all around you have tasted bitterness, and you have not even stopped to recognize it. That is why the people left."

The voice paused and then spoke once more. "Remember my servant Job. Remember my Son, Jesus. When have I promised an easy way out?"

And the preacher cried out, "Then, O Lord, what wilt thou give us?"

And the voice replied, "Myself."

And the preacher ran to the doorway and called the people back. And he mounted his pulpit, and one hundred faces looked up at him. And the preacher said in a cracked voice, "Let us give thanks that Christ Himself is with us, world without end!"

And one hundred voices cried out, "Amen!"

And there was joy in Heaven.

THE BEGGAR[32]

A beggar lived near the King's palace. One day he saw a proclamation posted outside the palace gate. The King was giving a great dinner. Anyone dressed in royal garments was invited to the party.

The beggar went on his way. He looked at the rags he was wearing and sighed. Surely only kings and their families wore royal robes, he thought.

Slowly an idea crept into his mind. The audacity of it made him tremble. Would he dare?

He made his way back to the palace. He approached the guard at the gate. "Please, Sire, I would like to speak to the King."

"Wait here," the guard said.

In a few minutes he was back. "His majesty will see you," he said, and led the beggar in.

"You wished to see me?" asked the King.

"Yes, Your Majesty. I want so much to attend the banquet, but I have no royal robes to wear. Please, Sir, if I may be so bold, may I have one of your old garments so that I, too, may come to the banquet?"

The beggar shook so hard that he could not see the faint smile that was on the King's face.

"You have been wise in coming to me," the King said. He called to his Son, the young Prince. "Take this man to your room and array him in some of your clothes."

The Prince did as he was told and soon the beggar was standing before a mirror, clothed in garments that he had never dared hope for.

"You are now eligible to attend the King's banquet tomorrow night," said the Prince. "But even more important, you will never need any other clothes. These garments will last forever."

The beggar dropped to his knees. "Oh, thank you," he cried. But as he started to leave, he looked back at his pile of dirty rags on the floor. He hesitated. What if the Prince was wrong? What if he would need his old clothes again? Quickly he gathered them up.

The banquet was far greater than he had ever imagined, but he could not enjoy himself as he should. He had made a small bundle of his old rags and it kept falling off his lap. The food was passed quickly and the beggar missed some of the greatest delicacies.

Time proved that the Prince was right. The clothes lasted forever. Still the poor beggar grew fonder and fonder of his old rags.

As time passed people seemed to forget the royal robes he was wearing. They saw only the little bundle of filthy rags that he clung to

219

wherever he went. They even spoke of him as the old man with the rags.

One day as he lay dying, the King visited him. The beggar saw the sad look on the King's face when he looked at the small bundle of rags by the bed. Suddenly the beggar remembered the Prince's words and he realized that his bundle of rags had cost him a lifetime of true royalty. He wept bitterly at his folly.

And the King wept with him.

---

1. "Storytelling is not only our oldest art, it is our oldest way of casting out demons and summoning angels. The story is, quite simply, an essential part of our humanness," says Jane Yolen in "Storytelling—An Art for All Ages," by Norma J. Livo, *Media & Methods,* September, 1983, p. 25. Don't you find yourself agreeing with Michael Hague: "Imagining and believing are the only forms of magic left in the world"? (Ibid., p. 24.)

2. Russell Hoban, *Ridley Walker* (New York: Summit Books, 1981).

3. James A. Michener, in his best-seller, *Space* (New York: Fawcett Crest, 1982), has one of his characters suggest a reason to read science fiction: "Mott pointed out that of all the engineers he had known, practically none had bothered with science fiction, whereas almost all the scientists had. 'Why is that?' he asked his two visitors.

" 'I think you were always preoccupied with how to do it,' Pope suggested. 'The scientists were always far out, setting goals to try next' " (p. 492).

4. Frank Herbert, *Dune* (Radnor, Penn.: Chilton Book Co., 1965).

5. This teacher used a section from *The Jesus Incident,* by Frank Herbert and Bill Ransom, reprinted on page 204.

6. Margaret Laurence, *The Diviners* (New York: Bantam Books, Inc., 1975).

7. Dr. Seuss, *Yertle the Turtle and Other Stories* (New York: Random House, Inc., 1958).

8. Stephen R. Donaldson, *The Wounded Land,* Book One of the Second Chronicle of Thomas Covenant (New York: Ballantine Books, 1981), p. 471.

9. Robertson Davies, *The Manticore* (New York: Viking Press, 1972).

10. Harold Fickett, *Mrs. Sunday's Problem and Other Stories* (Old Tappan, N.J.: Fleming H. Revell Company, 1979), pp. 39-49.

11. *The Gospel Blimp and Other Stories,* © 1983 by Joseph Bayly, David C. Cook Publishing Co., Elgin, Ill. Used by permission.

12. William Golding, *Lord of the Flies* (New York: Pittman Publishing Group, 1978).

13. Madeleine L'Engle, *Walking on Water* (Wheaton, Ill.: Harold Shaw Publishers, 1980), p. 30.

14. Bruce Lockerbie, *The Timeless Moment* (Westchester, Ill.: Cornerstone Books, 1980), p. 68.

15. Earnest Hemingway, *Old Man and the Sea* (New York: Scribner Book Companies, Inc., 1952).

16. Burgess, *The New York Times Book Review,* Feb. 5, 1984, p. 37.

17. John Calvin, Institutes of the Christian Religion, as quoted by Samuel F. Rowen in *Moral Development Foundations,* ed. Donald M. Joy (Nashville: Abingdon Press, 1983).

18. Dale Vree, "Sex in the Service of Capitalism," in *New Oxford Review,* May, 1983.

19. From *The Silmarillion* by J. R. R. Tolkien. Copyright © 1977 by George Allen & Unwin (Publishers) Ltd. Reprinted by permission of Houghton Mifflin Company.

20. Reprinted by permission of the Berkley Publishing Group from *The Jesus Incident* by Frank Herbert and Bill Ransom. Copyright © 1979 by Frank Herbert and Bill Ransom.

21. Hermann Hesse, *Steppenwolf* (New York: Bantam Books, 1969), pp. 169, 170. Used by permission.

22. Lockerbie, *The Timeless Moment,* p. 108.

23. Robert Farrar Capon, *The Third Peacock* (Garden City, N.Y.: Image Books, 1972), pp. 12, 13. Used by permission of the author.

24. Ibid., pp. 13, 14.

25. Aleksandr I. Solzhenitzyn, *The Gulag Archipelago* (New York: Harper & Row, 1973). From pp. 451, 452, 458 in *The Gulag Archipelago, Two,* by Aleksandr I. Solzhenitzyn, translated by Thomas P. Whitney. Copyright © 1974 by Aleksandr I. Solzhenitzyn. English language translation copyright © 1975 by Harper & Row, Publishers, Inc. By permission of the publisher.

26. Jeanne Walker, "Rev. Algebra B. Coons Was a Lover," published in *Christian Living,* a class-and-home weekly for senior high students.

27. Isabel Anders, "The Rules and the Stories: Imagination and Scriptural Language" (Master's degree thesis, Mundelein College, 1980).

28. Eileen Lageer, "Palm Sunday." Reprinted by permission of *His,* student magazine of Inter-Varsity Christian Fellowship, © 1970.

29. Gloria Durka and Joanmarie Smith, "Is Art Necessary?" in *Religious Education,* Jan.-Feb., 1981.

30. I've written quite a number of parables on assignment. One request had me stumped. I mulled it over until deadline time was upon me. Then I remembered that I had once put together some parable starters— the ones printed here. This is how I concluded my parable starter, "Lazy Sylvester":

Sylvester rushed out with all of the other horses to welcome the newcomer. But before he finished neighing his *hello,* the farmer said, "He'll be using your stall, Sylvester. I'm putting you out to pasture."

Sylvester's nose turned an embarrassed red. He didn't even turn to say good-bye to his fellow workers, and none of them trotted after him to say they were sorry to see him go.

After he got over his humiliation, Sylvester began to like the pasture. It was great fun to run free in the field, and for days he alternated between eating fresh grass and running from one fence to the other.

"I'm having a wonderful time," he told himself many times a day; but finally he had to admit that he was bored with eating and running. His life didn't have a purpose any longer. He tried to keep himself from looking at the horses working in the fields. They made him feel more useless.

"If only I had another chance to show the farmer I've changed," he thought. "I would make him so proud of me."

---

31. Richard Hunter, "You'll Never Guess What Happened in Church This Morning," © 1965, *Presbyterian Life.* Used by permission.

32. "The Beggar," by Ruth A. Walton. Reprinted by permission of *Eternity Magazine,* © 1972, Evangelical Ministries, Inc., 1716 Spruce Street, Philadelphia, PA 19103.

CHAPTER 9

Discussion: A Learning Imperative

If you gain the whole world and lose the mind of the world, you will soon discover you have not won the world. Indeed it may turn out that you have actually lost the world.

—Charles Malik

Can learning take place without students interacting with the content? Of course. An excellent lecturer can present whole bodies of content in short time spans. The listeners assimilate the material. They learn. But how much more students learn when they take an active part in the class, when they add comments, ask questions, and answer the questions of their peers. When students share aloud they become more sure of what they believe, and more confident about their abilities to live what they believe. They also hear the wisdom and experience of more than one person, traditionally the teacher. The impact is multiplied.

By the time students have been in a Christian education program for seven or twelve or twenty years, they know most of the facts. Yet they have barely scratched the surface of what it means to become like Christ.

The Bible stories remain the same, yet their impact on students changes as the students' questions grow more complex and their life decisions less obvious. They need to verbalize what is happening to them on their faith journeys. They need to get excited over the successes others share. They need to grapple with ethical questions in a secure situation in preparation for the less secure life settings.

Discussion in the Sunday school classroom is a lot more than just talk. Very few educational methods can stand alone without it. Consider roleplay, for example. A class of adults has been considering what happens in a neighborhood where property values are falling. Issues of Christianity, racial and economic prejudice, zoning, and corruption in small-town governments have all played a part. Roleplay ends. Unless there is a debriefing time—a discussion where students talk about the implications of this roleplay—the class may have only had a lively time. But after the roleplay, the real issues must surface. "I was a lot less prejudiced before I sank every last cent I had into a house." "But what happens if Christians try to infiltrate our city government? That's certainly not what I see Jesus doing. What should be our reaction to power?" Discussion is part of any good teaching plan; discussion may be generic to youth and adult learning.

Students can benefit from discussion in a number of important ways:

1. *Discussion stimulates interest and thinking, and helps students develop the skills of observation, analysis, and logic.*

2. *Discussion helps students clarify and review what they have learned.*
For example, after an adult class has studied the life of Christ, students might break into small groups to discuss one major emphasis they found in Jesus' teaching and how that emphasis should affect Christians' lives today. Through this discussion students would organize their thoughts and gain new insights into the life of Christ which they may have previously overlooked. A few may actually learn new facts about Christ's life. But the primary purpose of a discussion is rarely to teach new factual information. Unless students have a base of knowledge from which to talk, their comments often have little significance.

3. *Students can sometimes solve their own problems through discussion.*
"My girl friend's father is trying to rape her," a student in my high school class announced. The unit was on crisis situations teens face, so her statement fit. My first response as a teacher was to panic. I had never been faced with this problem before, and here it was in the middle of a class of eleven boys and two girls. The students were silent, dead silent. "What are some of the suggestions you would make?" I gulped at the class. "Remember the principles we've been studying." I'd often said to those kids

that if God wasn't big enough to handle their problems, He, or rather their concept of Him, was too small. The fellows' reactions were interesting, ranging from nervous, very inappropriate humor to genuinely thoughtful comments. By the time the class period ended, the girl knew she had the prayer support of the rest of her class. They had also presented her with some helpful ideas. After the class period, the girl and I talked further, making sure she had a plan of action and the support and feedback of several adult Christians.

4. *Discussion allows students to hear opinions that are more mature and perhaps more Christlike than their own.*

There is no guarantee that once these comments are heard, students will be able to adapt them to their own situations, but at least they will be able to draw from a larger body of information.[1]

5. *Discussion stimulates creativity and aids students in applying what they have learned to everyday situations.*

For example, a teacher could give each student a foot long piece of thin florist's wire. Students are asked to pretend that the wires are time lines of their lives the previous week. Every time students remember failing God, they should put a bend in the wire. After a few minutes, most of the students' wires should be twisted. Class members might then form pairs and discuss some of the problems they have that keep them from living in uninterrupted fellowship with God. The Bible study might center on God's solution to this dilemma. Yes, the teacher could skip the wire and go directly to the discussion. After all, the discussion is the important part of the situation. The two methods together, however, allow students to first think in new patterns, group their thoughts in a new way. People who think in symbols or who think best while manipulating materials will be prepared to talk through what they have done. The creative melding of the two methods will make the learning process more successful.

6. *When students verbalize what they believe and are forced to explain or defend what they say, their convictions are strengthened and their ability to share what they believe with others is increased.*

DISCUSSION STARTERS

The question or comment a teacher uses to start a discussion is very important because it sets the direction for what lies ahead. Discussion starters that begin with the words "Why?" "Explain," "What do you think?" are usually good because these words indicate that there is something to discuss.

225

Consider this discussion starter: "Retell the story of the feeding of the 5000 from the small boy's perspective." The student response might provide the class with a creative review, but the question probably will not start a discussion. However, on the same story, the teacher might ask, "When Jesus fed the 5000, He proved that He could feed a lot of people on a very low budget. But what does this story mean to us Christians who seldom see obvious miracles like this happen today?" Here the students must do more than repeat facts they have learned. There is something to discuss. Not only must they mentally review the story, but they are forced to analyze what it means.

Again, students may interact as they answer, "Name Christ's 12 disciples and tell one important fact about each of them." But their comments only indicate that they have been listening to what you have said. The question, "How were Jesus' 12 disciples a lot like we are today?" asks students not only to review what they have been taught but also to analyze how what they have learned applies to their contemporary situation.

The following discussion starters are very general. They can be adapted for use in many different lesson situations:

- "If Christ were here today, what illustration or parable from contemporary life do you think He might use to help those around Him understand today's lesson? Explain your choice."
- "Let's discuss different ways we could put the lessons we have learned in today's Bible study to work this week."
- "How would you explain this passage to a non-Christian? To an elementary child?" (Young teens often differ greatly in their abilities to understand. When they are asked to explain something as if they were explaining it to a younger child, they are actually helping to teach those who are not as mature mentally as most in the group. It's a way of simplifying the content without teenagers feeling you are treating them like babies.)

WRONG LESSON

Occasionally something will be said in a discussion to alert you to a need a student has that will not be met by the lesson you had planned. Because students always take precedence over lesson plans, you should switch the emphasis of your lesson to help meet that need. Suppose that during a discussion on living the Christian life, a high school girl says, "I don't feel I can participate. I don't know Christ, and I'm not sure I want to. I just don't understand what's involved." The girl has not been shy about her feelings, and a wise teacher might pick up on the girl's implied questions without embarrassing her. "Good point. How would some of the rest of you respond to the question, 'What does it mean to have Christ as part of our lives?' "

Sometimes it's not just the direction of the lesson that will need to be switched to meet needs; it will be the entire lesson. "Tommy was the second boy to die in the high school in two months," said a senior. "The first had been killed in an automobile accident, and Tommy was electrocuted when he threw a stone with a string attached over a live wire. We had our Bible club meeting the night it happened, and lots of kids came who weren't usually interested. Our leader didn't find out about the second death until he came through the door. He just ditched all the games and fun things we usually did and we talked about death. We kids had a lot of questions, and that was all we wanted to talk about. It was an awful meeting, but it was good to be able to talk about stuff." That youth leader realized that he must meet the immediate needs of his high schoolers. No matter how good the event he had planned was, he would have failed as a leader if he hadn't dealt with Tommy's death.

Sometimes the subject will take the teacher by surprise. How many teachers are perfectly prepared to talk about any subject that might come up? There is nothing wrong with: "I don't know the answers, but I'll do some studying between now and the next time we meet." This is also a perfect opportunity to point out that the teacher isn't the only one who can dig into Scripture. Students can learn how to use their Bible concordances.

THE PARTICIPANTS

No two people in a discussion are exactly alike. Each has biological and psychological needs, drives, patterns for living, past experiences, and creative abilities. Each should be encouraged to contribute in personal, unique ways.

Some students will hesitate to speak in class because they are shy or feel their contributions are less valuable then those of their classmates. Draw them into the discussion by directing a question at them. Consider having them elaborate on something someone else has said, or ask them to share their opinions about a specific subject. "Marian," a teacher might say to a shy, but intelligent student, "how do you feel about our local theater showing previews of restricted films before a feature that is designed for general audiences?"

Nearly every class has at least one member whose contributions do not seem as valuable as those of the rest of the class. Students should learn from your example how important it is to show respect for each person's comments. Sometimes a nod or a smile is all that is necessary to let the speaker and the rest of the class know you appreciate the contribution. Or, it may be possible to salvage something worthwhile from what the person has said and ask another student to comment or elaborate on that point.

No one should be allowed to monopolize the conversation. If it becomes obvious that this is happening, the teacher should politely cut that student's remarks and direct the conversation to another person: "Thank you, Mr. Johns, for your contribution. Mrs. Sylvana, how do you feel about this point?"

Even if all students are participating, a discussion cannot be totally successful unless you maintain an atmosphere of freedom and inquiry. Each person must know that he or she is not required to make a "Sunday school response." Rather, students should be able to share their true feelings and opinions during the discussion, even if those opinions differ from traditional positions. Those opinions stretch the teacher and other students: "What logical person could believe the Incarnation?" "How can you say that God is love when He allowed six million people to die?"

In a free discussion, you must assume the role of guide and participant rather than the role of an instructor or dictator. You steer, rather than shove, to keep the discussion relevant to the morning topic.

A CONDUCIVE CLASSROOM

The success of a discussion depends on the people involved and the topic they are discussing, not on external variables such as the room arrangement. Even so, the leader should try to make the classroom as conducive as possible to discussion.

Circles or semicircles make the best seating arrangements because they eliminate the seat of authority. Students react directly with each other. No longer is the teacher the central figure in the room through whom all comments and questions must pass. Also, in these arrangements, each person is able to see all classmates' expressions and reactions. This adds an additional dimension to the discussion.

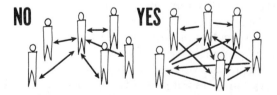

In a healthy class situation, students interact with the leader and with each other. The leader does not become the pivot point from which all discussion must be directed.

There is no room situation that cannot be adapted to discussion. Of course, some of those adaptations will be a little more effective than others. The worst situation I've ever faced was at a Sunday school convention in California. The workshop was billed as a participative dramatic workshop. I was hoping for a large room, a rug, and not many chairs. I got seats nailed to the floor in rows and 300 people. I can remember sending up a quick prayer for help and promising myself that if God got me through this session, I would stop overusing the word *creative*. We did a few "up front" illustrations and placed our bodies in circles for discussion and roleplay. "Circles" were formed by three people in one row turning backward on their chairs to interact with the three lucky people who got to sit normally. It worked, not excellently, but adequately.

Some adult classes are rather large. People who are scared to speak out in a class of 30 people feel less frightened by smaller groups of five or six. A room could be set up like this, allowing for good flexibility.

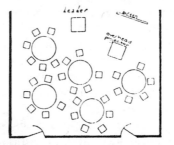

Be aware that if students are comfortable, they are more apt to enjoy interacting. Make sure the room is as comfortably furnished as possible, well lighted, and moderately warm.

STRUCTURE A DISCUSSION

There are many different ways to structure a discussion. All have group interaction as their goal. All provide an opportunity to share in the learning process. But using different structure can add surprise to a discussion. It can mix people in unique ways. It can allow new people to talk.

Total Class Discussion

In some small classes, all students are able to participate in one effective discussion. It can build a sense of class unity, and it allows everyone to hear the wisdom of peers. But in most groups, total class discussion by itself is unsatisfactory because there is usually time for only a few to contribute.

Buzz Groups

Small groups of three to ten people are assigned any topic for discussion. They quickly select a chairperson and a secretary. The chairperson is responsible for keeping the discussion on the track, and the secretary records the group's ideas and reports the relevant ones to the total class.

Brainstorming

Students, usually in small groups, are presented with a problem and asked to come up with as many different solutions as possible. The emphasis here is on quantity, not quality. Quantity often breeds quality. It's easier to modify a creative idea than it is to beef up an uncreative one. Participants should withhold judgment until all suggestions have been offered, or until about two-thirds of the time allotted to the brainstorming session has been spent. After a short break, the group should pick the best contribution from those suggested (or perhaps combine several different ideas) and refine it. (For additional information, review the brainstorming process as it was presented in Chapter 2.)

Each brainstorming group will present its solution in a total class discussion. If class action is indicated, the students may want to decide which idea they would like to further refine and act upon.

Consider using brainstorming problems like these:

- "Assume that we as Christians want to make an impact on our government. We have only the resources available to us that actually exist in this class. How can we best make this impact?"
- "We feel strongly that as Christians we are responsible for the poor and are required to make some active response to better their condition. What can we do?"
- "We would like to build better communications with (parents, children, neighbors, other churches). How can we go about doing this?"

Forum Discussion

Forum discussion is especially valuable when:
1. The subject is difficult and the students would not be able to participate in a meaningful discussion without quite a bit of background.
2. People with special training or experience have insights which would not ordinarily be available to the students. Depending on the topic, it

230

may not always be necessary for those participating in a forum discussion to be Christians.

Each forum member should prepare a three- to five-minute speech, and be given uninterrupted time in which to present it. Then students should be encouraged to interact with the speakers, either directly or through a forum moderator—usually the teacher.

Adapt the following forum outlines to your class by substituting suggested participants with people available in your church and community.

- Forum on drugs:
    1. Person who has tried and rejected the use of drugs
    2. Doctor or policeperson having experience with people on drugs
    3. Friend/parent of person who is/was on drugs
- Forum on sex:
    1. Pastor or youth leader
    2. Christian doctor
    3. Christian parents (both a father and a mother, preferably with teenage children)
- Forum on futurism:
    1. Business person
    2. Scientist who works in a quickly changing field—space, genetics, etc.
    3. Reader who has read several of the books on futurism
    4. Christian with a strong background in what the Bible has to say about the future

You will probably want to make your forum topics more specific than the ones provided here. Slant them so the speakers deal with problems that will help students better understand how the topic specifically applies to them. The forum, when used as part of the Sunday school hour, should, of course, deal with the Scripture that is being studied. For example, if the Scripture study deals with the apostle Peter's difficulty accepting Gentile Christians, you might plan a forum on changing neighborhoods around the church. You would then assign speakers specific topics that would directly apply Scripture.

- Forum on Changing Neighborhoods Around Our Church
    Aim: To help us live together and minister to each other effectively during this time to change.
    1. Minority leader (Topic: What we new people in the neighborhood can bring to this church and what we need to receive from it)
    2. Class member (Topic: Why I am proud of this community and this church)
    3. Majority leader (Topic: Areas in which I suspect we may have problems and my suggestions for dealing with those areas)

231

Sometimes it is impossible for a person who could make an important contribution to your forum to be present. Suppose you wanted the head of the juvenile narcotics division of the city police force to participate in a forum for junior high and senior high students, but the officer had duty on Sunday morning. During the week before the forum, you or a student could interview the officer and record what he or she says. This is not an ideal situation, of course, because the officer won't be present for the response discussion. But students will have the benefit of his or her insights, along with those of the other "live" members of the forum. (In some situations it may be possible to videotape a contributor, rather than simply doing an audio tape. This can be extremely effective.[2])

Panel Discussion

Panel discussions are held in much the same way as forum discussions, but they are less formal. Members from the audience may interrupt the speakers at any time after they have been recognized by the moderator. And members of the panel may interact with each other.

Debate

Occasionally a lesson subject lends itself to debate. There are many ways to structure a debate, but during the Sunday school hour the following pattern is quite effective. At least a week before the debate, those participating should be given the debate topic, stated in the form of a resolution. Examples:

Resolved: Our church should take an active stand in this community on the public housing issue.

Resolved: Our class should begin a youth ministry centered outside the church to reach teens who would never participate in the organized church program.

As students prepare before class for their parts in a debate, they should remember that it is the affirmative side's responsibility to prove that the resolve is correct. The negative has to prove that it isn't. Of course, the negative may also want to present an alternative proposal.

For example, in the youth ministry debate, the negative may counter the affirmative position with an objection like this: "Our class members who would work in this ministry are not strong enough in their faith to stand up to street-smart kids. They might end up being influenced by the negative leaders rather than influencing them for Christ." Or the negative may want to first discredit the resolve and then offer another suggestion: "We believe we can initiate an extensive church sports program that would attract kids to our church. There would be immediate identification with who we are and what we stand for."

Debaters should give their speeches in the following order:
1. First affirmative speech
2. First negative speech
3. Second affirmative speech
4. Second negative speech
   (Brief break while each side discusses and plans its rebuttal.)
5. First negative rebuttal
6. First affirmative rebuttal
7. Second negative rebuttal
8. Second affirmative rebuttal

Since the burden of proof lies with the affirmative team, these people have the advantage of presenting the first and last speeches. Debate winners are determined by the ability of debaters in presenting their positions. Simply stated, to win, the affirmative team must prove that the resolve is correct. To win, the negative team must prove that it isn't.

In a classroom debate it is often good to open the floor for comments and questions following the last rebuttal. The moderator should help direct these student remarks.

Floating Panel

Sometimes you have a topic to which almost everyone in the room would have something to contribute, for example: marriage, love, work, getting along with people. For a change of pace, announce that you will have a floating panel; four or five people whose names are chosen at random (from a hat, perhaps) will become "experts" for several minutes. These "experts" sit in the chairs in the front of the room while you and other class members ask them questions. These questions should be anecdotal (experience related). When the panel has been in front for several minutes, enough time for each person to make several comments, draw other names and replace the original members.

Suppose the panel is on getting along with parents and the members are from a senior high class. Questions to which almost every student could respond include:

- "In your opinion, what are some of the qualities a perfect parent ought to have? Explain your choices."
- "When you think about the special things your parents have done for you, what is one specific thing that pops into your mind?"
- "Why do you think kids often have difficulty getting along with their parents?"
- "When your children are teens, what is one thing you are going to do to make certain the lines of communication stay open?"

233

Mixed-Group Discussion

Often the Sunday school hour is so age segregated that teens don't get to interact with their parents and other adults. The teens miss friendships that might build between them and the adults, and they are not exposed to the wealth of experience adults have. Adults miss the fresh ideas and approaches and the enthusiasm teens often have in abundance.

Consider planning a mixed-group discussion when the aims of both groups' lessons are similar. For example, you might use the following mixed-group discussion idea or structure one like it for your adult and teen classes.

Parent-Teen Wisdom Exchange

(Adults who are not parents of teenagers should participate in the discussion in the way they would if they actually were parents of teens. Perhaps they might "adopt" for that Sunday teens whose parents do not attend the adult class.)

The dual aim for this program is to engage adults and teens in meaningful discussion of contemporary problems, and to develop greater understanding and appreciation for each other and for the wisdom recorded in the Book of Proverbs.

Participants should be challenged before the session to be honest with their comments and to come prepared to participate.

For the first part of the meeting, students should remain in their individual class groups. Give each group the same list of references on parent-child relationships and ask students to review them. The list may include: Prov. 3:12; 10:13; 13:22, 24; 15:5; 19:18, 26; 20:7; 22:6, 15; 28:7; 29:15-17; 30:11-17; Eph. 6:4.

While they are still in their separate class groups, both groups should discuss how they would complete statements like these:

• "The lesson stressed in these references that is most helpful to me right now is . . . because . . ."
• (Adult class) "If I could teach a teen one lesson from these verses, I would teach . . ."
• (Teen class) "If I could teach a parent one lesson from these verses, I would teach . . . in the following way . . ."

Following the segregated discussions, the groups would get together for summarizing how they answered the questions. Then the mixed-group discussion is ready to begin.

The discussion leader must direct questions toward both teens and adults. Otherwise the session is likely to degenerate into a lecture aimed at the teens rather than a sharing time. The teacher may want to use questions like these to start discussion:

- "Parents, in what areas do your kids still need instruction? How could this be given in a way the teens will accept?"
- "Teens, in what problem areas of your lives do you feel parents and Christian adults can be most helpful to you? Why and how?"
- "Teens, what types of correction do you feel are most helpful to you? Why?"
- "Parents, does your responsibility to correct ever end? Support your answer."
- "Teens, what is the ideal relationship between parents and teens? What things often keep that ideal from becoming a reality?"

Teens and adults may want to interact with each other's answers. Allow this discussion to continue for about ten minutes. Then reverse roles. Ask teens to pretend they are adults, and adults to play the role of teens. (Groups may need a few minutes at this time to review the Proverbs verses.)

The session should be concluded with a review of the discussion given by both adults and teens. This summary could state what content has been learned or reviewed, and in the opinion of those speaking, what the parent-teen exchange has accomplished.[3]

Interview

The interview can be used by a teacher in several effective ways.

The interview as homework

Ask students to interview someone during the week and present what they learned in the form of short reports the following Sunday. In the simplest homework interview, the students ask the person they are interviewing a single question that has been supplied by the teacher. Then they write or verbally report in just a few sentences the responses they received.

A lot of the success of this mini-interview depends on the type of question the teacher assigns. It should be designed to force people being interviewed to give paragraph answers rather than single word or phrase answers. Adapt the following ideas to fit your lesson aims.

- Talk with one person in our church neighborhood who does not attend church and ask him or her what that person's opinion of our church is and on what that opinion is based.
- Interview someone who works on a volunteer basis in our church. Ask that person about his or her job and how we could make that job easier.
- Interview someone whose Christian life you admire. Ask that person to share what led up to him or her allowing Christ to have control.

Older teens and adults are capable of doing more complete, in-depth interviews, but usually, because class time is limited and so is students' time commitment to homework, the single-question interview is the more effective teaching tool.

The interview in class.

Occasionally it is profitable to schedule an in-class interview, perhaps with a visiting missionary or with someone who has unique insights to share with the group. An interview can often be more valuable to the class than a lecture given by that person, because, first of all, an interview demands student participation. And second, when students ask the questions, they are alerting the visitor to areas in which they have both interests and needs.

One person can take charge of the entire interview, structuring and asking questions. But whenever possible the entire class should take part. Each student should write a question to ask the guest. Again, questions should require that the speaker talk in depth about the subject, and, whenever possible, deal with specifics rather than generalities.

A student could ask a short-term missionary, "How did you share the Christian life-style, as opposed to the Western life-style, with people in your host country?" Or the class might benefit from knowing a foreign student's answer to, "What special problems do Christians in your country have?"

Members of large Sunday school classes could consider interviewing each other. They would set aside five minutes each class period in which to ask questions of a different classmate each week. It's an interesting way to get to know one another better.

The in-group interview

Divide the class into groups of three, called triads. Supply all groups with the same question or discussion topic. A in the group interviews B while C listens. Then B interviews C while A listens. Finally C interviews A while B listens. Each interview should take from one to three minutes. When the triads return to the total class situation, each person reports on what he or she heard rather than said.

Questions like these can be used in triad discussions:

• "Which story in the Bible means the most to you today? Explain why."
• "What problem do you think Christians your age struggle with most, and what solutions can you suggest?"
• "What can our church do to make singles feel more welcome, especially those singles who are heading up single-parent households?"

Evaluate

Following every class period in which you use discussion, ask yourself these questions to help determine the success of your discussion time:

1. In what ways did this discussion contribute to my students' understanding of today's lesson? (Consider each student individually.)
2. In what specific ways did the students teach themselves during the discussion?
3. If each person was not involved, what can I do next week to correct the situation?
4. In what ways did content play a role in the discussion? (I.e., people were not simply sharing off-the-top-of-their-head opinions.)
5. What follow-up, if any, should be made on the discussion? (For example, if students showed a lack of knowledge or misunderstanding in some area of Scripture, you may want to cover this subject soon during the class hour. Or, if students discussed decisions they were making or projects they felt the class should be involved in, follow-up outside the class hour may be necessary.)

1. Lawrence Kohlberg has been a primary secular name in the field of moral development. According to his initial claims (which are currently being reevaluated by educators and Kohlberg himself), people are attracted to mature reasoning slightly more developed than their own. As adolescents, for example, hear other students and adults sharing more abstract ways of thinking through decision making, they may begin to participate in a more mature reasoning process. Kohlberg makes the assumption that people have a natural tendency to be drawn to higher reasoning, and therefore perhaps more mature actions. As Christians, we believe that each individual cannot find for himself or herself, in a total life experience, what is morally good. Donald Joy, professor of human development and Christian education at Asbury Theological Seminary, Wilmore, Kentucky, said, "I have criticized Kohlberg; I also thank him. He has offered the first model in what must become a panoply of theological models needed in the marketplace where moral development is a top priority." Joy points out that Martin Luther said the papists made him a good theologian. We might also say that Kohlberg, in forcing Christians to look at moral development, may be making us good developmentalists.

2. With over three million video tape recorders in the country, many of them in churches, we need to find more creative ways to use them. In a survey by the Corporation for Public Broadcasting and the National Center for Education Statistics, statistics showed that over 15 million of the nation's 45 million elementary and high school students regularly receive instruction from teachers who use television in their classrooms. (The survey

went on to show that many of these teachers are using television poorly.) Some students are learning to read pictures and sequences of pictures more skillfully than they do words. Our command is not to "Go, and make readers." It is to make disciples, and if a video recorder can help, we'd better begin developing our skills.

CHAPTER 10

Case Study: Chunk of Reality in the Classroom

It is not enough for one to say he is a disciple of Jesus because he reads, studies, or memorizes Scripture. It must be translated into a life-style.

—Herbert E. Epp

I grit my teeth at Madeleine L'Engle's comment about Sunday school in *Walking on Water*, but perhaps many of our schools deserve the kick she delivers:

> I was fortunate (in the strange way in which tragedy brings with it blessings as well as griefs) because my father's deteriorating lungs dictated an unusual schedule; he worked best in the afternoon and evening, and slept late into the morning. Therefore there was no one to take me to Sunday school. I have talked with such a surprising number of people who have had to spend most of their lives unlearning what some well-meaning person taught them in Sunday school, that I'm glad I escaped![1]

We need to train our students to think. We must challenge them to deal with the more difficult aspects of the Christian life. The truth of the Gospel is simple, but never simplistic. The Christian life is filled with conflict, multi-faceted decisions, and issues that remain poorly defined. If our students are not growing in their ability to handle the complex, we will lose them to a secular world that will challenge their thinking. Or, pathetically, we will stifle mental and moral development in an atmosphere that allows only questions for which there are predictable answers and simplistic responses.

Case studies challenge our students to think, to deal with an increasing range and complexity of life experiences, and, within the Christian frame-work, deal with increasing personal intentionality and responsibility.

WHAT IS A CASE STUDY?

Paul Lawrence, of Harvard Business School, states, "A good case is the vehicle by which a chunk of reality is brought into the classroom to be worked over by the class and the instructor."[2]

A case study is not simply an example of what might happen or has happened in a given situation. It's not just a slice of life, nor a situation in which all details are presented like a photograph. A good case is not a guessing game for the right answer, in which the teacher asks which course of action the students should study, A or B—and then announces, "No, you're all wrong, the correct answer is C."[3]

A case must be a true situation in which a problem is presented. Names and some places may be changed, if necessary, but the essential facts must remain the same. The problem is not a simplistic one. In real-life situations there is rarely any difficulty in telling whether or not God wants us to shoplift. So a simple situation in which a teen struggles with lifting a lipstick from the cosmetic counter isn't a good case for discussion. God's rules leave little doubt here.

However, there are those gray areas where our kids stumble, and where we stumble, too. A case study is a short dramatic situation based on actual facts involving actual characters who are faced with actual problems that need solving.

Consider the first few paragraphs of the following case, "A Matter of Life and Death" by Robert Evans.[4] See if you could finish reading this without thinking about your own position, and the ramifications of your position on this girl and her baby, if she were in your Sunday school class.

The antiseptic smell of a hospital had always made Sue Ann Thomas feel sick to her stomach. As she waited alone in the cold reception room, her mind flashed back to two weeks ago when she had told Danny she was pregnant. He wasn't so much angry as he was confused and kind of dazed. They talked about what she could do.

Sue Ann was 16, a junior at Central High, and she was afraid to tell her folks about the baby. Danny had finished high school last year and had a pretty good job in a garage in south Chicago about 15 miles away. Together they could get up the $175 for an abortion.

Do you want to stop? Not if you're like most readers. You want to know if this girl is a Christian, if she has considered Biblical and pastoral teaching. You want to know more about her parents. You want to help her make the right decision and live through the difficulties that will follow that decision. You're hooked on a case.

In a case study, the class reads the case (or hears it read) and discusses it. Christianity becomes alive to students who have only considered Bible stories and the principles they contain in abstract ways. Roleplays give practice for what could happen in real life, but case studies are the experiences of real people. Case studies are field experiences that allow students to apply their Christian values.

Both teens and adults react positively to case study. Probably the most often stated examples of case study education are the Harvard Law and Business Schools. The business school is almost 100 percent case study. People learn by solving real problems and in doing so, they learn the problem-solving steps that will service them when they are in the business world. They also learn to use the sources that are available to them.

High schools are beginning to use case study, too. At Newton High School in Massachusetts, an economics class tried case study as its approach to learning. Suddenly young people who couldn't relate to textbooks were excited about economics. The story approach captured them. Economics ceased to be a subject in school and became a true-life detective story that they had to solve.

Students and teachers involved in case studies enter what is called a willing suspension of disbelief. The literary phrase simply means that those involved are not totally logical about the situation. They are willing to forget that by the time the case has come to them a solution has already been chosen by the real participants. Sue Ann, for example, has made her decision (the case is several years old). But young people and parents in Sunday school classes are still grappling with her unwanted pregnancy. Students enter the case as if the decision had to be made this week; they become the people involved with it.

Would you like to know what Sue Ann decided and how that decision changed her life? So would hundreds of students who have used her story as a study tool, but none of us will ever know. One of the strongest aspects of a case study is that participants rarely find out what really happened.

Students are left to grapple with the issues. The participants say, "If that were me, I would have made this decision . . ." Or, "I would sure hate to be in her shoes. If I don't change the way I've been acting, I easily could be."

If each case had an ending and students knew it, they would also know that you could bring the discussion to a closure. Why should students worry about Sue Ann, if they know the teacher will tell them the "answer" at the end of the period? Why should they search the Scriptures for themselves if the last paragraph hands over the writer's solution?

This is the ending to "A Matter of Life and Death," the only ending we will ever get.

Getting an abortion had seemed like the only thing to do. It was all so easy. Sue Ann began to tremble. She wondered if the baby were a boy or a girl.

She dug her fingers into the bed sheets and began to feel the tears well up in her eyes. She had come this far. What would she do if she backed out? The social worker turned to Sue Ann and waited.

BENEFITS TO THE STUDENTS

When we use case study with adults and teenagers, we can expect some of the following things to happen as part of the teaching process.

● People will be exposed to others who have problems similar to their own, and realizing the similarities, they may apply the Biblical solution to their own problems.

● Students will reevaluate Sunday school. Case study can be a tool for real-world training.

● Students will hear opinions other than their own. It's easy for people to think there is just one possible solution and one possible ramification of that solution.

● Students will become more tolerant. When Christians discuss the situation which may have caused a teen to allow herself to get pregnant out of wedlock, for example, and explore the feelings that the girl and her parents have, they may never again feel as pharisaically smug about their own situations. The reminder, "There, but for the grace of God, go I," is one we all need from time to time.

● Scriptures become real to students who get involved in the total study. Just what did God say about this issue? Are there principles that need to be applied? When someone in a case makes a decision based on his or her understanding of the Bible, what responsibilities do the rest of us, as Christian family, have to that person?

"It says right here that God knew us before we were born. We were real people. Sue Ann can't even consider an abortion!"

"But then what happens to her? What if she wants to continue her education, and her parents won't help? What if they will, and she comes back to school? How are you going to treat her?"

"There's this girl in our school who is selling Tupperware to help support herself and her baby. Maybe our Sunday school class should throw a party."

"What do we want with Tupperware? She's the one who had the baby, and she's responsible for it, not us."

"Hey, let's hear your Biblical support for that crack!"

And the discussion goes on. The answers in good case studies are not simple, and they are never the fill-in-the-blank types.

- As with roleplay, people who participate in case study increase their decision-making skills. They learn to analyze the case, make a decision, and consider the consequences of that decision.

Consider the following two cases: "Justice for Whom?" and "Dance for Life." The first we will look at from a teacher's perspective. How would this case study be used with teens and adults? The second we will look at from a writer's perspective. Many cases follow a predictable pattern. If you have a bit of writing skill, you can begin structuring the cases you and acquaintances have lived and use them in your class.

GET THE CHARACTERS

The first thing a teacher will want to do with a case is read it at least three times, getting familiar with the characters. What are their personalities? What do they do in the case? With which characters do you sympathize? With which character will most of the students identify?

Begin to get to know the characters in the following excerpt:

Excerpt from
JUSTICE FOR WHOM?[5]

He was on his way home from a school yard pickup basketball game, dribbling his ball down Arthur Avenue in the Bronx, when a white teenager walked up and stabbed him once in the abdomen. The black boy was dead before he hit the ground.

It took the detective almost a month before he broke the case. At first it was a total mystery, with no apparent motive for the killing and no decent leads to work on.

243

He was 17 when he was killed, a senior in high school.

(Finally an eyewitness talked.) The killer was an 18-year-old who worked as a delivery boy for a local pastry shop.

The suspect lived with his aged parents in a two-bedroom apartment over a shoemaker's shop, not four blocks from the scene of the killing.

The boy's father answered the door. He was a frail, white-haired man in his 60's, and he spoke with a heavy Italian accent. Asked what he wanted, the detective said he had to speak to the boy about a crime that had been committed. As he stood there, the detective was embarrassed by the old man. He could see that the boy's father did not have the slightest inkling of what this was all about, and the detective had little stomach for what he knew was about to happen.

"It's a murder. A black kid was killed up on Arthur Avenue three weeks ago. I've got to talk to him about it."

"Are you here to arrest my boy?"

"Yes, I am," the detective said softly.

The old man looked hard at the detective. His eyes widened, but he seemed to regain control of himself. He called the boy's name.

The boy emerged from his bedroom and walked up to his father and the detective. He was short and slender, almost fragile in build, dressed in blue jeans and a white T-shirt. The boy looked straight at the detective and then lowered his eyes. He knew what this was all about.

The old man spoke first.

"This man says you killed a black kid up on Arthur Avenue three weeks ago."

The boy hung his head and began to cry. "Papa, I did it. I didn't mean to do it, and I wanted to tell you, but I couldn't. It just happened, and I'm sorry." The old man was in a state of shock. The three of them stood silently, and then the old man too began to cry. The detective waited a minute and then put the boy in handcuffs and led him away.

DETERMINE THE ISSUES

What issues are obvious in this case so far? If your students are from suburban or rural areas, with which issues do you think they will relate? Often a case study that is part of a curriculum will give you a teaching plan which selects the issues that are appropriate for the day's aim. If you are finding your own case studies in newspapers, magazines, or in the lives of people you know, you will need to select from the multitude of possibilities the one or two issues you wish to discuss in class.

In this study, let's grapple with the issue of justice. Just what does it mean to be just to all people in today's society? In some situations, injustice is obvious. It is wrong to judge people by their color, family background, or paycheck. It is wrong to climb over people to get to the top of the heap. It is wrong to snub others and cultivate a better-than-thou attitude. But sometimes in today's world, it is not so easy to know exactly which action is the most right, the most just, the most Christlike.

The situation in "Justice for Whom?" will probably be removed from most of your students' daily lives, but it will hit concepts with which they will grapple:

- What is the right and Christian response to the kid at school who has been in trouble with the law?
- What are some of the ways we "kill" others—at school or on the job?
- How do we learn to look at complete issues, rather than just the emotional bits and pieces of issues?

PREPARING TO TEACH A CASE

Some new teachers approach a case thinking that teaching it will be simple. Just read a story and get students to talk about it. Great way to cut down on study.

Not so. Actually it's quite difficult to teach a case because the teacher can never really be sure what direction the students will take. It's certainly more work than lecturing. As long as a teacher lectures, the teacher is in complete control. The teacher determines what material is being presented and in what order. In the case study method, however, teachers surrender their sovereignty while still maintaining control of the discussion.

Robert W. Merry, of Harvard Business School, gives this advice to teachers who are interested in teaching case study: "It would be a mistake for the new instructor to assume that he has only to read and reread the case and then go into the class and ask one or two leading questions. Rather he must be so thoroughly conversant with the case that he is ready to deal with any angles which the class may introduce, to modify his approach at any time, or suddenly to change his outline in accordance with new ideas which may not previously have occurred to him."[6]

Several years ago in an adult Sunday school class, I was teaching a case involving a family that had to make a decision about the father being kept on a life-support system. The class period was moving along well, or so I thought. Then about 15 minutes into the period, a new member said, "I wish we wouldn't talk about this case anymore. It's upsetting, and if it is continued, I'll leave." We stopped talking about the case. People are always more important than lesson plans. When he realized that we had heard and responded to his request, he was willing to talk. He had had a heart attack less than a year before, and the doctor had given him very little hope for recovery. Talking about death scared him. The whole class surrounded him with support, and, of course, much greater things than the continuation of my planned lesson were accomplished.

When a teacher is not prepared or has not prayed through the process, when he or she is not open to being a "failure" when the unexpected happens, case study is dangerous.

Not all teachers will teach case studies the same way. Each of us has individualized patterns that work for us, that are comfortable to us. But there are certain steps that every teacher needs to take to make the case experience successful:

1. *Master the facts of the case.*

2. *Consider specific things your students might want to bring up.* What you know about your students will be more helpful than any printed teacher's guide. You are the person God has chosen to use.

3. *Decide what your particular learning objectives will be.* You are the director of the case. In "Justice for Whom?" we could be talking about poverty or race. But for this discussion, we are considering justice. It's your job as leader to keep the discussion on track. Contradiction: It is also your job as leader to let the case get off the track if you perceive that the class has special needs that are not being met by the direction you chose before the session.

4. *Write questions for the case that will spark discussion.* If you're using a case that comes with a curriculum, questions will be provided. That's a great way to get started. It's also limiting when you find a story or article that is a case if you feel you can't use it because there are no accompanying lesson plans. In "Justice for Whom?" the writer in the original article provided no questions. It was simply an article printed in a magazine.

Here are some possible questions that could be used if the issue being discussed were justice:
- "What things can you know about the black teen? The white teen?"
- "Based on what you know about the case so far, how would justice best be served?"
- "What do you think will happen to the white teen? What are some just possibilites? Some unjust?"
- "Suppose this boy were to be tried by an all-black jury. What do you think would happen? Suppose the black jury were composed of Christians. What then?"

5. *Present the case to the class.* Again, a word from Merry to secular teachers is helpful to Christian education teachers, too: In the classroom, "something between these two extremes of tight control and no control at all is ordinarily called for. And the new instructor may find that he can most

readily achieve this objective if he can free himself from close reliance on his notes. Having worked out his detailed teaching outline, he may do well to put it aside in favor of a mere list of the critical areas—such a list as may fit on an index card or two, which the instructor may glance at during the class hour simply to make certain that no important areas have been slighted. For the details of development he will rely on the thoroughness of his own preparation."[7]

a. Use Scripture:

"Justice for Whom?" was printed in a secular magazine; no Biblical references accompanied it. Yet Bible study should be part of every Sunday school hour. In a class of highly motivated students with strong Biblical background, the students may pick their own Scriptures to emphasize their points. The whole class would then study the suggested Scriptures, making sure that the assumptions made about the verse are true and are developed in context. Consider how the following passage from Micah would help senior high students deal with "Justice for Whom?"

Hear now, heads of Jacob and rulers of the house of Israel: Are you not supposed to know justice, you who hate good and love evil? Hear this, you heads of the house of Jacob and rulers of the house of Israel, who spurn justice and twist everything that is straight, who build Zion in blood and Jerusalem in iniquity. Her leaders deal out judgment for a bribe; her priests teach for hire; her prophets divine for silver, and then they lean on the Lord, saying, "Is not the Lord in our midst? Evil shall not come upon us!" Therefore, for your sake, Zion shall be plowed as a field, Jerusalem shall be heaps, and the temple mountain shall become as a jungle hill (Micah 3:1, 2, 9-12).

Consider the next segment of the case:

The judge set bail at the modest sum (for a murder) of $15,000. It was raised within the hour. The boy walked out of the court after spending only one night in jail, and the case was referred to the grand jury.

The defense attorney acknowledged right away that his client was guilty and admitted he didn't dare take the case to trial. He had to plead his client guilty, and did not care what particular crime he pleaded to so long as it was not murder, which carried with it a mandatory life sentence. What he did care about was the sentence his client would receive, and in this regard he had two requests. Before discussing the question of sentencing he asked me to read a report on his client prepared at his family's request by a forensic psychiatrist. Then he asked me to meet the boy myself and size him up. I agreed.

The psychiatrist's report read, in part, as follows:

[The boy], whose English is, of course, fluent and unaccented, and who is very much a product of this society, is ashamed of his parents' heavy

---

accents, and what he described as their "foreign ways." On the other hand, [the boy] loves his parents deeply, and has great difficulty coping with this shame over their "old fashionedness."

. . . [He] has also had serious trouble in coping with peer-group pressure. He does not yet need to shave frequently, and his boyish appearance makes him the butt of a considerable amount of peer-group teasing. It is quite remarkable that he has done as well as he has in his studies. He is a B student, a fact that reinforces my own impression that he is both a sensitive and an intelligent young man.

. . . I have been seeing [him] for two months now on an intensive basis, and even in this short time there has been extraordinary progress. He has begun to discuss his feelings and has begun to face directly the problems that have so deeply disturbed him. His parents, who are deeply concerned, have cooperated fully in his therapy, and my sessions with them and the boy have been fruitful.

It is my professional judgment that with continued care [this young man] will become a well adjusted and valuable member of society. I view with horror the prospect of his going to prison. Such an eventuality would most likely destroy him.

Two weeks later the lawyer brought the boy and his parents to my office.

The boy asked me for permission to go see the parents of the boy he had killed. He wanted to seek their forgiveness, to tell them how terribly sorry he was for what he had done. I told them that it would be unwise for him to try to see the dead boy's family.

Most cases are quite long. This edited version is approximately half the size of the original. Because of their length, you will want to plan the entire period around most cases, using Bible study and discussion of Biblical principles throughout.

b. Interrupt case at different points for discussion:

You will also want to interrupt your reading of the case to your students with discussion questions or other group processes. (In some rare cases, you may have a Sunday school class in which students read a case before they come to class and are prepared to discuss it immediately. Great when it happens, but most teachers don't count on this homework miracle!)

Questions like the following could be used at this point in the reading.

- "How have your opinions of the characters changed?"
- "If Christ were the professional in the story, what do you think He would have done?"
- "Would being a Christian change the decision you think is just in this case?"

- "What if you discovered the black boy and his family are Christians? Would that make any difference in your tentative decision about the just outcome?"
- "What problems do you see with a harsh punishment? With an easy punishment?"
- "How might the prophet Micah have handled this case?"
- "Can you think of anything Jesus did or said that might shed light on how to handle this case? Read the passage, and share how it applies."
  Continue reading the case to your students.

That afternoon I spoke to the dead boy's father on the telephone, and arranged for him to come to my office the following day. We shook hands firmly, and he met my gaze with unwavering eyes.

When he spoke, it was with great force. He said he was not about to make things easy for me by telling me not to go hard on the white boy. As far as he was concerned "that white boy" had to go to jail for a long time and the longer the better. He told me their son's death had just about killed his wife. The death made her old before her time and he knew she would never be the same again.

And then there was their younger son. He had been doing really well in school, almost as well as his dead brother had been doing. But ever since the murder, the knowledge that his brother's killer was free had been eating at him. He was turning bitter, neglecting his studies, and for the first time had begun to get into trouble with the law. Was it right that their only remaining child be condemned to grow up with such hatred?

Then there was the question of race. He asked me whether a black kid who had senselessly killed a white honor student would be out on bail receiving such gentle treatment.

---

c. Interrupt case for learning activities:

After the previous breaks in the case, we talked about discussion questions that could be used to involve the learners. But discussion is not the only method that can be used with case study. Consider the following variations:

- The class could break into two sides and debate what should happen. The teacher could award points for good reasoning and effective use of the Bible.

- The class could take a hand vote and see which side has the most people for it. The groups could then have five minutes to try to convert others to their sides. I tried this with a group of college students. The sides were drawn—some for the harsh punishment and some for lenient treatment. One student stopped the whole process by announcing, "I won't participate. Obviously there aren't just two sides here. We're pretending

249

things are simple and they never are. There is no such thing as justice here. I know because one of my good friends is in jail. Let's talk alternatives and not debate."

• The class or the teacher could develop a test that would help students qualify how they feel. For example:

Directions: Mark the line with an X at the spot that best indicates how you feel:

Life/Death Sentence ————————————————————— Parole

• The class could roleplay how different people might respond. For example, roleplay how the father of the dead boy explains what he feels must happen in their family to his wife and younger son.

Roleplay works perfectly as a part of many cases. I was leading a case study workshop for doctors and nurses who worked at a hospital for terminally ill patients in New England. They played the family in the case, working through in roleplay some of the guilt, fears, sorrows that their patients' families might feel. Real tears came. The players explained that it was difficult not to block out emotions when they worked with pain and loss every day. It was important for them to remember, if only in an artificial situation, how people felt when the hurt was real.

Many cases would end at this point. Most cases that are written as case studies do end without giving solutions. Yet this case was first a magazine article, and the reader was given the ending. But perhaps this ending leaves the case more in need of Christian interaction than it was without it.

Over and over again, I asked rhetorical questions. Didn't I know what was going to happen to the boy in jail?

Didn't I know that 80 percent of the prison population was black or Hispanic? Once they find out what the boy is in jail for they would probably cut his throat.

When the time came I made a sentencing recommendation to the judge. Later, at the time of the sentence, he followed it.

The boy is currently serving a 15-year term in state prison. He will be eligible for parole in three years. Two months after sentence, the white youth's father suffered a stroke. He is now an invalid. The dead boy's brother is now under indictment, charged with armed robbery. There has been no noticeable decrease in the amount of crime or racial violence in the Bronx.

Following a case study, you will want to bring what has happened to a closure. Again, questions are an excellent tool:

- "Have you changed your ideas about justice for the killer? If so, how and why?"
- "If you personally had to make the decision, what would you decide?" (This question brings people out of the case into real life again.)
- "What injustices have not been righted by the decision that was made?"
- "How do you feel about the decision?"
- "Justice would be easier if everything were more simple. How dare Christians act in complex situations like this one?"

LEARNING TO WRITE A CASE

DANCE OF LIFE[8]

Introduction

Tears streamed down Tracy Graham's face as she blurted out her feelings to Dr. Adams. "I don't want to tell my sister that it's all right for her to die. But if I really love Sara, maybe that's what I have to say."

Transition

In talking with Dr. Adams, Sara's doctor, she wanted to piece together the events of the last few months to try to understand Sara's choice to leave the hospital. Without the artificial cleansing of her blood through dialysis she could live only a few weeks. If she continued the treatment, there was a chance that she could live for at least a few more years.

Flashback

Tracy, now 17, and Sara, who would be 16 next month, had always been very close. It was now almost six months to the day when Sara had begun to lose weight and get very weak. The family doctor said it was a kidney disease and had recommended Dr. Adams, a specialist. When both of Sara's kidneys failed, she was put on a dialysis machine which hooks up the blood circulation system and cleans the blood of impurities as the kidneys would. Dr. Adams began to look for a donor to give Sara a healthy kidney.

"Dance of Life" follows a typical case study pattern that is used by most case study writers. We'll examine that pattern throughout this short case.

Introduction

This is a short section, usually one or two paragraphs. It can be longer if it involves conversation.

251

The introduction starts at the crisis point. The case will work its way through the transition and the flashback until it returns to this crisis point once again. No resolution will be given, but by the time the case has worked its way back to the crisis point first presented in the introduction, students will know enough about the situation and people involved to deal with the complexities of the issue.

As the writer, you will usually want to use an expressive rather than an analytical style. You are telling a story. You are not simply outlining an issue or slicing a direct piece of life. You are picking pieces to add to your story, and that story must come alive. You have to make the students who will work on the case care about the characters in it.

Transition

This is not a long section. It's a bridge that writers use to lead the students away from the crisis point—the cliff-hanger—into the events that led up to the crisis.

There are a lot of phrases that will do this:

"The whole story started six months ago when . . ."

"To better understand the dilemma, let's go back to the beginning . . ."

The author in "Dance of Life" is quite polished in his transition. He sneaks it in, and most people will be unaware that they have been through a transition: ". . . she wanted to piece together the events of the last few months . . ."

Flashback

The flashback will be the bulk of your case. It is here that you share the story with your students. They must come out of this section feeling with the major characters of your story and being able to focus on the major events.

Consider this part of the flashback for "Dance of Life":

Tracy remembered the arguments with her parents. She wanted to be the donor, but her mom, dad, and Sara, as well as Dr. Adams, said no. A donor was at last found, the transplant made, but after ten days of waiting the signs were obvious that Sara's body would reject the new kidney. She was placed back on the dialysis machine. Tracy insisted again that she be the next donor. As there was a slightly better chance of her kidney being accepted, the girls' parents and Sara reluctantly agreed. Three weeks later Tracy's transplanted kidney was also rejected by Sara's body.

Tracy slipped into Sara's room. How still and pale Sara looked with all of the tubes and machines around her. There was hardly a sign of the laughing, joyous girl who had told Tracy from the time she was seven that she wanted to be a dancer.

Dr. Adams had called Mr. and Mrs. Graham and Tracy into Sara's room for a conference. He told the family then that some blunt realities had to be faced. "After two rejections, we should no longer consider a kidney transplant as a possibility at this time. In a few days when Sara is stronger, she will be able to go home and resume many of her normal activities. But she must return here to the hospital three days a week for six to eight hours to use the dialysis machine. If not, her own blood would poison her.

"At the present time there is no medication that can take the place of this machine. However, there is always the hope that through new medical advances we will learn how to combat the rejection of an organ transplant." Dr. Adams had told the family in confidence yesterday that Sara might live only a short time even with dialysis because of the possibility of several complications that could arise.

Step away from the case now, and look at the author's craft. He has chosen a focus from which to tell the story. He is giving the student enough facts to work with, but he's not throwing in the kitchen sink. Part of your skill as a writer will be to tell enough facts so students will be able to think about the issues, and not so many facts that they are bored before they get to the issues.

The best way to achieve this balance is to establish an aim for your case. Disregard anything that doesn't further that aim. Ask yourself, "Is this important to the story?" Get rid of everything that isn't. Everything! Weed out all those details, for example, about kidney machines and the effects of the disease. Everything that is not imperative to the case must go.

Be objective. This means that you may not be able to do a good job writing up a case you're too close to. Your best friend's marriage just broke up, and she has moved in with your family until she can face picking up the pieces. Yes, this might make a wonderful case, but you're probably too involved. Stay away from it, at least for a while. People reading your case need to grapple with issues and their own conclusions about those issues—not pick up your biases and affirm or disaffirm them.

Keep your cases short. Most are too long to be helpful in Sunday school or as part of evening Bible studies. For Christian magazines and most Sunday school materials, a case of about 1,500 words is appropriate. Of course, if you were writing a case to be used in a law school, you might take a book to retell it. But when you write, consider your audience—the people you want to read and interact with this case. And almost always, make your short case even shorter.

Continue with more of the flashback in "Dance of Life":

The Grahams began to make plans for the future. At this point the purchase of a dialysis machine was financially impossible for them, and in their part of the state none was available for rental. Thus because the family lived more than 65 miles from the hospital, Mr. Graham, who ran a small business in Oak Town, began to look for an apartment much closer to the city. Tracy knew that the medical costs for Sara had placed the family heavily in debt. The members of their village church, many of whom had been regular visitors at the hospital for the past few months, had spoken of their prayers for her and had already held two bazaars to raise money for Sara's expenses. The money had covered only a fraction of the actual costs.

Mrs. Graham, who spent her days with Sara at the hospital, had begun to take in secretarial work in the evenings. Tracy, now in her senior year of high school, said that she really didn't want to go off to school in the fall, but would rather postpone this and get a job instead.

Sara told Tracy how aware she was of the love and support of the family and their friends. She said she was most aware of the tremendous faith they had in things working out for the best. Recently Sara had spoken to Tracy several times of their common Christian beliefs and of her assurance of a life after death. Dr. Adams had told her how lucky she was to have access to the machine. But Sara confessed to Tracy that the idea of living through the machine was very hard to take, and right now to think about life without dancing and running was almost impossible.

Up to this point, the case has not contained a real issue for most Christians. Sara is underestimating what she can be and do. Life is not over because she can't dance. What she is asking for, in some people's opinions, is the right to commit suicide.

But in this next part of the flashback, the case takes on a new dimension. The issues aren't as simple as they were. Make certain that the cases you write are not just good stories with difficult, but possible solutions. A case must be a many-faceted story, one in which a number of opinions is possible.

Sara was quite thin and took many days to recover from her second surgery. She had gotten acquainted with Mike, a boy on the same floor, and had told Tracy about him. "He's just a little guy. He's really 12, but he looks about 9. He's waiting for a kidney donor, but unless one shows up pretty soon, he'll need the machine to make it. I even explained to him what the machine does. But I overheard two of the nurses talking. Right now there's no space available to schedule Mike for dialysis. Do you know that only one out of ten people who needs this machine gets a chance, and our hospital has one of the only machines like this in our section of the state?"

The flashback is over. It's now time for the writer to bring the students back to the point where the story began.

Crisis Point (Return to the introduction)   That was over a week ago. Then just this morning, Sara had turned to Tracy and in a clear, firm voice said, "Trace, I can't stand the thought of living the rest of my life tied to this machine. It's not living for me. I want to go

> home now—and not come back to the hospital. I've
> already told Mom and Dad. They are very sad, but I think
> they understand. But most important to me is that *you*
> understand and will support my decision."

The words of the first paragraph don't have to be repeated, but the action of the case comes right back to that first section in which the difficult decision was presented.

To review, most cases have the following four sections:

1. Introduction to crisis point.
2. Transition back to the starting point of the case, to the spot where the writer chooses to start.
3. A chronological body of material that tells the story from start to the crisis point. This flashback contains selected aspects that contribute to the focus of the case.
4. Return to the crisis or decision point.

This simple formula is easy to handle. Of course, there are more complex patterns (for example, "Justice for Whom?"). But until you have written several cases and feel secure in the regular pattern, don't experiment too far beyond the pattern.

After you've written your first case, have someone critique it. For the best results, pick someone who isn't obligated to like it because of your relationship with him or her. Pay attention to any suggestions, and if necessary, rewrite.

Because of the nature of most cases, it will be necessary to keep some names and identifying points confidential. Disguise is acceptable procedure, but make certain you are not changing the direction or tone of the story. For example, it would do little harm in the case "Dance of Life" if the girl had been a boy who didn't want to give up sports. The issues would have been as true and as important, but people who knew the real characters would have been less likely to pick them out. On the other hand, if both boys in the story "Justice for Whom?" had been black, some of the basic issues of the story would have been changed. It would still be a case, perhaps a very valuable case, but a different case. Unless the second story were true, you would be violating a rule in case study development—the essential story must be true.

If you are telling someone's story, you will need to get a release from him or her. All the lead characters should give their approval. For example, in "Dance of Life," you would want the parents' approval in writing.

"Most of the skills of a good case writer must be acquired on a trial-and-error basis," said Paul A. Lawrence, in "Preparation of Case Material." "One last word of advice would be that a new case writer would profit greatly from extensive experience with cases as a student and, if possible, as an instructor. Such experience gives a familiarity with cases and their uses for which no article like this can be a substitute."

THE QUESTION OF QUESTIONS

There are two opinions on writing teaching plans for case studies you have developed.

If you are publishing a case or adding one to your church library, remember that teaching plans limit the issues that will usually be discussed. You may decide not to include plans, but rather a list of possible subject areas for which users might develop their own plans.

If you're going to use your own case, you'll want to have an organized teaching plan. If you are writing a case study as part of a printed Sunday school curriculum you will want to develop questions for the teachers that will help them reach the lesson's aim. The curriculum writer's motto might be, "Give those teachers all the help they can get!"

Here are some questions that were actually used in "Dance of Life." The questions were structured for young adults participating in a life-style curriculum, "If I Should Die Before I Wake—A Christian Looks at Death, Dying, and Grief."

- "What are some of the theological assumptions or implications that showed up in this dialogue?"
- "Do you think Sara may not really be asking for approval of her plan to die after all? Is it possible that she is only testing her family to see whether they consider her a burden or really want her to remain with them?"
- "Does the commandment 'Thou shalt not kill' apply to a medical situation like this in which death will occur anyway without the life-support apparatus? (Remember the Karen Ann Quinlin case in 1975 when a comatose young adult's parents pleaded with a New Jersey court for the right to disconnect the respirator that kept Karen alive.)"
- "Jesus said, 'I am come that they might have life, and that they might have it more abundantly.' Does this have any bearing on the quality of life—Sara's or an old person's in a rest home?"
- "Is Sara's concept of sacrificing her life for Mike a Christian one?"

WHERE TO FIND MATERIAL FOR CASES

1. *Live a case.* This often happens, but the writer will rarely be the central figure in the story. It's easier to be objective if you are one of the people on

the edges of a difficult situation. For example, I was a member of an inner-city church in which a staff of people from very different economic and racial backgrounds was trying to demonstrate that twentieth-century churches don't have to be homogeneous. What happened when that situation erupted affected me, because I loved the people and the work we were all involved in. But I wasn't on staff; my life wasn't destroyed. I could look at the bits and pieces of the story more objectively than I could have if I had been on staff. The case that grew out of that experience follows the traditional four-point outline, so the following introduction is not only the first three paragraphs, but the crisis point to which the case, after a long flashback, will return.

CENTRAL CHURCH[9]

"Is the open church possible?"

The group of elders sat in silence after Daryl Fetter, chairman, asked the question. Then slowly Kenneth Russell stood to his feet.

In the past he had vocalized his belief in the open church, a church which modeled the love of Christ as people of all colors worshiped together and committed themselves to true brotherhood. He loved, respected, and had grown under the ministries of both the white pastor, Peter Jones, and the black pastor, Robert Thomas. Several weeks before this elders' meeting, Kenneth had said to Daryl, "As the only nonstaff black person on the board of elders, I realize my position is unique. I've got a white wife and a high-level position in a white Christian organization. I feel very visible at Central, very torn by all the polarization that's taking place between black and white members." Other board members had told him that his response to the current problem could determine the direction the church would take.

---

2. *Read articles that make good cases in secular magazines.* "Justice for Whom?" was first published in *Psychology Today* magazine.

3. *Newspapers are great case study sources.* Look for articles where the right decision is not obvious. "Students Boycott Classes" was taken from a newspaper article.[10] It is not a complete case, but it makes an excellent discussion tool. The questions were added by a curriculum writer.

WYOMING, Mich. (AP)—Six hundred students boycotted classes at a Grand Rapids-area high school Monday in support of teachers and counselors who lost their jobs in budget cuts.

Chanting, "We want our

teachers,'' the students milled in front of Wyoming Park High School and refused to return to class until the 10 staff members were rehired.[10]

- "Do you think Christians should take part in a public protest? Why or why not? What if you knew that the protest would help someone in need?"
- "Share a time when you were involved in a helping experience. How was it like or unlike this situation? Make a list of ways our class can help people in need."

4. *History is full of case studies.* Perpetua's story was researched by freelance writer, Judy Dodd.

Perpetua was a beautiful, rich young woman who went to jail because she believed in Christ. It would have been a simple matter, however, for her to get out. All she had to do was deny Him, and she had every reason to want her freedom. She had a small baby who needed her and a family who loved her and was in anguish. Her father came to visit her in the prison and begged her to reject her faith. Perpetua's answer to him is recorded in her diary, which dates back to 200 A.D.: "Can anyone call anything by any other name than what it is? So neither can I call myself anything else than what I am, a Christian." Perpetua was thrown into the arena and died as one of the early Christian martyrs.

- "If you had been Perpetua, what do you think you would have done?"
- "Roleplay the conversation Perpetua could have had with her family as she tries to explain the decision she is about to make."

1. Madeleine L'Engle, *Walking on Water*, p. 58.

2. Paul Lawrence, "Preparation of Case Material" (Harvard Business School).

3. "The 'example,' which goes back to the medieval exemplum, used by religious writers to express a moral precept, in my opinion, is not what a case should be. . . . And a case is not, I think, a sheer guessing contest—a kind of a blind thing in which you repeatedly ask a student, 'What is this?' or 'What do you do in this situation?' 'No, you're wrong.' That is the sort of thing where you say: 'Guess what I've got in my hand?' and after a number of people have guessed, you say, 'No, that isn't right; this is what I've got in my hand,' " says Malcom P. McNair in "McNair on Cases," reprinted from Harvard Business School Bulletin, July-August, 1971.

4. Robert Evans, "A Matter of Life and Death" (McCormick Theological Seminary). Used by permission. (Previously published in *Introduction to Christianity: A Case Method Approach*, John Knox Press, 1980.)

5. Steven Phillips, "Justice for Whom?" Reprinted by permission of Wallace & Sheil Agency, Inc. Copyright © 1977 by Steven Phillips. "Justice for Whom?" was condensed for reprint in the Sunday school class-and-home weekly, *Christian Living*, and a complete teaching plan for high school students was included in the teacher's guide. Portions not appropriate for general classroom discussion were omitted from the condensation (for example, homosexual rape in prisons), while editors carefully maintained the essence of the struggle.

6. Robert W. Merry, "Case Instruction for the Beginning Instructor," © 1954 by the President and Fellows of Harvard College.

7. Ibid.

8. Robert Evans, "Dance of Life," used by permission. (Previously published in *Introduction to Christianity: A Case Method Approach*, John Knox Press, 1980.)

9. Marlene LeFever, "Central Church," written as a class requirement for the Case-Study Institute Summer Workshop (The Association of Theological Schools), 1976.

10. Reprinted by permission of Associated Press, 50 Rockefeller Plaza, New York, NY 10020.

CHAPTER 11

Creative Writing: Helping Students Save Their Thoughts

If I read, and feel physically as if the top of my head were taken off, I know that is poetry.

— Emily Dickinson

"My students hate to write."

Maybe, but more likely, students are afraid to write. What will their peers think of their words? How will their teacher respond? They may also have fears about their spelling and punctuation. Writing in Sunday school class brings forth memories of school papers covered with red marks and an English teacher barking, "How do you ever expect to get along in this world if you can't tell a subject from a predicate?" Yet, I still advocate challenging students to do some writing in class. There are ways to break through their negative feelings to discover the joy of communicating on paper.

BREAK THROUGH THE NEGATIVES

• *Begin with a fun writing idea.* Keep it small, insignificant. This chapter will provide you with some starter ideas that you can adapt to your own teaching situation. The creative writing that happens in Sunday school dare not seem "schoolish."

• *Stress that writing in class is just talk written down.* Because writing takes longer than talking, people who need extra minutes to think through their ideas may suddenly find themselves important contributors to the class. Let people know that you are not expecting great writing, just individual sharing.

• *Give the option to write or think, and then share.* Take the pressure off. Sometimes people who begin with sharing verbally will write their thoughts without your suggesting it. "Hey, that was good," a listener responds to another student's acrostic. "Would you repeat it?"

"Oops! I forgot it already!" And suddenly people who never wrote before are writing.

• *Don't make negative comments about spelling or punctuation.* If a student asks you, you might go over his or her work outside of class. You may even want to take the best creative writing assignments and post them on a bulletin board. In that case, you might type what people wrote, or have them rewrite it. You will also want to correct any errors.

BENEFITS FROM SELF-EXPRESSION THROUGH WRITING

Students who consider themselves poor communicators on paper may change their self-opinion when they have a successful experience. Discovering their ability to communicate through writing gives students a sense of achievement that few other teaching methods can match.

• *Choose assignments that help students stabilize in their own minds what they believe.* Encourage students to write in the first person: "I believe," "I feel." This helps them communicate more personally and honestly, and forces them away from safe generalities: "We believe," "We feel."

• *Encourage students to keep many of these assignments as a permanent record of their thoughts, ideas, and decisions.* Of course, most writing which students do in class will not have lasting value, but when students create poems, songs, and prayers that touch the essence of their relationship with God, they will be able to keep those pieces. They may also polish some assignments and share them with others outside the class.

A group of teens, children of missionaries to Japan, did just that. Students wrote paragraphs explaining why they were proud of their fathers. Then all it took was a little polishing and a few transitional sentences to turn their paragraphs into an article they hoped would help other teens appreciate their Christian parents more. The following excerpt is from their article, "It Takes a Man," as it was published in a senior high Sunday school paper.

"My father is often a complete failure," grinned Mark DeShazer, a senior at a school for missionary children near Tokyo. "And I think that proves his courage, faith, and Christian manhood more than anything else.

"You see, it's no great thing to be dedicated to a job when the world says it's important and it applauds you verbally and financially. But sometimes he sees no results. The world sneers and says he's wasting his life and education on a fruitless task. His family goes without things other men can give their loved ones. When his only justification for being on the mission field is a command from God which the world discounts as foolishness, that's courage."

Eighth-grader Susie summed up the qualities of manhood necessary for success in God's foreign service when she described her father, Herb Murata. "My father is sort of a second fiddle. He does odds and ends which don't seem of real importance, but are, if everything in our ministry is to run smoothly. He honestly enjoys his work and does it well. I'm proud of him. I have a right to be, because in his attitude and understanding, in his love for God and the people God has given him to work with, my dad is the biggest man I know."

● *Students may be challenged to more original thinking as they hear how their classmates express themselves.* A new Christian may increase his or her knowledge about the Savior and have some ideas clarified and questions answered as that person reads what classmates have written. Students who have been Christians for a long time benefit from the enthusiasm and fresh approach which are often part of a new Christian's writing. A new Christian may not be familiar with the clichés many students use to express spiritual things, and so he or she often writes in a more personal and creative way.

A 15-year-old girl with little Christian background wrote how she felt about God in the following poem.

I am the grass in the field, Lord,
And You are the great, blue sky.
Wind tries to blow me down,
Rain hits me hard.
But I am trying to grow higher and higher
Into the blue Heaven, Lord.

• *Students can come to appreciate the different ways people learn to communicate.* Some students are comfortable sharing verbally; others will be more effective sharing on paper. People who communicate with words on paper may be overlooked in discussion or extemporaneous activities. When this happens, they may feel less important than their peers and the class is missing out on their important insights.

In I John 1:1, John talks about the ways people got acquainted with Jesus, the Word of Life. See what happens when each different way is accompanied by methods which we have available today. Each student, no matter which learning style he or she is comfortable with, should have the opportunity to learn about God in the most effective way.

"That which was from the beginning,
which we have *heard*

        lecture
        discussion
        roleplay
        group study

which we have *seen* with our eyes,
which we have looked at

        visual aids
        reading
        video
        viewer of mime, drama

and our hands have *touched*

        art projects
        creative writing

this we proclaim concerning
the Word of Life."

Hearing, seeing, touching: we need to involve our students as completely as possible in the process of Christian education.

• *Students preach to each other in stronger terms through their writing than you would ever be able to preach at them.* The writings of teenagers are strongly moral. Even if the writers make little attempt to meet their own standards, they reveal an awareness of right and wrong.

From a seventh grader:

One kind word
Returned for bad,
One sweet smile
To someone mad:
If these will make
Our Father glad,
Shouldn't we give
Good for bad?

One Sunday after class, an eighth-grade boy with perfect attendance wrote me a note and expressed his tension. "I had to get a new girl friend because of you. Last Sunday I invited the one I did have to come with me. You talked about dating. She decided we should do things the way you said God expected. I had to get another girl. And I'm sure not going to ever invite her to this class!"

When students speak or write of sins, they rarely use generalities. Instead, especially in the younger teen years, they are able to see their own situations honestly. Consider this eighth grader's written testimony: "After I gave my life to God, I thought I would never do bad things again. I was wrong. I lied to you last week, and I had to tell you."

A seventh grader wrote a story about a friend who had stolen a guitar book. The writer wasn't sure what his responsibility should be. The story ended with a question asking the reader what he or she would do. As it turned out, the tale was true. The author needed an answer to his problem, but he didn't think it was fair to his friend, the thief, to ask anyone directly.

● *Note the maturing.* When you work with young teens, you can almost see the maturing that takes place in them as they move from an acceptance of their parents' faith, through a time of questioning, to a personally mature faith. Clues as to where students are in this faith-shaping process can be easily spotted in their writing.

Young teens are often in a faith stage compared by Stephen Jones to membership in a club.[1] Preteens and young teens are affiliating with their faith. They belong to the church, the community of faith that together loves God.

As they mature, they move a step further in spiritual development. They personalize their faith. They are no longer members of the club; they own the club.

Very often the transition from membership to ownership is filled with questioning as teens try to make sense of all the bits and pieces of what they have been taught. This questioning helps students define for themselves what they have previously accepted only because people they respected told them it was truth.

Note the contrasts, the growth in questioning, that has taken place between writers who are in seventh grade and writers in eighth grade. Both age levels were writing letters to a man who was dying of cancer.

Seventh-grade notes:

(1) "God will take care of you. If you pray to Him, He will make you well again."

(2) "When bad things happen to me, I just pray, and God makes life brighter."

Eighth-grade notes:

(1) "I don't know how you feel, but I will try to imagine. I will be praying for you to have strength."

(2) "Sometimes it's hard to understand why God does things, but this must be according to His will."

The 13-year-olds were thinking in questions while the younger students were content to express themselves through platitudes. (This letter-writing project began in class and students finished their letters at home. The results were a vivid demonstration to the teens of how important words on paper can be. Over the course of three months, they sent the man over 150 letters. He had always wanted children and this class adoption project partially filled that need. Before he died he wrote to the children and told them that he had become a Christian, and their letters had played an important role in that decision. No teacher repeating Sunday after Sunday, "Write about your faith; write about your faith," could have made the impact his one letter did.)

Tension and rebellion are often a part of the youth faith development process. It is necessary for young people to move away, at least mentally, from some of the things they have been told all their lives so they can examine for themselves what they are willing to accept.

Debby Boone wrote about this stage in her development, as she moved away from what her parents believed. "I thought it was unfair. I was terribly embarrassed in front of my friends because I wasn't doing the things they were doing. I wasn't allowed to go to the places they always went to or see the movies they saw or wear what they were wearing. And when you get to that age, the peer pressure is so strong, and you want to fit in so badly, you're searching for your identity anyway; so I was trying to be anything but what my family represented."[2]

Note the obvious tension in the writing of a 13-year-old student who is just beginning to own her faith. After a test in Bible class where she'd been asked to list the Ten Commandments, the Japanese girl wrote, "Your Christ is a very hard God. I like His rules, but I will never live like that. I am not made like Him. I am sorry."

A teacher who makes creative writing a regular part of the teaching plan may be able to identify students who need extra time. If a young teen feels safe talking with a teacher, that teacher may receive "Help me!" notes from the student saying something like:

"I would never say this out loud, but I don't think I love God anymore. How can I tell?"

● *Homework.* Don't rule out creative writing homework assignments. They can help students prepare for lessons during the week so they arrive in class ready to participate and learn.

Now, let's not be idealistic. Many students just won't do a writing assignment, no matter how creative the idea is. Others will completely forget about it unless you give them a midweek call or postcard reminder. So never build the entire class around a homework assignment. Be prepared for the possibility that not one student wrote a word.

● *Outreach.* Use creative writing as an outreach idea. Parents who never attend class may read something their teenagers wrote, especially if it has been printed on the back of a church bulletin or in a Sunday school newsletter. Don't rule out sending an excellent piece of writing to your denominational magazine. Even secular newspapers might be interested in some assignments. Suppose a group of adult parents wrote two-sentence answers to how they are planning to raise moral children in today's secular, immoral society. The results could be edited and sent to the paper's religion editor, or even the paper's family or woman's page editors. (If you can possibly place an interview like this one on a page other than the one where religious news appears, do it. You'll get a wider readership, and perhaps pique the interest of people who skip the religion news.)

To recap, you should use creative writing in the Sunday school classroom because it can alert you to the problems and issues that are vital to your students. It can help your students appropriate Christian concepts into their own life-styles. It can give students a vehicle for communicating truth to others.

SHARING ALWAYS FOLLOWS WRITING

When students write in class, always give them an opportunity to share what they have created. Some may protest that what they have written isn't worth sharing, but that protest often means, "Beg me a little more." Sharing, for most students, is part of the learning process. Don't insist, but do encourage students to volunteer. We could all sit at home and write and study alone, but we learn more when we come together and open ourselves—and our written offerings—to others.

Because the sharing is important, you will want to allow time for this to happen. I was teaching a course at a seminary, and with over 20 students in the class it was difficult to allow enough time for "show and tell." One day I short-circuited the process by asking for volunteers to read original parables. When three brave students put up their hands, I announced quickly that they would be the only presenters. The next day one student came to me and said, "Bill wouldn't want me to tell you, but he wrote a great parable that he wanted to read yesterday. He lives off campus, so he doesn't get much opportunity to share with the rest of us. In fact, he was sick yesterday, but he came anyway because he wanted to read what he had written. Do you think we could take time today?" Absolutely!

POETRY

ROYALTY[3]

He was a plain man
and learned no latin

Having left all gold behind
he dealt out peace
to all us wild men
and the weather

He ate fish, bread,
country wine and God's will

Dust sandalled his feet

He wore purple only once
and that was an irony

Poet Luci Shaw said about her art, "Some Christians consider poetry a dispensable garnish for the meat-and-potatoes of religious communication. . . . In life we can either look at a window and see the streaks, the bubbles, and the fingerprints on it, or we can look through it to the three-dimensional world on the other side of the glass. God's full-orbed reality of experience is what's on the other side. And poetry can help carry us into that dimension."

Ottone M. Riccio, in his book *The Intimate Art of Writing Poetry*, says, "To become a fine poet takes a combination of talent, sensitivity, pride, and humility, knowledge and insight, and a fascination with the process of language as a living phenomenon. To become a great one requires also genius and the gift of prophecy."[4]

Many younger teens will not enjoy poetry, although they love limericks and humorous word turns and puns. They are able to deal with concrete, two-dimensional thought patterns. But they are not yet able to understand logic and the deepest aspects of the spiritual or metaphysical realm—that comes with three-dimensional understanding. For the middle and older teen and adult, poetry often helps him or her to understand the mysteries of this maturing, new life.

Students will enjoy playing with poetic forms and do so more successfully if they have been exposed to excellence. They need to read and hear excellent poems read.

When you are picking poems to read to your students:

● *Look for poems that share true emotion*, poems that have blood in their veins.

● *Don't rule out poems that aren't pretty.* Poet Chad Walsh sometimes has his students visit the local garbage dump and then write a poem about it. We need to get over the idea that poems are only about love and death and flowers and birds.

● *Look for poems that are fresh.* Consider the poem that began this section, "Royalty." Shaw captures us in her God poem without a single cliché or extravagant emotion.

● *Choose poems that teach* without their lessons sticking out in an ungainly fashion. Allow your students to do some of their own thinking about a poem, and its meaning will have lasting value to them.

● *Check the content against the age-level experiences and vocabulary of your students.* No matter how great the poem is and how closely it pulls together the aim of your lesson, if no one understands it, don't use it. Another caution. Read the poem aloud before you use it in class. Many poems that are easy to grasp on paper are difficult to understand when they are read aloud.

Emily Dickinson (1830-1886) wrote "I'm Nobody!", an excellent discussion tool for young teens who are working on their identity formation. Perhaps it could be a jumping-off point for them, a model from which they could write their own poems about their self feelings. However, for it to be effective, a teacher would need to make certain students understood the words *banish* and *bog*. The impact of the poem depends on knowing these words.

I'm nobody!
Who are you?
Are you nobody too?
Then there is a pair of us
—Don't tell!
They'd banish us, you know.

How dreary to be somebody!
How public like a frog
To tell your name the livelong day
To an admiring bog!

Most of the writing our students call poems will not in any honest sense be poetry. Poets who are truly poets are few. Poet Luci Shaw compares the writing of a poem to a birthing. She often goes through 40 to 50 drafts before she is satisfied. In class a teacher's goal is to give students a few minutes to express themselves around a pattern or a form. The form makes writing easier. It doesn't make a poem, but it lays the groundwork for students who have special talent in this area. Remember the goal—not to write poetry, but to give people an opportunity to share their ideas and feelings within a structured format.

Here's a simple form to play with: take your phone number. Write a poem to God thanking Him for something He has done for you between this Sunday and last. Each line must have the same number of words as indicated by the number in the same position in your phone number. Any O's should be single words of praise. The results are fun, a valuable teaching exercise for people who need a structure or unique idea to guide their words.

But just for poetic comparison, consider the real poem, "Cream," in which a poet expresses her feelings about the gift God gave her.

CREAM[5]

From the white depths
The poem's richness rises,
Clotting in thickened skins
Across my soul.

I rise and skim
The spirit-filled surprises
And fill with cream
The paper's empty bowl.

BIBLICAL FORMS

One of the most interesting ways to get students involved in poetic forms is to expose them to simple parallelism and acrostics, both important aspects of Hebrew poetry and especially Old Testament poetry. These patterns allow students to confirm and share what they have learned.

Hebrew poetry is perfect for class use with nonwriters.

First, it is built around a thought pattern rather than a rhyme or meter.

270

The authors can vary their line length—from short to long—and they don't have to worry about whether the words rhyme, a primary part of most students' definition of poetry.

Second, Hebrew language is filled with color and vitality. The verb, the action word, is very important. Metaphor and repetition are plentiful. Hebrew writers usually rejected abstract philosophical and theological pictures in favor of the more concrete and pictorial ones. Young people's writing, when they are not trying to make the sentences sound Christian, is often filled with colorful language and a delightful sense of self and God.

Third, parallelism is an essential feature of Hebrew poetry. There is a relationship between two or more lines in each verse. The statement that has been made in the first line may be repeated in slightly different words or contrasted in the second line.

Synonymous Parallelism

Even students who have done little creative writing will find developing synonymous parallelism a successful experience. The first line states a complete fact, and the second line expresses the same thought through the use of synonyms.

Study synonymous parallelism in Isaiah 53:6
Line 1—We all, like sheep, have gone astray,
Line 2 (note the synonyms repeat the message of line 1)—Each
of us has turned to his own way . . . .
Psalm 5:1 is another good example:
Line 1—Give ear to my words, O Lord,
Line 2—Consider my sighing.
If you gave your students the line, "I am ashamed before God when I sin," they might write synonymous lines like these:
"I bow my head before my Lord when I do evil in His sight."
"I shrink in sorrow before Christ because I failed Him."
Supply your students with first lines like these, and ask them to write synonymous lines:
1. "I will always love my God."
2. "It is important for me to do God's will."
3. "I'm a member of the family of God."

Antithetic Parallelism

In antithetic parallelism, the thought is made clear through contrast. Actually these are easier to construct than synonymous lines.
Consider Romans 6:23:
Line 1—For the wages of sin is death,

Line 2 (says exactly the opposite)—But the gift of God is eternal life. . . .

Proverbs 10:1:

Line 1—A wise son brings joy to his father,

Line 2—But a foolish son grief to his mother.

Psalm 30:5 demonstrates double antithetic parallelism:

Line 1—For his anger lasts only a moment,

Line 2—But his favor lasts a lifetime;

Line 1—Weeping may remain for a night,

Line 2—But rejoicing comes in the morning.

Have your students practice writing antithetic lines for the following sentences:

1. "When I know that I am in fellowship with God, I am happy."
2. "The person who doesn't follow God's way is in for big trouble."
3. "When Christians gossip, they ruin their testimonies."

Also encourage your students to write original antithetic parallelisms.

Emblematic Parallelism

(This form should not be used with young teens, because many of them are still struggling with symbolic language.) In this form the idea of the first or the second line is reproduced in the alternate line in symbolic terms.

Proverbs 26:21:

Line 1 (symbolic language)—As charcoal to embers and as wood to fire,

Line 2 (the point is driven home)—So is a quarrelsome man for kindling strife.

This form takes more time than the first two, and could perhaps be used as a homework assignment. The symbol in the first line should explain the truth or statement in the second.

1. Use a symbol to describe something about the Christian life. One student wrote:

Line 1—A train on its track will not crash,

Line 2—And Christians who follow Christ will safely move through life.

2. Use a symbol to say something about love.
3. Use a symbol to say something about your identity.

Synthetic Parallelism

In this form, the second and later lines enlarge or complete the thought in the first line.

Psalm 2:6:

Line 1—I have installed my King

Line 2 (the first line's thought is completed)—On Zion, my holy hill.

Psalm 19:7 is a double synthetic parallelism:

Line 1—The law of the Lord is perfect,

Line 2—Reviving the soul.

Line 1—The statutes of the Lord are trustworthy,

Line 2—Making wise the simple.

Try to complete the following synthetic parallelism by making a statement in one line and using the second line to complete or enlarge it.

1.   Start with a statement about the Church universal.

2.   Start with an idea about adult faith development.

3.   Start with advice to your peers.

ACROSTIC POEMS

In an acrostic, the words are arranged in a certain order so that specific letters in each line (usually the first or the last) form a pattern or spell a word or motto. A popular Old Testament poetic form, the acrostic was used by the psalmist.

Students can build acrostics by using the alphabet.

Single word example:

A—Always
B—Believe
C—Christ

Phrase example:

A—All my life I will praise You, Lord,
B—Because You have shown Your love to me,
C—Caring for me when I least deserve it.

Students can also identify the key word in a lesson or Scripture passage and build an acrostic around that word.

J—Jesus, You are always near;
O—Oh, how great to know
Y—You will never fail me.

The acrostic is an excellent tool to use with adults (who are perhaps ill at ease with putting their ideas in writing) because it gives them a structure to follow. Don't make too big a project out of the assignment. If they can't think of a word, phrase, or sentence to follow a letter, they should simply go on to the next line. Explain that students will be asked to share only a line rather than their entire acrostics. This is less threatening, and students will be willing to volunteer the single line they think is their best.

In large classes you will have a number of people who want to share each line they have written. Simply call out the letter and let all who wish to share do so. Then move on to the next letter. For example, with the word JOY, five students might share what they have written for J; when there is a pause, move on to O.

IDEAS FOR USING ACROSTICS IN CLASS

1. After the Bible study, divide the class into small Poem Power groups. Ask each group to develop an original acrostic built around the theme of the lesson: e.g., PRAYER, LOVE, SALVATION, PRAISE. Then have each group read its poem to the rest of the class.

This idea can be adapted for use with students who have reading or writing deficiencies. Write the acrostic word or phrase vertically on the chalkboard. Have students suggest phrases to follow each letter, and you write them on the board. The finished poem can be just as meaningful to students as ones they write completely by themselves.

2. Use an acrostic at the beginning of a lesson and at the end to provide a study in contrast. For example, if the lesson is on Christ's solution for sin, the class could begin by writing acrostics using and defining the words SIN or EVIL. The period could end with the students expressing thanksgiving to God for His solution by writing acrostics from the words SALVATION or GOD.

Or the contrast could be obtained by using the same word. For example, at the beginning of an Easter lesson, students could write acrostics explaining what that holiday means to non-Christians:

E—Each of us buys something new to wear.
A—All the children get candy-filled baskets.
S—Sing about the Easter bunny.
(Etc.)

After studying the Christian's reason for celebrating Easter, students could write what it means to them:

E—Every time I think of Christ's resurrection
A—And remember He was raised for me, I am thrilled!
S—Surely I participate in true Easter, the Resurrection.
(Etc.)

3. As a homework assignment for teens, ask students to write an acrostic around the Bible story they will be studying the following week. This is a unique way to get students to review the story. When they get to class, they can quickly share their acrostics and be ready to study the lesson on a deeper-than-story level.

In the story of Samuel and Eli, the acrostic could be built from the name SAMUEL.

> *S*—Softly, in the middle of the night, the Lord delivered His message to a boy,
> *A*—And Samuel, because he trusted God, rose to take the message to Eli.
> *M*—Much sadness must have filled Eli's heart.
> (Etc.)

4. Guide students in developing an outreach acrostic. This poem should be written in class for a specific outreach. If students are interested in using an acrostic to help them witness, they might write God's plan of salvation using the motto, "God Is Love." Consider reproducing copies of the poem for each student. Some may want to promise God that they will share their poem and their testimony with at least one non-Christian in the coming week.

Or, an adult class might plan an acrostic around the sentence, "We Will Save You a Seat," and print it in the church bulletin as an invitation to all adults who don't attend Sunday school.

These four ideas started with the basic acrostic. As you read other suggestions for student writing projects, try to think of at least two creative ways you could use each of them in your class.

WRITING PRAYERS

Many students are hesitant about talking aloud to God, yet they want to participate in group prayer. When they write their prayers, they have time to organize their thoughts. Gone is the worry about what words they will speak next. They are free to concentrate on what they are saying to God.

The following poem and prayer were candid, honest thoughts written and read to God by seventh graders following a lesson on spiritual battles.

POEM:
> I'm in the Army
> The Lord is my Captain
> We went to war with Satan.
> My Captain charged while I napped.
> The Lord came back all beaten and worn.
> He stopped in front of me and said,
> > "You lost."

PRAYER:

> Lord, I just lost my fight.
> I found that I didn't really want to win.
> Help me, Lord.
> My battle is homework.
> I hate it, and I'm so lazy.
> I really don't want to work.
> Help me, Lord, to be on the job.
> Next time make me sit down.
> Don't let me goof around.

Most lessons call for a response from students, and often an immediate and valuable way for them to respond is by writing prayers to God.

When you structure written prayer into your lessons, follow these guidelines:

1. *Let students know they will not be asked to share their prayers aloud unless they wish to do so.*

2. *Suggest they write their prayers using the same language they use when they talk.*

3. *Challenge them to pray honestly.* Sometimes teachers encourage dishonesty by assuming everyone in the class is ready to write a prayer to God. Most students will pretend to write something even if they do not really believe, simply to avoid being conspicuous. So always supply an alternate writing activity. A teacher could ask students to write thank-You notes to God following a lesson on thanksgiving. At the same time the teacher might suggest that those who don't honestly feel thankful and those who don't yet have a prayer relationship with God write the ending to the sentence, "The most important thing I learned from today's lesson is . . . ."

4. *Encourage students to pray as specifically as possible.* For example, instead of praying that the Lord bless all the missionaries, a student might bring to Him a request from missionary Ed who needs a new mule for his work in central Mexico.

Notice how specific the seventh-grade writer was in the following prayer:

> Dear Lord,
> I have this problem.
> I can't control my temper.
> Yesterday in the basketball game,
> I had a technical call on me.
> I told the ref off.
> Help me, dear Lord. Help me at practice tomorrow.

---

5. Develop ways in which students' written prayers can continue to be part of their learning experience after they have shared them with God. They might take their prayers home and read them several times during the week. They might exchange prayers with a friend and promise to pray for each other every day this week. The group could begin prayer notebooks in which they record prayer requests and prayer answers.

As your students are writing prayers, you may want to suggest they use the prayer subjects used in the Psalms. No universally accepted classification of the Psalms exists; however, the following list from *The New Bible Dictionary* (InterVarsity Press) will get your students started:

- Prayers petitioning God for blessing and protection.
- Praise for specific examples of God's mercy, God's majesty as revealed in creation, worship, and adoration.
- Pleas for divine intervention or deliverance in sickness, calamity, danger.
- Confessions of faith that God is Lord, Creator, King of the nations, Judge, moral Ruler of the universe.
- Penitence for sin.
- Intercession for the king, their own people, other nations.
- Prayer for judgment on the enemies of God's people.
- Spiritual and religious instruction.
- Psalms that deal with God's providences that are hard to understand and questions about future life.
- Extolling of God's Word.

Psalms deal with the personal experiences of the writer, but they also deal with the collective experience of the group. Try writing a class psalm prayer. Perhaps students could praise the Lord for His hand in the lives of this small part of the church family.

Usually you will encourage your students to write simple prayers to God, but occasionally you may want to involve students in one of the following more involved prayer experiences:

1. Suggest students write acrostic prayers or share their thoughts with God through a mixture of parallelisms. This type of prayer would be best developed by students at home as part of their daily devotions.

2. Prayer promises are often an effective life response. For example, following a lesson on living the Christlike life, a teacher could ask students to write prayers to God asking Him to help them change a problem area that is hindering spiritual growth. Students who wish to participate should seal their secret prayer requests in an envelope and put their names on the outside. Then they should make a pact with God to continue to pray and work on the problem area for one month. The teacher would then collect the envelopes. At the end of a month, the unopened envelopes should be

returned to students. The prayer would serve as a reminder of their promises and as a help in evaluating how much they have grown.

3. Prayer can be used in an object lesson. After an adult class had studied God's forgiveness, the teacher gave students an opportunity to write private prayers confessing specific sins to God and asking His forgiveness. Then the teacher said, "If you honestly believe Christ has forgiven your sins, tear your confession into little pieces and throw it away." The prayer served as both a response to God and an object lesson to each student on God's complete forgiveness.

PARAPHRASES

"How do you think David would have written the Twenty-Third Psalm if he had lived in your apartment?" The inner-city teacher was asking students to paraphrase a Scriptural passage, not only into contemporary language, but also into a contemporary setting.

Students, no matter where they live, will show by what they write just how much they understand a particular passage and its principles.

> The Lord walks guard beside me; I won't panic.
> He keeps me cool like I was under a streetlight.
> He leads me down safe alleys.
> He turns up the heat and puts glass in the window.
> He don't let me do nothing to shame Him.
> The Sharks got knives, my friends got needles, but
>   I'm clean.
> I got Jesus with me. He never cuts out.
> My enemies see me full without busting no heads or
>   rolling no dice or stealing no wheels, and I tell them
>   Jesus done it. I got joy.
> The joy will just keep on coming the rest of my days,
>   and I got me a pad with Jesus forever.

Consider a twist, perhaps after students have grasped antithetic parallelism. The assignment would be to take a portion of Scripture and write it the way modern Christians or the secular world is living it. What students write will indicate how well they understand the positive message of the passage.

The author of the following contemporary Twenty-Third Psalm is not known, but the antithetic message is all too apparent.

> The TV is my shepherd,
> My spiritual growth shall want.

278

It maketh me to sit down and do nothing for His name's
    sake,
Because it requireth all my spare time.
It keepeth me from doing my duty as a Christian,
Because It presenteth so many good shows that I
    must see.

It restoreth my knowledge of the things of the world
And keepeth me from the study of God's Word.
It leadeth me in the paths of apathy
And doing nothing in the Kingdom of God.

Yea, though I live to be a hundred,
I shall keep on viewing my TV,
for it is my closest companion.
Its sound and picture, they comfort me.

It presenteth entertainment before me,
And keepeth me from doing important things with my
    family.
It filleth my head with ideas,
Which differ from those set forth in the Word of God.

Surely, no good thing will come of my life,
Because my TV leaveth so little time to do the will of
    God.
Thus I will dwell in the house of idleness . . .
And sloth forever.

Because most students will need at least 15 minutes to prepare their contemporary versions, you may want to make this a homework assignment the week before the familiar passage will be studied in class. Caution the students to thoroughly study the Bible passage before they begin writing so they will be sure to capture the feeling and the message the author intended—or the effective reverse.

Allow enough time the Sunday the assignment is due for all students to share what they have written.

LETTER WRITING

One of the simplest and least used forms of writing in the Sunday school is the letter. Of course, there is often not enough time to complete the letter in class, but if students begin a project they consider worthwhile, they will usually complete it on their own.

Consider a project in which your students would write letters to:

- Missionaries or children of missionaries, especially those who are away from their families, attending boarding schools.
- People in homes for senior citizens.
- Shut-ins.
- Servicemen and women and those at school or away from home for the first time.
- People who don't often get thanked for the work they do in the church (organist, custodian, Sunday school superintendent).
- People who have just lost someone they love.

It is sometimes helpful to suggest several things students might want to include in their letters. Of course, the suggestions will vary with the different people who will be receiving the letter.

- Tell a little about your family.
- Share something fun you did this week.
- Tell why you are writing this letter.
- Share what Christ means to you and one way He interacted with your life this week.

Remind all students that they are writing a real person who should read their letter and get to know another real person better. The more facts and paragraph stories writers can include in their letters, the more alive the correspondence becomes. The fewer facts and personal touches, the more ineffective communication is.

"There was a lady who always sent me the complete outline of her pastor's sermon," said one single missionary. "She paid the postage week after week. Never once did she tell me who was having babies or who was dating whom or what new buildings were being considered for our area. I wasn't real to her and she wasn't real to me. I know I should have been grateful, but when I'm honest, I know I wish she hadn't bothered. Week after week I was reminded of all the things I wanted to know from back home. She added tremendously to the adjustment problems I was having my first two years overseas."

The following letter was written by a junior high student as part of a class project:

Dear Mr. Myers,

I don't write many letters because my handwriting isn't so hot. We are having a class party this evening. We're going to put cookies into little bags for children in the hospital. We are also going to put in stories telling of Jesus' love for them.

My parents are Christians, so people expected me to be one, too. But I knew I wasn't a Christian just because people believed I was. I thought hard about belonging to Christ. I really am happy that I finally followed Him. I know I will have lots of troubles, but there is always Someone who can help me now.   Jan

---

A WORD ABOUT PROJECTS

Ideas like letter writing are really projects that demand time and out-of-class participation by students. Projects are important parts of our teaching and a wise teacher is always looking for the one that is just perfect for his or her class. In projects teens and adults actually give part of themselves; these projects may be the most significant things students remember when they look back on what they gained from your years of teaching.

Consider this comment on projects from Jewish writer, Helen Epstein. The personal illustration she gives was from her elementary years, but the impact of projects does not lessen as we grow older.

The Hills of Judea were unlike any mountains I had ever seen. Bent and broken with age, their sinews swelled out one from the other like the muscles of an old man's back. They seemed not only indestructible but also infinitely fertile, able to nourish new growth even after centuries of erosion. Whole new forests had been planted in the gray, powdery ground and those woods of young trees touched off in me memories of bringing dimes to Sunday school and receiving a stamp imprinted with a leaf for each dime. We had a large poster of a tree in our classroom—that was one of the few things I remembered of those Sunday mornings—and, one by one, we children would lick our stamps and stick them on the empty branches until the tree was green and lush with leaves. Our dimes went to plant a tree in Israel, we were told then, and when I saw the forest rising out of the mountainsides, it was as if I saw my own family tree magically restored and growing.[6]

In a study ordered by the National Board of Junior Acheivement (1980), researchers found that young people of the '80's are suffering from a lack of an exciting frontier. This lack, said the study, is the number one issue of youth for this decade. The study recommended that Junior Achievement carve out a larger mission for itself by putting forth the world of work as the next frontier.

What an exciting opportunity for the church to increase the concept of work to include service projects, significant service to others that cannot be done without commitment, time, effort, and the help of the Holy Spirit.

What projects would work in your class?

- Letter writing.
- Fund raising—only the money earned by students specifically for this project should be accepted.
- Muscle work for people in the church and community who are unable to do house and apartment tasks for themselves and are unable to pay for the service.
- Volunteer work with home missions and overseas groups.

Of course, the best projects are those that students come up with on their own.

FINISH THE STORY

Introduce creative story writing to your class by setting up "what if" situations for students to complete. Use some of the ideas suggested here or develop your own. Allow about ten minutes of class time for this writing activity.

1. What if the little girl Christ raised from the dead had kept a diary? Write what you think her entry might have been on the day after He healed her.

2. What if you had been one of the people visiting Jerusalem on the day of Christ's crucifixion? You had never heard of Jesus before, but out of curiosity you followed Him to Calvary and watched Him die. Write a letter to your friends back home telling them what you saw and how you felt about the experience.

3. What if you were a Roman newspaper reporter who had been given an opportunity to interview Paul during his house arrest in Rome? Write the first few paragraphs of that story. Include what you learned about him and how you felt about what he said.

Often students can finish a story as a homework assignment. Homework story starters can be more involved than "what if" situations done in class. It is ideal if each student can have a copy of the story starter to take home.

The following example would make an excellent homework assignment for students to bring to class Easter Sunday morning.

ON GUARD

What if you were one of the Roman guards assigned to guard Jesus' tomb? While you were on duty, there was an earthquake. Someone dressed in white clothing—with an appearance like lightning—rolled the stone away from the tomb's door. The Roman seal was broken! You were so afraid that you and the other guards became like dead men.

Later the high priest paid you money and said, "You will tell people His disciples came while you were sleeping. They stole the body."

You were frightened and did what you were told. But years have passed, and now you are faced with another decision concerning Jesus. *Julius paced the floor of the barracks.*

"Settle down," his friend Marcus advised. "What are your new orders? How could they possibly upset you this much?"

"I've been ordered to round up Christians because they are enemies of the state."

"And good lion food," Marcus laughed. "That's not so bad. You've had worse assignments than this. Weren't you a guard over their Leader's tomb?"

"I wish I'd never heard of Jesus," Julius said. "Marcus, I'm going to tell you a story that could make lion food out of me. Then I'm going to ask you what you would do about these orders."

He turned to his friend and said, ". . .

FINISH THIS STARTER

BIBLE REVIEW NEWSPAPER

After your young teen students have completed a large unit of study, perhaps on the life of Christ or the Patriarchs, plan a Bible newspaper competition to help them review.

Divide the class into two or more newspaper staffs. Explain that each staff will be competing against the others to give the most complete and interesting newspaper coverage of events they have just studied.

One teacher did this as an interest-center activity. The newspapers contained Biblical jokes (junior high style), recipes for fig, date, and camel casserole, and excellent articles on the Biblical events in Abraham's life. The young people enjoyed adding their personalities to the assignment.

OTHER WRITING PROJECTS TO TRY

Adjust these quick writing assignments to your own situation:

1. *Take an adage, cliché, or poem and ask students to make the same statement in an original way.* For example: "Remember the story about the two bricklayers who were asked what they were doing? One said he was making a wall, and the other said he was building a cathedral." Change the imagery, but keep the meaning. A student might write: "Remember the story about the two coaches who were asked what they were doing? One said, 'I call the shots,' and the other said, 'I model Christ before teenagers.' "

2. *Boxed love.* Place a box in front of each student. Then give every student the same number of slips of paper as there are students in the class. Ask everyone to write a "You are special because . . ." sentence for each other person in the class and put the slip in that person's box. Students take home their boxes and read only one sentence a day. (This idea works best with older teens and adults who will be aware of the hurt an unthinking remark could bring.)

3. *Exchange prayers.* Each student writes and then exchanges an important prayer request with another person. The two promise each other that every day for the next week they will remember to pray for their exchange requests.

4. *Graffiti Wall.* Cover one wall or section of a wall with newsprint and invite students to write their comments about a specific topic (God's love, God's presence, being a Christian, etc.) on it. Encourage them to record original slogans, Bible verses, and relevant thoughts. A graffiti wall makes an excellent pre- and postclass activity. The idea works with teens, but don't rule it out for adults. Once they get used to the idea, many adult students will enjoy this.

5. *Sharing Box.* Place a box in the classroom and invite students to put into it questions, problems, and comments they would like to share with you. These may be signed or unsigned.

6. *Key verse.* Give students time to copy a key verse from the lesson onto a 3 x 5-inch card. Suggest they place the card where they will see it every day and be reminded of the truth it contains.

7. *Proverbs and mottoes.* Have students restate the lessons they have learned in the form of proverbs or mottoes. For example, after a lesson on Christian conduct, a student might write: "God specializes in helping me pass life's tests" (proverb), or "My Christian Goal—Zero Defects!" (motto).

8. *Spiritual geography.* Post a large map of the world, country, or area where you live, and supply students with little paper flags and straight pins. Ask them to write their names on their flags and pin them on the map at the places where important events in their spiritual lives took place. Give opportunity for students to share what happened at certain "flags." This is a great way for mobile adult classes to get acquainted with each other.

9. *Humorous couplets and limericks.* Suggest students write humorous rhyming couplets or limericks to emphasize an important point in the lesson. For example:

Wearing clothes all squeaky and new
Doesn't make God impressed with you.
      Or,
A fine Christian man once said, "Hey,
Our country's going the wrong way.
Of course, I don't vote!"
He cleared his deep throat,
"Instead I sit home and pray."

---

10. *Chain reaction story.* Give each student a piece of paper and ask him or her to write an ending to the sentence you will give. Students should then fold their answers back so no one else can see them and pass their papers to the person on their right. This person will finish the second sentence you give, fold the answer under and pass the paper to the next person. The process continues until the story is finished. Then students unfold their stories and read them to the class.

For example, if the lesson is on the problems of living for Christ in a secular school situation, a chain reaction story might be built around finishing the following sentences:

- "Joel became a Christian because . . ."
- "The biggest problem he will face in his Christian life in high school will be _____, because . . ."
- "One way Joel can get help with problems in his Christian life is by . . ."
- "Joel asks you what you think the secret to a successful Christian life is, and you say . . ."

1. Stephen D. Jones, *Faith Shaping: Nurturing the Faith Journey of Youth* (Valley Forge: Judson Press, 1980).

2. Debby Boone, *Debby Boone—So Far* (Nashville, Tenn.: Thomas Nelson Publishers, 1981).

3. Luci Shaw, "Royalty," reprinted from *Listen to the Green* by Luci Shaw by permission of Harold Shaw Publishers. Copyright © 1971 by Luci Shaw.

4. Ottone M. Riccio, *The Intimate Art of Writing Poetry* (Englewood Cliffs, N.J.: Prentice-Hall Publishers, 1980).

5. Elizabeth Rooney, "Cream," from the chapter, "Elizabeth Rooney," by Luci Shaw, in *Bright Legacy*, ed. Ann Spangler (Ann Arbor, Mich.: Servant Books, 1983), p. 102. Rooney explains the arrival of her poems: "Mine seem to come like butterflies, and I try to net them and get them on paper without knocking too many bright bits of color off their wings. My problem is to know how to improve them without destroying them. . . . I do hope they can open to me more friendships . . . and chances to tell people about the Lord to Whose love we all respond" (p. 105). "Cream" was used by permission of the author.

6. Helen Epstein, *Children of the Holocaust* (New York: Bantam Books, 1980), pp. 233, 234.

CHAPTER 12

Joyful Noises

Most historians feel reasonably comfortable in drawing on literature, visual arts, and architecture to supplement their work, but usually shy away from using music. Thus an important dimension of human expression and creativity is ignored.

—John W. Barker

"For the sake of mission, at least some Christians are obligated to learn the musical language of the youth culture until it becomes their natural expressive medium. The younger generation is already producing this kind of art as an organic product of its Christian experience. Today, at the same time that secular popular musicians are repeating themselves or searching aimlessly for new modes of expression which move beyond the high-water mark of the last decade, Christian musicians are breaking new ground."[1] This challenge comes from Richard F. Lovelace. Music plays a part in our worship experience, and it should also be playing a positive part in our teaching process.

Picture this situation. Your adult students enter, and you are playing Christian artist Tom Howard's song, "We All Mean Very Well."[2]

We all mean very well
Sometimes it's hard to tell
We mean to live as brothers
To love and help each other
But the vision can be lost from time to time.

The church is in the middle of making an important decision—whether or not to build a new sanctuary. Opinions have been very strongly expressed. How might you use this song to help adults deal with their feelings? Here are some suggestions:

- Discuss what you as a church have to learn from this song.
- Instruct your students to write a second verse sharing what would happen in your church family if you never get beyond the phrase: "We all mean very well."
- Encourage your students to write a vision for your church by using synonymous parallelism.
- Use mime to symbolically show the problem suggested by this song and the solution as students envision it.
- Set up some roleplay situations which allow you to practice how to live as loving brothers and sisters during this decision-making time.

Music is a language. It's learned, and many adults and most teenagers today "speak" it without an accent. But there may be a problem. Over 70 percent of the human ear develops between the ages of three to seven. The sounds the ears hear in those early years are the native sounds that will not be erased by subsequent experiences. This means that some teachers, particularly in youth classes, do not speak the same musical language as their students. As we adults use music as a teaching tool, we must be aware of our prejudices and examine them carefully, if we do not wish to turn off our students to the possibility of developing their talents for use by God.

WRITE A SONG

"I would use more group singing as part of my class hour," one teacher said, "but I can never find songs that are perfectly suited to the lesson." Throw the problem to the class, and ask them to come up with original words to familiar melodies. Start with a simple melody. "Faith of Our Fathers" is good, or you could use a contemporary tune, if everyone in the class knows it.

Talk about the content that you want to put into the song. Perhaps the lesson is on accepting people who are different from ourselves. Perhaps

288

it's on developing our individual creativity. You know of no songs that really fit those aims.

The class can either work together to write the song or work in small groups to produce many stanzas. The process is simple. Students softly hum the song one line at a time. They brainstorm possible sentences and phrases that would fit the musical score and finally pick the ones which say best what they want their song to communicate. If students really enjoy a song they have created, they might want to perfect it and sing it to the rest of the Sunday school or congregation.

The following words were written to the melody of "Faith of Our Fathers" to praise God for our creativity:

I am creative
I have no doubt
Since I'm your child
And You're guiding me.
I will reflect You,
Creator, I know,
As I hone skills
You want me to grow.
I see new patterns,
New ways to serve
Right brain and left—
My praises flow.

No, it's not poetically excellent, but it does speak to the issue of the lesson. Students may want to use their song as the hymn of the month and sing it each Sunday. If they write original words to one song a month, they could compile their songs into a class hymnal at the end of the year. (Caution: if your class uses music that is copyrighted, and the class wishes to reproduce its songs, you must get written permission from the company that holds the copyright.)

CHORAL READING: WHEN YOU REALLY CAN'T SING, TALK

"Even today as one walks through some of the ultra-religious sections of Jerusalem, which are in many ways attempts to perpetuate traditional Eastern European life, one hears a chorus of voices reciting and studying the holy texts together," says Barry Chazen, of the Hebrew University of Jerusalem. "To some ears it is noise; to others it is a symphony of a community."[3]

Choral reading for anyone, singer or not, is a wonderful way to share praise with each other as a class and with the entire congregation as part of the corporate worship service. In a choral reading people talk, rather than sing. They have most of the options a singing choir has. There can be duts, solos, total choir. Each of the aspects of a singing choir, as outlined by Connie Fortunato in *Music Is for Children,* is true of the speaking choir:

> Music is language, too. It is capable of communicating substance as well as feeling, atmosphere, and emotion. And music is made up of many intricate parts. . . . There is always a tone or melody. . . .
>
> Harmony provides the supporting structure for that tune. It adds the dimension of depth. And rhythm is the heartbeat or pulse, recurring with such precision that before long you're tapping your foot or wiggling your finger in time to the music.
>
> Timbre is the personality of sound. It distinguishes the sound of a trumpet from the sound of a violin or piano. Finally there is the aspect of pitch. Although this involves the vibrations of sound per second we all recognize poor pitch when we hear a sour note.
>
> The amazing thing about music is that an intellectual understanding of each of these parts—or any of them—is not needed to enjoy it.[4]

SCRIPTURAL CHORAL READING

Guide your students in writing and presenting an original choral reading developed from Scripture.

First, choose a passage which deals with the lesson topic. Usually limit the readings completed in class to only a few verses. You will need a chalkboard or large sheet of paper and a student scribe to write what the group suggests.

Make sure each student has a copy of the passage. Ask each one to read it silently three times. On the first reading, the student should try to grasp the general content. On the second reading, he or she should decide which lines are most important. If possible, the student should find the key phrase. On the final reading, the student tries to feel the emotion the writer must have felt—for example, sorrow, joy, boldness, fear.

Now students are ready to study the passage. You can use any Bible study method. Many people who participate in choral readings, and especially Scriptural choral readings, skip this step. It is not necessary to the presentation. It is possible to do a wonderful choral reading based on Psalm 98 without ever studying the content. But the goal in using a Scriptural choral reading in class is twofold:

- First, you want your students to study God's Word for themselves.
- Second, you want to give students a vehicle for sharing what they have learned with others.

Neither of these goals can honestly be met if students don't become personally involved in the passage.

Consider Psalm 98, the inspiration for the hymn "Joy to the World" and a powerful statement about the relationship between music and worship. This psalm may convince us that if we are not using music in our Christian education programs, we are ignoring a vehicle for worship which God has given us. Throughout the Bible, there is a relationship between music and prayer and praise. Israel was a nation of musicians. Few family feasts were without music. Music was part of every ceremony, every rite. God was praised with the harp, with trumpets, and with the braying horn. We don't know much about the actual sound of Jewish music, but we do know that the voice, usually in unison, was important. The music wasn't written, so we can assume that there was room for improvising.

In Psalm 98, a teacher might begin guiding the development of a choral reading by asking questions like these:
- "What musical instruments best express your praise of who our Lord is?"
- "Imagine you are hearing the kind of music described in the psalm. Use a simile to share how it would make you feel. 'It makes me feel like . . .' "
- "Someone asks you, 'What is the place of music in worship?' Use Psalm 98 to answer."

After students have read and discussed their surface findings about the psalm, you might want them to participate in a simple inductive Bible study. They should record all the things they know about the Lord based on this passage. They should not only look for things that are obvious ("The Lord is righteous") but they should also look for things that can be induced from the passage.

Students should limit themselves to this Scripture. It's not part of this Bible study method, for example, to look at David's appointment of the Levites to minister with harps and lyres, cymbals and trumpets in I Chronicles 16:4-6. This limitation will help students dig deeper.

Most of the time on the inductive study should be spent looking for attributes of God. But toward the end of the study time, students should come up with original titles for the psalm that would differentiate this passage from all others in Scripture. Finally, students should spend a few minutes talking about what the passage means to them today.

Only after students have studied the passage is it time to begin working on a choral reading.

Explain that in a Scriptural choral reading, students cannot change the words of Scripture, but they can vary the word order and repeat phrases for emphasis.

Give students an opportunity to decide what key phrase, if any, they will use and with which phrase in the Scripture they will begin. For example, "Make a joyful noise" might be an excellent key phrase with which to begin and to repeat several times throughout the reading, even though it only appears once in the psalm the students are scripting.

Now the scribe is ready to begin.

As different members suggest how the phrases and sentences should be arranged in their reading, the scribe records their suggestions on the chalkboard. He or she should leave a large left-hand margin and double-space between each section of copy.

(If time is limited, you may want to write a choral reading for your students ahead of time or select a committee to do it. Then reproduce a copy of the reading for each student. As on the chalkboard, double-space and allow wide left-hand margins. Even if the total class doesn't become involved in writing the choral reading, have them read the passage three times and study it, as previously explained.)

After the body has been written, students are ready to assign parts. Explain to them that vocal combinations used in singing groups are also possible in choral reading. They should let the text help them decide what combinations would be best. If the reading is on the majesty of God, large groups, strong male voices, or deliberate female voices might be emphasized. If the passage is on sorrow, solo voices or duets may better capture the mood.

Finally, students should underline the words they wish spoken with special emphasis. They should mark the volume and, when necessary, the expression they feel would most effectively convey the message.

For example, if a class did a Scriptural choral reading on John 3:16, 17, it might choose "So loved" as the key phrase and develop a reading something like this one.

JOHN 3:16,17

FEMALE SOLO:	(softly) So loved.
FEMALE DUET:	(gathering strength) So loved.
ALL:	For God so loved the world, that he gave his only begotten Son,
MALE SOLO:	That whosoever believeth in him should not perish, but have everlasting life.
MALE SOLO:	So loved?
FEMALE SOLO:	Everlasting life?
MALE SOLO:	(emphatically) So loved.
FEMALE SOLO:	(emphatically) Everlasting life.
MALE SOLO:	(joyfully) So loved.

MALE AND FEMALE:	*(joyfully)* So loved! Everlasting life!
ALL:	For God sent not his Son into the world to condemn the world;
DUET:	*(joyfully)* But that the world through him might be saved.
ALL:	*(loud)* For God so loved.
ALL MALE:	*(slightly softer)* So loved the world.
FEMALE DUET:	*(fading)* So loved.
FEMALE DUET:	*(whisper)* So loved.

REVIEW

Before you try to develop a choral reading with your class, go through the whole process by yourself:

1. Study Scripture (use Psalm 98)
2. Consider how you might write the basic choral reading (or if this is your first time, use the one provided here).
3. Mark sections for emphasis. Assign parts in a way that you think would most effectively communicate the message.
4. Practice with your students. Make adjustments.
5. Present your choral reading to a group outside your class setting. Evaluate their response to hearing Scripture in this form.

Using these steps, now work through Psalm 98 (KJV):

(Assign parts here.)   **PSALM 98**

_____ Oh sing unto the Lord a new song
For He hath done marvelous things:
His right hand, and His holy arm,
Hath gotten Him the victory.

_____ The Lord hath made known His salvation:
His righteousness hath He openly shewed
In the sight of the heathen.

_____ He hath remembered His mercy and His truth
_____ Toward the house of Israel.

_____ All the ends of the earth have seen
the salvation of our God.

_____ Make a joyful noise unto the Lord all the earth.

_____ Make a loud noise,

_____ And rejoice,

293

_____ And sing praise.

_____ Sing unto the Lord with the harp;
With the harp, and the voice of a psalm.

_____ With trumpets and sound of cornets
Make a joyful noise before the Lord, the King.

_____ Let the sea roar and the fullness thereof;
The world, and they that dwell therein.

_____ Let the floods clap their hands.

_____ Let the hills be joyful together

_____ Before the Lord;

_____ For He cometh to judge the earth:
With righteousness shall He judge the world,
And the people with equity.

_____ Oh sing unto the Lord a new song;

_____ Make a joyful noise unto the Lord.

_____ Make a joyful noise

_____ Unto the Lord.

Music can be used with choral reading. Consider one or a combination of the following ideas:

- Ask a musician in your class to play music that fits the mood of what is being spoken.
- Students could find records that could be played as appropriate background music to the spoken words.
- Students could write a chorus that would be sung several times during the choral reading. The chorus should be Scripture only. This is an excellent way to commit Bible passages to memory.

We speak and sing psalms in good company. The pilgrims offer one model from the past as they set out for the new world. This is Edward Winslow's moving account of their leave-taking:

They that stayed at Leyden feasted us that were to go at our pastor's house; . . . where we refreshed ourselves, after tears, with singing of Psalms, making joyful melody in our hearts as well as with the voice, there being many of our congregation very expert in music; and indeed it was the sweetest melody that ever mine ears heard.[5]

---

1. Richard F. Lovelace, "The Evangelical Muse," in *Dynamics of Spiritual Life: An Evangelical Theology of Renewal* (Downers Grove, Ill.: InterVarsity Press, 1979).

2. Tom Howard, "We All Mean Very Well." Used by permission: Copyright Joyful Road Music.

3. Barry Chazen, "Holy Community and Values Education," in *Moral Development Foundations*, ed. Donald M. Joy (Nashville: Abingdon Press, 1983), p. 80.

4. Connie Fortunato, *Music Is for Children* (Elgin, Ill.: David C. Cook Publishing Co., 1978), pp. 11, 12.

5. Edward Winslow, *Hypocrisie Unmasked* (1646), cited by Margaret P. Hannay in " 'Psalms Done Into Metre': The Common Psalms of John Milton and of the Bay Colony," in *Christianity & Literature*, Spring, 1983, p. 20.

Chapter 13

Art:
What Colors Are in God?

Our parents were inclined to laugh a lot and examine everything for the fingerprints of God.

—John Updike

"I hate Bible studies!" My husband Jack slammed his notebook shut and made no effort to catch his pen as it rolled off the table. "It's fine for someone like you who loves books and words, but my thought process is different. I could tell you what colors are in God, but no one ever asks questions like that."

What colors are in God? I picked up his pen and thought, "I wonder what his answer would be. I could learn something about God by asking Jack that question." Jack is an artist and he communicates in colors and textures and forms. He doesn't like writing answers to Bible questions in straight lines across white pages. But if there were such a thing as a color study of the Bible . . .

God is creative. He makes different patterns across His sky every day. His snowflakes are an extravaganza of design. He had fun putting bumps and stripes on animals. And have you ever noticed how many different kinds of noses He puts on people? We allow Him those areas of creativity. Why not mind creativity? Our minds are different, and some of us would benefit from studying God's Word in different ways—in color, form, and pattern.

This chapter suggests ways for you to use color and form in your teaching. Teachers may need to allow others the opportunity to show us the colors in God. Because we are teachers, most of us are quite verbal, and we tend to pick methods for our classes with which we are comfortable. Verbal methods feel more right. Perhaps our choices are saying to students in our classes, "You don't think the same way I do; you're wrong—or at least not as right." We limit ourselves and our students when we use only familiar, safe ways to teach.

"Look, Jack," (I can imagine God's smile) "take My colors and share them. I had fun making you."

A Color Study for Teachers

A good way to expose yourself to color is to participate in the following color Bible study. It's designed for adult teachers. Of course, there are ideas in it that you might want to use with your students some day, but for right now, you will need your Bible, crayons, and seven sheets of white paper.

Directions:

1. Read Acts 4:32-37; 5:1-6 three times.
2. Then draw your answers to the following seven questions—one answer on each of your seven sheets. Your color choices and the pattern or design you scribble should work together to express moods, emotions, and attitudes.
   a. Read Acts 4:32. Pick a color, and use an uninterrupted line to express how you think the early Christians felt about their situation.
   b. Read Acts 4:33. Pick a color, and use four straight lines to express how you think people hearing the salvation message for the first time felt.
   c. Read Acts 4:34-37. Pick a color, and using any pattern, express how you think Christians today feel about giving to the church.
   d. Read Acts 5:1-6. Pick a color, and use one straight line to describe Ananias's personality.
   e. Decide what Ananias's sin really was. Pick a color and a design that describes how Christians should feel about that sin.

f. Pick a color that describes how you think Christians felt when God killed Ananias. Express that feeling in circles.

g. Read Acts 5:7-11. Pick a color and symbolic design that shows the correct way we should give to God.

Now comes the hard part. Share what you've done with another verbal person. Explain your thinking. Verbalize how you felt as you were working through this project. Consider your students. Which students do you think would benefit from this activity?

Using "Real" Art

Most of us do not use enough genuine art in our teaching. In the younger age levels, teachers show pictures of what a sheep looks like and how the Tabernacle was covered. But as students get older, we use visualizations less and less as part of the teaching plan. A few posters may dot the walls to create a mood. But often reproductions of great art and the newer reflections of our culture play insignificant roles.

We forget how right Alice was in Lewis Carroll's famous children's story when she said, "And what is the use of a book without pictures?"

Karen Mains tells about an experience that helped develop "artistic seeing" for her:

Whenever I feel the need to escape, I flee to the art museum. I am one of those odd people who does not have to be pressured or threatened or wheedled into spending time in any of the world's warehouses of great paintings. I suppose this is because I once made the amazing discovery that these supposedly inanimate works of art had a life of their own. I only had to watch long enough to see it. Some pieces became so real, they actually seemed to breathe.

I remember the day when I escaped to the Art Institute of Chicago. A special exhibit was being displayed of the works of Georges Braque, a French artist. Along with Pablo Picasso, in the early 1900's he developed a new style of painting called cubism. I am not particularly inclined toward these geometric dissections, but I was determined to see if under my scrutiny, they too would begin to breathe.

The life in a painting can't be detected until one has looked for at least 15 minutes. So I plunked myself down on a bench and devoted a half hour of looking to the first picture that caught my fancy At first glance, it appeared to be a room which had been violently disordered by a hurricane.

But sure enough, after a while, I had entered into the being of that picture. There was order here, among these seemingly disparate angles and bunched boxes and shattered rectangles. The disorientation suddenly became focused, and the picture breathed.

Captivated by this metamorphosis, I fixed my attention all the more and wished, "Oh, if only a guide would come who could teach me more about this, more about what these paintings mean!"

As if by command, another group shuffled into place in front of a painting across the room. "In this piece, Braque was attempting to . . ." a voice boomed. They were students being led by a teacher. "Observe the relationship of the forms within the picture to one another," he continued. The young people yawned. They pulled on their winter coats. They shuffled their feet. They longed for lunch in the cafeteria.

Here was the answer to my wish. I rose, slipped quietly to the edge of the distracted group, and mimed a question, "May I join you?" The teacher smiled and nodded his permission. We proceeded down the long side of the hall, then doubled back.

Finally, we came to the picture which had so recently captured my long attention. "What do you think the artist was attempting in this painting?" the teacher inquired. No answer. "Well, then," he persisted. "Let's break it down into pieces. Do any of you have a feeling about what this object in the corner is? What is this in the background?" No answer again.

My compassion was challenged. I bailed him out. After all, I had looked at that painting, really looked at it. "That's an old-fashioned tool for winding yarn in the corner. The object in the background of the canvas, through what looks like a distorted window—that's a church steeple." The yarn winder had come into focus some 20 minutes into my private viewing. The room at 15 minutes. The window and the steeple at 30.

Soon the tour was over. The reluctant students were dismissed and quickly dispersed. The teacher turned to me with relief. "Would you have the time," he asked rather shyly, "for me to take you on a tour of Braque?" All teachers love appreciative audiences.

Of course, I responded favorably. So we began at the beginning, and when we were done, I knew the work of Georges Braque, as well as its secret life, in a way I would never have dreamed possible. It not only breathed. It had begun to sing.[1]

Among the tools God can use to breathe life into our teaching is art. We must be careful not to limit ourselves and our students to art that requires no thought, no effort to understand.

There is an old parable about a tourist who was visiting a British art gallery. The lady passed a famous painting and paused for a moment. She then turned to the curator standing nearby. "Why so much fuss about that painting? It doesn't look so great to me." "Madam," said the curator coldly, "it's not the painting that's on trial."[2]

We verbal teachers don't often go to the opposite extreme—from "There's not an art gallery in the country I haven't yawned in" to "Only the masters and not one brushstroke less." But perhaps that position is worth mentioning. Consider the lesson the potential art snob learns in this excerpt from *The Manticore* by Robertson Davies:[3]

There was a picture on the wall, a perfectly hideous thing in vivid colours, of a Boy Scout looking the very picture of boyish virtue, and behind him stood the figure of Christ with His hand on the Scout's shoulder. I was making great game of it for the benefit of some other boys when I became aware that Father Knopwood was standing at a little distance, listening carefully.

"You don't think much of it, Davey?"

"Well, Father, could anybody think much of it? I mean, look at the way it's drawn, and the raw colours. And the sentimentality!"

"Tell us about the sentimentality."

"Well—it's obvious. I mean, Our Lord standing with His hand on the fellow's shoulder, and everything."

"I seem to have missed something you have seen. Why is it sentimental to suggest that Christ stands near to anyone, whether it is a boy, or a girl, or an old man, or anyone at all?"

"That's not sentimental, of course. But it's the way it's done. I mean, the concept is so crude."

"Must a concept be sophisticated to be a good one?"

"Well—surely?"

"Must the workmanship always be superior? If something is to be said, must it always be said with eloquence and taste?"

"That's what they teach us in the Art Club. I mean, if it's not well done it's no good, is it?"

"I don't know. I've never been able to make up my mind. A lot of modern artists are impatient of technical skill. It's one of the great puzzles . . . ."

"A real artist never does anything gratuitously or simply to be puzzling," he would say, "and if we don't understand it now, we shall understand it later."

This was not what Mr. Pugliesi said in the Art Club at school. We had a lot of clubs, and the Art Club had rather a cachet, as attracting the more intellectual boys; you were elected to it, you didn't simply join. Mr. Pugliesi was always warning us not to look for messages and meanings but to take heed of the primary thing—the picture as an object—so many square feet of painted canvas. Messages and meanings were what Father Knopwood chiefly sought, so I had to balance my ideas pretty carefully. That was why he got after me for laughing at the Boy Scout picture. He agreed that it was an awful picture, but he thought the meaning redeemed it. Thousands of boys would understand it who would never notice a Raphael reproduction if we put one in its place.

How much we miss by not training ourselves and our students to look at what's being said on canvas about our society. Isn't our responsibility to identify the cries within it and learn to answer those cries with the Gospel? Today's art is an "art of anguish and guilt, of isolation and emptiness, of doubt and damnation. Contemporary art has rediscovered the irrational—

in the depth of the demonic! Yet our art, as the art of no other generation, has the meaning of freedom, of courage, of inwardness and honesty."[4]

We need to be responding to our generation, not only in words, but also in our own participation. We need to encourage youth and adults who are talented artistically to increase their skills, to be Christians who are artists. An artist who grew up in a large church where his father was one of the pastors expressed his frustration in his elementary and youth years. "Everyone knew I liked color; I could draw. So I was asked to do posters for special meetings. But nowhere in the church community was I challenged to grow as an artist. Art was never a part of the teaching process during the 12 years I was forced to attend Sunday school—never once. I can remember waiting for our subscription to *Reader's Digest* like I looked forward to none of the Christian magazines we received. I loved the back covers. To my untrained eye, they were great art, and month after month, I would reaffirm my commitment to learn to make pictures like those."

Grand Reynard wrote:

Christians will do well to spend more time in raising their level of appreciation. Art, whether that of the great masters or the humbler efforts of lesser talents, belongs to those things God has given us to enjoy. And in its truest integrity it exists for the glory of God. We need architecture that fittingly houses places of worship, music that worthily praises God the Father and brings men closer to God the Son, pictures on the walls of our homes that, while not necessarily religious, are examples of good art. We need Christian artists of dedicated talent who will extend their horizons in humility and devotion to the true praise of the Giver of talent, who is best honored by faithful use of his good gifts.[5]

WHERE TO FIND ART TO USE IN CLASS

● *Be aware of artwork that is included in curriculum teaching aid packets.* Quite often the poster art is of excellent quality. Instructions are usually given for using the poster as part of the teaching plan. Sometimes great religious pieces are reproduced. Occasionally contemporary pieces of secular art are reproduced with a poster caption. One Christmas a full-color oil painting of Christmas balls, entitled "Epilogue," by Joyce Stillman-Myers, was printed with a caption, "Is your Christ only an ornament?" The caption was used in class, but it stood apart from the reproduction so the picture could be cut out and framed.

● *Many libraries have a lending service.* Prints can be checked out free of charge for a three-week period. Choose paintings that illustrate your unit's theme. Or, you might have different class members pick paintings for the classroom walls. Each time there is a change, students should share the reasons for their choices.

● *Most museums have postcards of their most popular paintings.* Start a file that can be used when pictures complement your lesson aim. The National Gallery in Washington, D.C., for example, has small-poster-size reproductions for only 35 cents each.

● *Watch the reduced table at bookstores.* Very often art books are reduced after they have been on the shelf for a year or two. At less than half their original cost, they become good teaching aid investments. If you mount pictures on heavy cardboard, you'll insure their long-term use.

● *Subscribe to art magazines designed for art teachers.* You'll get ideas for class projects, and often excellent reproductions. For example, *Arts & Activities* usually includes an 8½" x 11" reproduction along with information about the painter and a teaching plan for helping teachers and students interact with the painting—making it breathe.[6] Use the magazine's notes and add questions with which you'd like your Christian students to struggle. For example, with the reproduction of Hans Hofmann's "Smaragd Red and Germinating Yellow" is his statement, "At the time of making a picture I want not to know what I'm doing; a picture should be made with feeling, not with knowing . . ." A Christian teacher might ask questions like these: "Some people say that representative art, great brushstrokes of color that make no attempt to represent a recognizable form, is wrong, even sinful. How do you react to that position and to Hofmann's painting?" Or, "How would you use the color and texture in this painting to explain symbolically the personal aspects of your Christian life?"

HOW TO USE ART IN CLASS—AN ILLUSTRATION

Consider the following poster art. How might you use it in a teaching situation? Come up with two or three ideas before you read the ideas that follow.[7]

● *Discussion of the three blocks is an obvious place to start.* Questions like these will get students involved:

"What might the symbols on these blocks mean?" (Actually, the artist intended this to be a representation of redemption. In the first block is the world as God made it. In the second block, the world and God are separated by sin. In the third block, the completeness of God takes on a different form as Christ breaks the sin barrier. If students don't give the blocks this meaning, don't be upset. In symbolic drawings there is room for many interpretations—none better or of lesser importance than others.)

"No drawing can totally depict the whole redemption story. What parts are missing for you?"

"A Christian manager of a large Chicago restaurant had the artist airbrush these blocks for his office. Why do you think he did this? What do you think secular business people would see in these squares?" (Roman Vishniac, author of *A Vanished World,* a photographic record of Eastern European Jews 50 years ago, speaks of the importance of the person who views the work of art: "When you are showing images, the image shown is not as important as the reaction of a person to it. Abstract compositions cannot move human beings. People don't think in the abstract. A picture must evoke something in the human mind."[8])

● *That last question could lead to a roleplay.* Roleplay what you think might happen if someone asked a Christian who had these blocks displayed, "Say, what do those things mean, anyway?"

● *Students might write the initials of people they are praying for on the second drawing.* When those people come to know Christ as Savior, students could scratch off the initials and write them on the little circle in the third square.

● *Students could do a mime that represents the same message as the blocks.* How would they show separation from God?

● *Students could participate in a Bible study to learn exactly what God says about each of the conditions represented on the posters.* They could start with a week's study on the world as God intended. The second week, they could study the effects of sin, separation from God. The final week could be a study of salvation and the way God chose to interact with our world.

● *Students could develop their own symbolic posters, or even large banners.* The students' work would say the same thing as the squares but use different symbols. Banners could be hung in the sanctuary. Simple posters could be reproduced and used as block prints on Christmas or Easter cards.

- *The blocks might stimulate a writing experience.* As students look at the forms, they might write their own personal experiences with the break Christ made in their personal sin barrier. This writing project could be expanded in many ways. For example, students might pick a word that represents where they are on their faith journey and build around that a praise acrostic thanking Jesus for their spiritual freedom.

GO AHEAD! DABBLE!

Artists give us new eyes. We may think, as word people, that we have read the whole book, but artists show us whole new pages filled with footnotes that proclaim just how much we will miss without them. As teachers, we may not feel competent playing with color and form, and so we skip those pages, or worse yet, clip them out and throw them away as useless. Our students come to the conclusion that those pages, those colorful ways of proclaiming our message, just don't exist.

Betty Edwards in her helpful book, *Drawing on the Right Side of the Brain: A Course in Enhancing Creativity and Artistic Confidence,* asserts that most of us are left-brain people. By that she means that we have cultivated the function of language and language-related capabilities, our intellect, our objective, analytic abilities. In the process, we have not been as concerned with feelings, intuition, and subjective insights. As Edwards says, "Half a brain is better than none, but a whole brain would be better." Research and debate on the specialized brain hemispheres continue,[9] but in the process, they have drawn our attention to the parts of us that go largely untaught—the artistic, imaginative parts. Have you ever had a course in visualization, creativity, intuition, or inventiveness?

Our lack of training in these areas does affect our artistic development. Edwards claims that most of the adults in the western world have not progressed past the artistic level of development they reached at nine or ten. The bridge years to adolescence signal the increased need for peer approval. Youngsters are concerned with how others perceive them. They now understand the distance between their skill level and their own desire for excellence, an excellence that will gain that approval. They quit trying. So while children draw like children, so do most adults. We give up aspiring to higher artistic levels, and for most of us, the Christian home and church environment does not challenge that loss.

What could you assume about the family of this artist, Tricia Merrill? She drew this picture when she was five. Many children do very individualized drawings until they become concerned about peer approval. Then they try to make their pictures look like everyone else's. An elementary Sunday school teacher can identify talent. A youth and adult teacher can give opportunities for students to use talent and gain the affirmation and respect of those whom they care about.

Joseph telling Mary, "It's time to go to Bethlehem now."

When we dare to use colors and artistic materials in class, we will certainly not be training students artistically. There isn't time in the Sunday school hour, nor are most Sunday school teachers qualified guides to artistic excellence. What we are doing is allowing truly artistic students to shine, to contribute "right-brain" wonders to their "left-brain" peers. As our artistic people are given affirmation, they may be willing to continue growing and serving God with their talents. And other students can have fun expressing themselves in ways they had never considered.

In her postscript in *Drawing on the Right Side of the Brain*, Betty Edwards quotes researcher David Galin. He assigned three tasks to teachers, and we as Christian educators can enlarge them for use in our own classroom situations:

Teachers have three main tasks: first, to train . . . not only the verbal, symbolic, logical . . . which has always been trained in traditional education, but also the spatial, relational, holistic . . . which is largely neglected in today's schools; second, to train students to use the cognitive style suited to the task at hand; and third, to train students to be able to bring both styles . . . to bear on a problem in an integrated manner.[10]

THE ART PROJECT

In one corner of the classroom, several students were studying a Bible atlas. Other groups were making lists of materials, drawing diagrams, discussing who in the congregation might be resource people. They were preparing to build a model of the city of Jerusalem in Christ's day. Just one week before, the class had sat silent, polite, disinterested, uninvolved with the lesson or each other. Miss Root, their teacher, was determined to unite the class and get them excited about the Bible as a living Book. Easter was just a few Sundays away when she had an idea. She was teaching the life of Christ. Why not have the students reconstruct the city of Jerusalem, Calvary, and the garden tomb as part of the Bible study, and display what they made to the whole church on Easter morning? However, she knew that to be a worthwhile project, the building of the city had to be more than an exciting activity. Of what real value was the art project?

A successful project must blend with the lesson aim and be part of the ongoing teaching process. To help evaluate her idea, Miss Root made a list of the benefits her students would receive from making the city:

- Become involved in inductive Bible study.
- Learn to work together in small groups and as a class.

- Learn to use reference material.
- Remember the events in the last week of Jesus' life and the significance of those events. They will also be able to mentally place those events at their correct location, so they will seem more real.
- Decide what their relationship to Christ is based on accompanying Bible study and discussion.
- Gain a sense of satisfaction on completing a project and displaying it for the whole church.
- Possibly serve as a catalyst to get families who don't attend church to come to see what their teens made.

Her list left no doubt as to the project's value to her class.

Many different projects are suggested below. Evaluate each one's worth to your students before you incorporate it into your class time. The following questions will help you guide your evaluation:

1. Can you adapt the project to the age level and the capabilities of your students?
2. Does the project fit your lesson's aim so students will be learning as well as participating? Does the project give them an opportunity to grow spiritually?
3. Does what the students learn justify the amount of time the project will take?

4. Will the project hold the students' attention? It is unrealistic to always expect 100 percent participation, but aim for the highest possible student involvement. By using a variety of teaching methods, you can boost student interest—for example, complete an art project one quarter, write original songs the next, and perhaps develop and present a mime drama the following quarter.

5. Have you prayed about the project and the students who will be involved in it? Projects should never be busywork. They are important tools teachers can use to introduce and involve students in the Christian life and to help them better understand how they can work for God as members of His family.

Coat of Arms

Have students draw the outline of a coat of arms and divide it into four areas.

Ask them to fill in the areas with drawings, words, and symbols that emphasize their identities. Point out that coats of arms identify allegiances and how others recognize those allegiances. Each should then share what has been placed on the coat of arms with at least one other person in the class.

Adjust the specific area of identity to the lesson aim. Here are some age-graded ideas:

Junior High: Draw who you were last year on an "antique" coat of arms and who you are today on a new coat of arms.

Senior High: Identify yourself as a student in your high school. What four things would you choose to show how you are similar and different from other students?

Adult: Plan two coats of arms. On the first, draw the coat of arms for the church the way you suspect the neighborhood sees it. On the second draw it the way we members see it.

Color Game

Develop an original color game for your class. You will need lots of color blocks cut from construction paper. You then need to write questions that have to be answered by students after they pick a color. They must also give an explanation of that color. Here is the way a color game might be structured to go with a Christmas lesson:

- "Pick a color that illustrates the most wonderful gift God has given you this year."
- "Pick two colors that you would mix to describe Joseph's feelings on that first Christmas night."
- "Pick a color that explains how you feel when you are singing praises to God."
- "Pick a color that symbolizes a gift you are willing to give to God in this next quarter. Exchange your block with another person. Place it where you'll see it often and remember to pray for the person with whom you exchanged."

Mathematical Puzzler

This 12-piece mathematical shape can be used in many different ways. In fact, it was first sent to me by a high school math teacher who said, "Why don't you brainstorm how your students might be able to use this in Sunday school?"

For example, cut a large puzzler apart and use the pieces to develop a symbolic pilgrim's path that illustrates the Christian journey for people of their age.

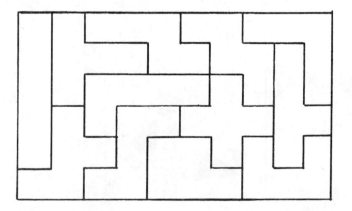

Tangram Art

A tangram is a square of any size that has been cut into seven pieces in this way:

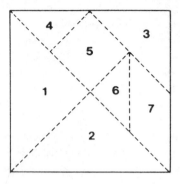

These pieces can be arranged to form many different designs.

Cut the tangrams before class and place each in an envelope. If possible, use colorful construction paper, although any type of paper can be used. Size will vary according to the size of the background pieces of paper on which each student will arrange a tangram. For example, a 3½-inch square would fit nicely on a 9 x 12-inch background sheet.

A tangram project can be an extremely effective teaching aid. First, it equalizes students by giving all the same seven pieces with which to work. Each student uses the pieces to create a realistic picture or symbolic representation. Interestingly, word people very often create tangrams that are more realistic. This one, for example, illustrates a Christian visiting the sick; it is easy to see the picture.

The more at ease a person is with this process, the more likely he or she is to use some symbolic structures. In this tangram, the student is showing a person (realistic) reaching up toward God (symbolic) as God is responding to the person.

Second, a tangram is an effective aid because it forces students to think through what they have learned, and how they can best illustrate that learning in a way others will understand.

Third, as students explain their pictures to their classmates, they gain experience sharing with others about God and their faith in Him.

I was using tangrams in a training meeting for teachers. One woman had brought her twelve-year-old son along and he participated in the activities right along with the teachers. The assignment I gave was aimed at adults: "Use your tangram pieces to illustrate Christian education." The best tangram and explanation came from the boy, and not the adults. "My picture shows a church on the left and a home on the right. That's me in the center. Because my parents are Christians, I learn about God in both places."

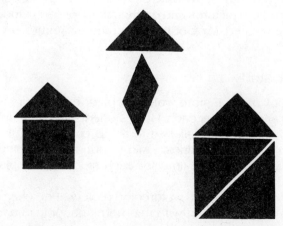

The first time you use tangrams in class, explain what a tangram is and show an example that you have created. Allow about five minutes for students to arrange their pieces and tape or paste them on their background sheets. Allow enough time after the tangrams are finished for each person to explain a creation.

Here are some tangram assignments to get you started:
- "Illustrate something you would like to tell the world about Christ's love."
- "What story in the Bible means the most to you right now? Illustrate it with your tangram and be ready to share your story and the reason for your choice with the rest of the class."
- "Use your tangram to explain to a non-Christian one important thing about God's plan for our future."
- "Illustrate something for which you would like to thank God. Or, think of an attribute God has—such as justice, mercy, understanding—for which you have never thanked or praised Him. Illustrate that quality and write a thank-You prayer beneath your illustration."
- "Each Christian has been given special abilities to use in God's service. Illustrate one area of Christian service in which we as individuals or as a class could get involved."

Torn-Paper Designs

A torn-paper design helps students think through what they have learned and communicate those lessons to others in much the same way as a tangram does.

Supply each student with a background sheet of construction paper. Put paste and many sheets of paper to be torn within easy reach of all students (no scissors allowed). Students should tear and paste a design on the background and be ready to explain their finished pictures. Explain that the finished design may be realistic or symbolic. Allow about five minutes for the creation of the pictures and enough time for each student to explain what has been created. (Any of the trangram assignments will work with this idea.)

Watercolor Study

Supply a box of dime store watercolors for every four students and a sheet of paper and brush for each. Have students read a Scripture passage and then work in complete silence to try to capture the feelings of that passage with color and lines. Allow about five minutes for the watercoloring and additional time for each student to explain his or her painting.

You can vary the basic watercolor project. For example, place a number of references dealing with the morning's topic in a box and have students choose one at random to study, paint, and explain to the rest of the class.

Or, assign each verse of the study section to a different student. A student would read the entire section, but illustrate only the feeling in one verse. For example, if the class were studying Psalm 100, a student illustrating verse 1 might paint a green circle in the center of the picture to represent the world. Coming from that circle would be wide orange brushstrokes which indicate the feeling of joy all the world could have if it realized that the Lord does rule.

Paper Sculpture

Students should find or draw pictures that illustrate a concept they are studying—friendship, salvation, spiritual growth, relationships. These are pasted on pieces of cardboard and fitted together to form a sculpture that could be displayed during the entire study. If the sculpture is well done, it could be given to a student at the end of the study, perhaps one who memorizes the unit's Scripture passage or one whose name is drawn from a hat.

A simple base can be built from two identical rectangles. Students slip one vertically from the bottom center to the middle of the rectangle. They slit the other vertically from the top center to the middle and then the two pieces will slip together and stand.

Students can add other pieces to their sculpture by slitting each piece and fitting it over another. A finished sculpture may look like one of these:

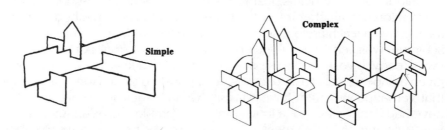

Junior high students will enjoy this project. Most senior high students will not, unless it is combined with a service project—some reason beyond the development of the sculpture itself. (They might enjoy creating them for a senior citizen's banquet to be used as centerpieces, as displays in children's hospitals, or as thank-you trophies for church support workers.)

This project should not be done in class time. It's too time consuming.

313

Symbolic Diagrams

High school and adult Sunday school lessons often deal with concepts. Suggest students draw diagrams illustrating a concept with the use of lines, symbols, and a few words. Students will learn from organizing their thoughts into diagrams and explaining what they have drawn to their classmates. Their diagrams could also alert you to any misunderstanding they might have.

Some possible concepts for students to diagram:
● "Diagram Christ as mediator between God and people."
● "Diagram the Holy Spirit's function in the lives of Christians today."
● "Diagram Christ's plan for the end of the age."

Have students use crayons rather than pencils. Their diagrams will be freer and others in the class will have less difficulty seeing them.

Identity Tag

This activity is effective on the first Sunday a new group of students meets. It can also be used with adults to help them "de-formalize."

Place straight pins, tape, construction paper, string, and other odds and ends in the middle of the floor. As students arrive, they should make their own identity tags. The tags are not important. It's what people are willing to say about their tags that can make the friendship difference.

Paper-Clip Sculpture

This activity grew out of the tangram idea. I had often cut tangrams into the middle of many nights, just to have them ready for a Sunday school convention or a teacher training meeting. I had to find a method that was as effective a teaching tool, and more time effective for me. The paper-clip sculpture was perfect. I needed only to buy a box of small paper clips, and I was ready to go. It works like this. At the end of a lesson, each person is given a paper clip and asked to twist a response to the lesson. You will find that verbal people often have difficulty with this activity. That's fine; they have had center stage for a long time! For example, the assignment might be, "Twist the clip into a message you would like to give the world about God." People who haven't developed their artistic abilities often will twist the clip into a well-known symbol such as the cross. Or, they will twist a letter, such as S and explain that it stands for salvation. Artistic people, on the other hand, can come close to developing a whole theology with a single clip! Listening to them is a growth experience for the class, and an affirmation of their own thinking patterns. Here are some other ideas for using the clip:
● "Twist the clip to illustrate community."

- "Twist the clip to illustrate the positive and negative features of our secular society."
- "Twist your clip to demonstrate your position on religion in public schools."
- "Twist the clip to illustrate one way to teach values in a Christian family."
- "Illustrate a message of your favorite parable."

Photography

In nearly every class there are students who enjoy photography. Involve these students in projects that will increase the impact of your lesson on the whole class and give these students opportunities to use their abilities to serve Christ.

For example, following a lesson on prayer, suggest students make prayer cards to remind themselves to pray for church missionaries, church leaders, sick people, students and service personnel away from home, etc. The photographers should take pictures of the people the class decides to especially remember in prayer and have a copy reproduced for each student. Prayer cards could be made from construction paper that has been cut to approximately 4¼ x 9 inches and folded in half. On one side students should mount the picture and write the person's name, address, and phone number. On the other side, they should write specific prayer requests for this person. As they pray, students should record God's answers on the inside of their cards. This idea could be expanded into an all-church project if students made cards available to anyone who would promise to pray for the person on the card.

Scripture Lesson with Slides

About six weeks before you want to use a Scripture and slide presentation, select a committee to study your lesson's Bible text. Ask the group to work with a class photographer to find ways to illustrate the mood and message of the verses. After the pictures are taken and processed, the photographer and reader from the committee should work together to coordinate the Scripture reading with the pictures.

Consider how a slide presentation might make a familiar passage like Ephesians 6:10-13 come alive to students.

(Verse 10)	*Be strong in the Lord, and in the strength of His might.*	1. Mountain 2. Large tree 3. Person sitting alone on ground with back to camera

315

(Verse 11)	*Put on the complete armor that God supplies, so you will be able to stand against the devil's intrigues.*	4—6. Crowd scenes
(Verse 12)	*For our wrestling is not against flesh-and-blood opponents, but against the rulers, the authorities, the cosmic powers of this present darkness, against the spiritual forces of evil in heavenly spheres.*	7—8. Out-of-focus crowd scenes 9—10. Out-of-focus blurs of people's faces
(Verse 13)	*Take up, therefore, the whole armor of God so that you may be able to stand when you have done all the fighting.*	11. Grass blowing in wind 12. Tree blowing in wind 13. Person from shot 3, standing, back to camera, arms outstretched, feet apart, expressing joy, victory

After students have successfully used this method in class, they may want to share what they have done with others. Suggest they build a slide presentation around the pastor's sermon Scripture and show it during the morning worship hour. Or, encourage them to plan an original Christmas or Easter program in which they use Scripture and slides to share with others.

LAUGH A LITTLE

We don't do enough with humor in our Christian education programs. Kierkegaard put the connection between humor and faith into perspective: "It is true without exception that the more thoroughly and substantially a human being exists, the more he will discover the comical."

Years ago I wrote an article for junior high teens called "The Mummy's Mustache and Other Fun Ways to Learn." It guided young people through a series of do-it-yourself cartoons on Biblical concepts. Several weeks after the article was published, I got a letter from a seventh-grade boy from

316

Baltimore. He wrote, "I never thought about using my cartoons in the church. I'm going to have a cartoon strip someday, and now I know that the lead character is going to be a preacher." He enclosed some of the cartoons he had done. They were preachy, but fun. The boy obviously had skill. We kept in touch. Six years later, he was teaching his own junior high class and using his cartoons as part of his teaching plan. He was also in art school. I fully expect to one day open the newspaper and find in the comic section the polished version of that preacher looking out at me.

Obviously the easiest way to use cartoons in class is to keep a file of them and when a lesson is on a filed subject, bring your cartoons to class and post them or pass them around.

File topics could include:

- Family
- Consequence of actions
- Temptation areas
- Categories that deal with specific areas of difficulty: lying, stealing, selfishness, etc.
- School (or work) situation
- Male and female roles
- Life-style
- Self-image

The next easiest way to use cartoons in class is to find ones that have something to do with your subject and cut off the captions. Let the students fill them in.

I did this with graduate students who were studying for the ministry. The results were fun. For example, in one picture, a poor, quivering man was answering the Devil. The answer had been cut off. Students suggested these captions: "Eve made me do it." "I said my name was Frouts, not Faust."

In another, two men were carrying signs announcing the end of the world. Captions I liked best were, "What translation are you using?" and "But what if social security does run out beforehand?"

One more. The cartoon showed two men in prophetlike garb. A huge crowd was bowing before them. Captions by the students read: "I love being in the ministry, don't you?" "O.K., Moses. I've warmed them up. Sock it to them." "This new praise-ercise fad is really catching on."

These cartoons were not used as part of the teaching plan. They were a tone-setting activity for a study in creativity. I wanted the cartoons to say to the students, "Yes, we'll work in this class, but it's just fine with me if we have a little fun at the same time."

Sometimes a cartoon is so perfectly targeted to your aim that you can ask students to write responses that can actually be used in the lesson. This cartoon was used in a junior high lesson on stewardship:

Students can draw their own cartoons. Sometimes you'll find a real cartoonist who can draw humorous cartoons as part of his or her class preparation and participation. I had a seventh-grade student who cartooned one of the psalms as a Bible assignment. There was his picture of God sitting on His throne dressed in the adolescent uniform of the day—jeans and a rope belt. Twelve-year-old Jim had not meant to be disrespectful or sacrilegious. An overview of his cartoon series made that obvious. He was simply in the process of getting to know God better. And for him at that stage in his development, he pictured God as a friend with whom he could totally relate.

Jim had special talent, but nearly everyone can do stick figures. They can give students a new perspective of a Bible story. What would happen, for example, if students drew stick figures of David dashing away into the hills with Saul in hot pursuit. S. Thomas Niccolls in his article, "The Coming Vision and Stories of David," suggests that the results might remind people of the type of gaggery we enjoy in the Keystone Cop series. The humor fits. What a mess Saul was making as he tried to kill God's appointed. Niccolls says, "The humor is rather like those clown routines that remind us of our all-too-earthy existence."[11]

Before you throw out the idea of using stick figures yourself and getting your students involved, try the following Bible study exercise:

1. Begin by reading Acts 6:1-7, the story of choosing people to help the disciples with the daily distribution of food. It's a familiar story, and it's easy to rush through it to get into something less familiar. But like a paraphrase or a new translation, when we approach a familiar story in a new way, we often learn a surprising amount.

2. Use stick figures to answer the following questions:
● In a stick-figure cartoon, illustrate the problem the church had.

- For any problem, there are a number of solutions. Some are good, and some are just awful. What would have been a solution the people might have chosen had they not been willing to listen to the advice of their spiritual leaders? Cartoon your suggestion.
- Draw a cartoon illustrating the feelings of the people involved after the solution had been adopted.

3. Consider: What did I learn from this process? What might my students learn?

1. Karen Burton Mains, "The Day Braque Breathed," from the course for high school juniors and seniors on the Book of Acts, "Nothing's Been the Same Since," **Christian Growth Electives.** Karen related her experience with artistic seeing to spiritual seeing: "The Christian holds within his grasp another great work of art. It is the dual effort of the supernatural and the human—the Scripture. This book has a marvelous, secret life all its own, but most of us shuffle through its pages and never notice when the wind whirls or the fire strikes the altar. We make appropriate comments, attempting to sound spiritual; we grab our little pieces of holiness—but we are tragically unaware that the words on these pages can actually breathe their own breath and blow those life-giving vapors into our souls.

"There are two ingredients which invariably bring the Scripture to life. One is looking, looking at its meaning for long periods of time. We must discipline ourselves to stop shuffling through this gallery, to pause before one passage long enough to understand before going on to the next.

"The other ingredient is to recognize the presense of the Guide who is none other than the Holy Spirit. How often we yawn and long for lunch when instead we should recognize the fact that we are following a Teacher whose skills have no rival.

"Two tools—concentrated looking and an adept Guide—these are the guarantees we hold that will bring to life seemingly inanimate objects."

2. Dr. Earnest A. Fitzgerald, "Communication: Risky to Be a Judge," in *PACE* (Piedmont Airline's magazine).

3. From *The Manticore* by Robertson Davies. Copyright © 1972 by Robertson Davies. Reprinted by permission of Viking Penguin, Inc.

4. Finley Eversole, *Christian Faith and the Contemporary Arts* (New York: Abingdon Press, 1962), p.11.

5. Grand Reynard, "Christians and Art: A Painter's View," in *Christianity Today.*

6. *Arts & Activities*, 591 Camino de la Reina, Suite 200, San Diego, CA 92108. The magazine is designed for art education in grades K-12.

7. Symbolic pieces developed by Rich Nickel Design, Wheaton, Illinois.

8. "From Abroad," *W,* February 10-17, 1984, p. 23.

9. In "How the Brain Works," *Newsweek,* February 7, 1983, p. 43, Daniel Weinberger of the National Institute of Mental Health was quoted: "A lot of old theories about the right brain and the left brain are nonsense. Things are not as localized as we thought." We do know that the brain's left side controls the right side of the body and vice versa, but scientists are not as clear about how the two sides divide up mental tasks.

"No matter what the research eventually concludes, the fact remains that we have done a lot less with those developmental areas previously assigned to the right hemisphere than we have with those assigned to the left."

10. Betty Edwards, *Drawing on the Right Side of the Brain* (Los Angeles: J. P. Tarcher, Inc., 1979), p. 196.

11. S. Thomas Niccolls, "The Coming Vision and the Stories of David," in *Encounter, Creative Theological Scholarship,* Summer, 1981.